Affirming Diversity Through Democratic Conversations

Edited by

Victoria R. Fu

Virginia Polytechnic Institute and State University

Andrew J. Stremmel

Virginia Polytechnic Institute and State University

Merrill,
an imprint of Prentice Hall
Upper Saddle River, New Jersey   Columbus, Ohio

Library of Congress Cataloging-in-Publication Data

Affirming diversity through democratic conversations / edited by Victoria R. Fu and Andrew J. Stremmel.

     p. cm.

     Includes bibliographical references.

     ISBN 0-02-339833-7

     1. Pluralism (Social sciences)—United States. 2. Conversation. 3. Storytelling—Social aspects—United States.   I. Fu, Victoria R. II. Stremmel, Andrew J.

  E184.A1A36 1999

  302.3'46—dc21   98-7064
                                                               CIP

Cover art: © Dian Ong/SuperStock
Editor: Kevin M. Davis
Production Editor: Linda Hillis Bayma
Design Coordinator: Karrie M. Converse
Text Designer: STELLARViSIONs
Cover Designer: Brian Deep
Production Manager: Laura Messerly
Electronic Text Management: Marilyn Wilson Phelps, David Snyder, Karen L. Bretz, Tracey B. Ward
Director of Marketing: Kevin Flanagan
Marketing Manager: Suzanne Stanton
Advertising/Marketing Coordinator: Krista Groshong

This book was set in Garamond Light by Prentice Hall and was printed and bound by R.R. Donnelley & Sons Company. The cover was printed by Phoenix Color Corp.

Excerpt from "Little Gidding" in *Four Quartets*, copyright 1943 by T.S. Eliot and renewed 1971 by Esme Valerie Eliot, reprinted by permission of Harcourt Brace & Company.

Photo credits: Photos on pages 130, 131, 133, 134, 136 supplied by C. B. Claiborne. Photo on page 138 © Time Inc. Reprinted by permission.

Printed in the United States of America

10 9 8 7 6 5 4 3 2

ISBN: 0-02-339833-7

Prentice-Hall International (UK) Limited, *London*
Prentice-Hall of Australia Pty. Limited, *Sydney*
Prentice-Hall of Canada, Inc., *Toronto*
Prentice-Hall Hispanoamericana, S. A., *Mexico*
Prentice-Hall of India Private Limited, *New Delhi*
Prentice-Hall of Japan, Inc., *Tokyo*
Pearson Education Asia Pte. Ltd., *Singapore*
Editora Prentice-Hall do Brasil, Ltda., *Rio de Janeiro*

In memory of my father,
Dr. Shang-Ling Fu,
who believed education and conversation
build understanding. V.F.

For Arthur Wilson,
Gerald Laughman,
and
Daniel Flickinger,
the classmates who first taught me
about diversity. A.S.

The Authors

Katherine R. Allen is a professor of Family and Child Development at Virginia Polytechnic Institute and State University in Blacksburg, Virginia. She is a core teaching faculty member of the Women's Studies Program and a faculty affiliate of the Center for Gerontology. She is the author of numerous journal articles on family diversity over the life span. She has written two books, *Single Women/Family Ties: Life Histories of Older Women* (1989, Sage), and *Women and Families: Feminist Reconstructions* (with Kristine Baber, 1992, Guilford). Currently, she is co-editing (with David Demo and Mark Fine) the *Handbook of Family Diversity* (Oxford University Press). She received her Ph.D. from Syracuse University in 1984.

Mary Cherian heads the Planning Division of the National Council of Social Service, Singapore. Her portfolio includes strategic planning and research within the non-profit social service sector. She has a Ph.D. in Family and Child Development from Virginia Polytechnic Institute and State University, and also was the child development specialist of the Virginia Cooperative Extension Service.

C. B. Claiborne currently teaches marketing classes in the School of Business at James Madison University in Harrisonburg, Virginia. His teaching focus is consumer behavior and product development and innovation. His research interests include quality-of-life issues, the roles of minority coaches, and consumption. He received a B.A. degree in engineering from Duke University, M.A. from Dartmouth, M.B.A. and Ph.D. in business from Virginia Polytechnic Institute and State University. He especially enjoys photography and travel and teaches aikido at James Madison University.

Karen DeBord is assistant professor and extension specialist in Child Development at North Carolina State University. Karen received her Ph.D. from Virginia Polytechnic Institute and State University. She was a state extension specialist in Virginia and Missouri. Her professional interests include supporting communities in programs for children, youth, and families, and developing learning networks among diverse audiences.

Elizabeth B. Farnsworth is a licensed professional counselor in private practice at Total Life Center in Lynchburg, Virginia. She holds a Ph.D. in Family and Child Development from Virginia Polytechnic Institute and State University, where she received the Outstanding Dissertation Award on Issues in Diversity. She specializes in processes in grief and adjustment to losses and transitions over the life span. She is currently a research associate for the Center for Gerontology at Virginia Polytechnic Institute and State University and an adjunct assistant professor at Lynchburg College and Central Virginia Community College, where she teaches courses in human development and human relations. She is the author of a book titled *Journey Through Grief* and numerous articles and chapters on bereavement and reflexivity in teaching.

Victoria R. Fu is professor of Family and Child Development at Virginia Polytechnic Institute and State University. She received her Ph.D. from the University of North Carolina at Greensboro. Her recent research and writing include social constructivism and reflexivity in teacher problems. She is interested in issues involving the complexity of teaching and learning, and exploring ways the Reggio Emilia approach informs teaching research and practice in the United States.

Jim Garrison is a professor of philosophy of education at Virginia Polytechnic Institute and State University in Blacksburg, Virginia. His specialty is the philosophy of John Dewey, and he has recently published a book on Dewey titled *Dewey and Eros*. Jim is interested in issues involving educating the emotions, the social construction of mind and self, and the difficulties involved in talking across differences.

Lynn Hill has an M.S. in Child Development from Virginia Polytechnic Institute and State University and is currently working on her Ph.D. She was a social worker for 10 years, working primarily with children in foster care. She founded a nationally accredited child development center and worked for 10 more years as the administrator. She is currently an instructor and curriculum coordinator in the College of Human Resources at Virginia Polytechnic Institute and State University. She has a passionate interest in teacher education and in creating extraordinary programs for children.

Stephanie L. Kimball is a former classroom teacher who has worked with emotionally disturbed and learning-disabled students. She has a Ph.D. in curriculum and instruction from Virginia Polytechnic Institute and State University. Her ongoing research and publications are on the topics of listening and agentic positioning. She is now in private practice as an educational consultant.

Doris Martin teaches undergraduate classes in the School of Education at James Madison University in Harrisonburg, Virginia. Her focus is on child development, issues of diversity, and qualitative research. Her research has been primarily in the area of social and emotional development, including training classroom teachers and counselors in the use of Theraplay. She received her undergraduate degree in Secondary English from Millersville University in Pennsylvania, her M.Ed. from the University of North Carolina at Greensboro, and her Ph.D. from Virginia Polytechnic Institute and State University. She enjoys travel and pottery, and teaches aikido at James Madison University with C. B. Claiborne.

Wallace Scott is the director of counseling at Family Service of Roanoke Valley. He has worked in the helping professions for more than 16 years. He has had positions in social services, residential care, mental health, and court services. He has worked primarily with children, adolescents, and families, and has most recently focused on the area of treatment of trauma and dissociation. He is an adjunct faculty member in the School of Social Work and Department of Counselor Education at Radford University. Wally has a doctorate in Marriage and Family Therapy from Virginia Polytechnic Institute and State University. He is a licensed professional counselor in Virginia, a clinical member and approved supervisor for AAMFT, and a member of the Association for Play Therapy. His orientation to therapy is solution-focused, collaborative, and narrative.

Tamara J. Stone is a child and family outpatient clinician. She is president of the board of directors for the Blacksburg New School, an independent parent–teacher cooperative elementary school. She has a Ph.D. in Marriage and Family Therapy from Virginia Polytechnic Institute and State University and an M.S. in Child Development from Texas Woman's University. Her doctoral dissertation is titled "Family Conversations about Sexual Orientation: Interviews with Heterosexually Married Parents."

Elizabeth Strehle is an assistant professor at Berry College in Rome, Georgia. Her interests are in developing literacy strategies that link theoretical concepts with classroom instruction. She is currently working with an elementary school in designing a curriculum for pre-service teachers that enhances the understanding of teaching through observation and participation in elementary classrooms. This yearlong project involves the alignment of Curriculum and Methods classes with the activities and instruction of three elementary classes in grades K–2. This project was made possible through the collaborative planning of the college instructor and the classroom teachers.

Andrew J. Stremmel is an associate professor in Family and Child Development and director of the Child Development Laboratories at Virginia Polytechnic Institute and State University. He received his B.A. from Pennsylvania State University in 1978 and his M.S. and Ph.D. degrees from Purdue University in 1981 and 1989. In between graduate degrees, he was a head teacher in the Purdue Child Development Laboratories. His recent research interests have focused on issues of early childhood teacher education, particularly the use of Vygotsky's theory in early educational settings, and intergenerational exchanges between preschool children and older adults. He also has published articles on diversity and the development of multicultural awareness in teachers.

Preface

Stories and narratives, whether personal or fictional, provide meaning and belonging in our lives. They attach us to others and to our own histories by providing a tapestry rich with threads of time, place, character, and even advice on what we might do with our lives. The story fabric offers us images, myths, and metaphors that are morally resonant and contribute both to our knowing and our being known.[1]

JOURNEYS IN SEARCH OF CONNECTIONS

A few years ago, we attended a three-day conference on "multicultural education" that left us feeling frustrated. Connection was lacking between what we were "told" by the experts presenting at the conference and the perceived realities of our lives. We also felt that socially constructed "expert" and "nonexpert" positions separated rather than encouraged the building of connections in trying to make sense of the meanings of multiculturalism. The tone of the conference conveyed that there are correct ways to think, feel, and act. This tone, in spite of its good intentions, we believe structured silence and inhibited democratic conversation. How can we build bridges and connections without being able to talk across differences? How can we achieve better relations when overgeneralizations are not challenged? How can we affirm diversity when selected views are allowed to be voiced, while others are silenced? Is it easier to tell others how to feel and what to do rather than join in a democratic conversation, so that we can work together to construct our notions of multiculturalism?

We decided that we had to find ways for us and for others to explore the meaning of multiculturalism as a lived-experience. The way to find meaning and to affirm diversity emerged when we—Andy and I—and our friends and colleagues got together regularly to explore the meanings of multiculturalism as a part of our lives as teachers, researchers, family members, friends, and citizens. We believe that meanings need to be socially constructed through conversations, and lived stories provide the contexts for constructing knowledge of self and others. Conversations promote understanding and break down stereotypes and myths about the unknown. As true to any good conversation we told and listened to each other's stories. In this process, we created a tapestry rich with threads of time, place, and character that provoked us to reflect and discuss our different points of view. This was the

---

[1] C. Witherell and N. Noddings, *Stories Lives Tell: Narrative and Dialogue in Education* (New York: Teachers College Press, 1991), p. 1.

beginning of our individual and collective journeys "to our knowing and our being known." Our stories were the threads that created caring connections among us.

Stories of our biases, fears, and doubts took us on journeys through a range of emotions and situations—hurt, healing, pain, comfort, anger, sadness, happiness, and celebration. Our lived-stories varied according to our backgrounds, experiences, and sense of self. Selective storytelling helped us define ourselves as individuals living in a diverse society. We were also aware that selective storytelling, in any situation, may be a reflection of our own intentions, willingness, or readiness to share particular parts of ourselves with others. All these feelings and concerns were respected, and along the way a caring community of friends had developed.

In time, we felt a strong need to share our stories with other people. We have been telling our stories and listening to other people's stories in many places, among a diversity of people—in the classes we teach, among our friends and families, and at professional meetings. Stories always lead to more stories that help us redefine ourselves. These experiences have culminated into this printed volume to be shared with a broader audience. We believe that a collection of essays, based on stories of diversity can encourage others to explore the nuances of diversity through democratic conversations.

Being academics, we tried to ground our experiences in theories of human development and interaction. However, we are aware that people-created theories are often too neat and restrictive to make sense of our complex lived-stories. Maybe our individually constructed personal theories of our lives are better frameworks for us to explore the meanings of living in a multicultural society. These personal theories of life are reflected in these essays. As Bruner said, "narratives are acts of meaning and telling stories is a way of knowing."[2] And life is a journey of finding meaning and knowing about ourselves in relation to other people.

Some stories are difficult to tell because they reflect our fears and vulnerabilities. However, we believe that they need to be told. As one of the authors said at the beginning and again at the end of this venture, "If we don't tell our story, who is going to tell it? At some point you have to tell it in a heroic way." We wish to thank all the contributors for the privilege of sharing their stories in this book. These are authentic stories told in their own voices, and we made no attempt to change them. Otherwise, we would have inadvertently committed the error of "structuring silence." We have learned with our friends the meaning of affirming diversity, that there is a time to speak, a time to listen, a time to learn, and, always, time to be thoughtful and caring.

The reviewers believe that this book offers a unique perspective and breadth of coverage, a strong theoretical base, a focus on feminist and micro-interaction issues, and is relevant to a broad range of practitioners of diversity. Their perception of the book is congruent with our intended purpose of the book. *Affirming Diversity Through Democratic Conversations* is a book of readings for senior-level undergraduates, graduate students, and practitioners in diverse fields. It is to be used in seminar classes and classes that encourage students to discuss and learn through active discourse. It is not intended to be used as a textbook for introductory courses in multicultural education. True to social constructivism, we believe affirming diversity is an ongoing process of evaluating, deconstructing, and reconstructing our knowledge through social discourse and interactions. Thus, we, as editors, avoid drawing our own conclusions at the end of each essay so we would not violate the underlying assumptions of social construction. The essays invite and challenge you to reflect on our voices and stories, and in so doing, share and reflect on your own stories and perceptions with others, and to deconstruct and reconstruct your notions of diversity.

---

[2] J. Bruner, *Acts of Meaning* (Cambridge, MA: Harvard University Press, 1990), p. 35.

We invite you to read our essays and listen to our voices. We hope that you will use our stories in your conversations with others—as teachers, parents, friends, colleagues, therapists, and social workers. More important, we hope you will join in our continuous conversation by telling your stories.

THE ESSAYS

In the first four essays (chapters) found in Part One, "Conversations in Diversity," the contributors propose practices that promote democratic conversations and ways of knowing. Victoria R. Fu invites us to join in a democratic conversation by creating opportunities to share our stories and listen to other people's stories, that is, "The Stories of We the People." Stephanie Kimball and James Garrison persuade us to engage in hermeneutic listening in multicultural conversation. They suggest that "our identities are constituted by our prejudices," and when we engage in hermeneutic listening we put our identities at risk because we challenge our views of other people, our culture, and ourselves. Katherine R. Allen examines family diversity from women's perspectives. She reminds us that we must acknowledge a history of "institutionalized oppression," "economic injustices," sexual repression and exploitation, and violence against women and children; and we must also take responsibility for resolving them. Karen DeBord relates the effect that community leaders' perceptions of "the meaning of community," "respect for diversity," and their own personal characteristics have on "building multicultural communities."

The chapters in Part Two, "Practices in Diversity," examine policies and practices that can either empower or silence in different situations. William R. Scott examines the formation of a therapeutic relationship, in which the therapist and client search for and co-create points of connection. He suggests that if therapists are client-focused and sensitive to differences in their own and their clients' stories, if they refrain from writing the clients' stories, then the clients become the authors of their own stories. Andrew J. Stremmel offers that if teaching–learning environments are to be compatible with diverse cultures a "responsive teaching approach" must be taken. In this approach the teachers must be able to assess and meet the needs, abilities, and interests of a diverse group of children, drawing from a repertoire of teaching strategies. Victoria Fu and Andrew Stremmel recognize that parenting and teaching are ever-changing, dynamic activities that invite us to commit to a pedagogy of caring and thoughtfulness. They ask us to listen to the voices of children, reflect on them, make sense of the meanings they convey, and respond to them. Doris Martin and Mary Cherian, through reflections on stories of their childhood and adulthood, make the case that "discrimination by social class" is often not acknowledged in our discussions of diversity. Yet children of all ages are affected by the social class of their families, especially in the context of schooling, and the place to start to effect change may be in teacher education.

The five chapters in Part Three, "Journeys in Diversity," take us on the authors' personal journeys to define and situate themselves in a world that challenges the essence of diversity. These stories are catalysts to promote democratic conversation and multicultural understanding in various contexts. C. B. Claiborne takes us on his personal, lifelong journey to explore the meaning of multiculturalism. He intimates that, "The meaning of multiculturalism is to have a personal myth that carries you beyond your historical values, beliefs, and circumstances. . . . Myths have a strange way of becoming reality." His narration of the "heuristic journey" along with the photographic images create the tone and the setting that invite us to reflect and invite others to converse on the meaning of multiculturalism. Tamara J. Stone and Katherine R. Allen share with us their courageous story of living in a world that, more often than not, threatens and silences lesbian families. They remind us of the risks they are taking in telling their story of strength, honesty, and openness in constructing their identities together based on love, commitment, and having "room for one more." They remind and educate us that the privileges taken for granted by the majority of our society must be afforded to all, regardless of sexual orientation. Lynn Hill's journey toward a more multicultural perspective in her personal and professional life and Andrew Stremmel's reflections with her on this journey lead us through a story of collaboration and co-construction of knowledge. Their story shows us the power of conversation that is built on trust, sharing stories and hermeneutic listening. Elizabeth Strehle takes us on a journey of learning to become "good teachers" who care, listen, and "hear the voices of those they teach," and in this process good teachers grow and change and become a part of the students' world. Elizabeth B. Farnsworth shares with us a therapist's use of personal experiences as "threads of meaning and influence" in building a "connected practice" that encourages individuals and families "to discover their own ways of making change."

This volume, with authentic stories, reflects in a limited way the breadth of diversity that can be found in the "Stories of We the People." For many of us, putting our stories and thoughts in print is a painful process because it reveals our vulnerability. But our underlying wish is that you will pay attention and listen hermeneutically to our voices, tell others about our stories, and tell your stories that make you who you are in a diverse society. Maybe you will join us in believing that creating opportunities to telling and conversing on "Stories of We the People" can bring us further down the road of affirming diversity for us and for those who will come after us.

> We shall not cease from
>   exploration
> And the end of all our
>   exploring
> Will be to arrive where
>   we started
> And know the place
>   for the first time . .
> T.S. Eliot

ACKNOWLEDGMENTS

The authors wish to thank the reviewers of this text: Sarah G. Gabby, Colorado State University; Gladys J. Hildreth, Texas Woman's University; Nazli Kibria, Boston University; Patrick C. McHenry, The Ohio State University; Brij Mohan, Louisiana State University; Kimberlee L. Whaley, The Ohio State University; and Emmadene T. Winston, Grambling State University.

Victoria R. Fu
Andrew J. Stremmel

Contents

PART **One**

Conversations in Diversity

CHAPTER 1

Stories of We the People

An Invitation to Join in the Conversation on Diversity in a Democracy

VICTORIA R. FU

Metaphors of the United States abound. The following is a sampling of these metaphors: "melting pot," "gorgeous mosaic," "salad bowl," and "patchwork quilt." Each metaphor reflects a different perspective on our democracy and the rights and privileges of its citizens. Diverse groups and individuals, embracing competing perspectives, try to make their voices heard and understood. Conversations on the timeless tenets of U.S. democracy continue to affirm the dynamic ethos of the democracy that includes the principles of freedom, tolerance, equality, justice, choice, and loyalty as integral parts of our society.

None of the metaphors adequately captures the feelings and beliefs of the diverse peoples of the United States of America. Hence, there is a continuous effort to create metaphors that recognize the inclusion of everyone. However, the image of the melting pot remains dominant. This could be due in part to the status it has accumulated over the years as an integral part of our social history, endorsed by the majority of people who identify themselves with its ideology and empowerment. The idea of giving up something that defines a group's sense of power, exclusiveness, and affiliation could be painful. The melting pot metaphor continues to be pro-

3

moted by politicians and conservative activists to justify the inclusion of some and the exclusion of others.

The seductiveness of the melting pot idea is reflected in the speech of people who question the underlying meanings of other metaphors. The source of this metaphor, the play *The Crucible* (Miller, 1953), embraced people of European heritage, while excluding all people of color. A white male student in one of my classes reflected on the viability of the melting pot. He said it was an ideal that we should all strive for in a democracy. "I don't see why some people don't want to be melted into the melting pot," he said. Another student pointed out that as it is described in *The Crucible,* the melting pot would exclude her, a Korean–American, and others of color. The first student ignored her voice and also questioned the use of hyphenation in describing different groups, saying that we are all Americans, so why designate diversity through the use of hyphenation? Another white student supported him by referring to an article indicating that such usage promotes separation. The issue of group identification among more marginalized groups was difficult for those in the majority to understand.

The above story illustrates the complexity of affirming diversity in our society. Issues of power, voice, silence, and belonging are central to this conversation. These issues are also central to all conversations on diversity in this country. The questions to be considered are the following:

■ "Why don't some people want to be melted into the pot?"
■ "Assuming that the notion of the melting pot is accepted as ideal, who will decide who will be melted into the pot?"

Concerns over the use of hyphenation in describing one's original cultural/national heritage as opposed to using *American* to describe everybody raise other questions to be explored in our conversation. How does affiliation enhance and empower a sense of identity while one is struggling to be accepted as an American? A group of exchange students from Germany were amazed at how easily people assumed they were Americans. They recalled many students who commented, "But you look American" and accepted them readily. I wonder whether their European origin, easily identifiable with those who were originally designated as part of the melting pot, had anything to do with their instant acceptance as "Americans"? Many of us people of color who are U.S. citizens and whose families have been citizens for generations are still being asked on occasion: "Where are you from?" "Are you Chinese?" "Where did you learn to speak English? You speak so well." These questions provide entry into conversation by sharing our diverse stories of being American.

Different ideologies or interpretations of democracy are, in fact, inferred "realities" of lived-lives of people from diverse cultural, economic, and educational circumstances. The dynamic ideological nature of democracy encourages us to look to the future. It encourages us to continuously engage in arriving at the meaning of democracy in changing social and political contexts. A model of universally accepted "perfect" or "ideal" democracy has never existed, nor will it ever exist. If an ideal does exist, in the minds of any group of people, it defeats the basic principle of democracy itself. Democracy is a blueprint of the ecology of human development that reflects a shared assumption among people of "how things could be." As with all blueprints, it could be in error and needs to be evaluated, deconstructed, and reconstructed in the public space.

'STORIES OF WE THE PEOPLE'

I propose another metaphor of the United States of America that reflects my view of democracy: "Stories of We the People." This metaphor reflects the stories of the struggles of the peoples of the United States in the context of historical and social changes. Stories are metaphors that are told in the context of daily living. The Stories of We the People are voices of human hopes and fears, love and hate, joys and sorrows, triumphs and failures, power and oppression, and so on. A rich repertoire of stories exists about successes, voices heard, and voices that silence. On the other hand, a wealth of stories are of voices struggling to be heard and to be understood: stories of caring, stories of helping others to be heard.

Lived-stories (narratives) are catalysts for conversation (dialogue), and conversations are the catalysts for change. Life stories of family members, friends, colleagues, students, and strangers prompt us to reflect and understand different standpoints in the contexts of life. From a multicultural perspective, I agree with Greene (1993) that it is crucial for us to provide opportunities for people to tell their stories and for us to listen and interpret what we have heard "woven into the fabric of American plurality" (p. 17). Lived-stories are "acts of meaning" (Bruner, 1990), for they deal "in human or human-like intentions and actions and the vicissitudes and consequences that mark their course" (Bruner, 1985, p. 98). Embedded in these stories are reflections of one's culture, beliefs, gender, and life history (Witherell & Noddings, 1991).

Every life is a story that is worth telling. We grow up listening to stories told by our parents, grandparents, neighbors, and friends. We also share our lives with them by telling our stories. We need to feel and believe that our own stories are worth telling. Noddings (1992) says, "Stories have the power to direct and change our lives" (p. 157). Thus, in telling and listening to stories, we find meaning in our lives and invent our lives. In telling our stories we are challenged to reflect on our experiences and their meanings, and hence, master the "ways of knowing" about our own and other people's perspectives (Greene, 1993).

Telling my stories has helped me construct and reconstruct my perspectives on democracy, diversity, and the power of conversation; and it has helped me make sense of other people's perspectives. I remember stories of my grandmother told by herself and other people, such as my grandfather, mother, father, aunts, and uncles. I cannot remember which story was told by whom, or which parts were the products of the imagination of a young granddaughter. But this is not important, for each story, as remembered, adds to my construction of an image of my grandmother. Stories brought her to life and contribute to my knowing of her—a woman in China, at the turn of the century, in a season of social and political changes, living and dreaming ahead of her time. She was a wife, a mother, a physician, an educator, and a revolutionary; but above all, she is remembered as a caring person in all her relationships. Caring, for her, took the form of providing health care and meeting the basic needs of the indigent; of advocating social justice for the oppressed (e.g., the concubines owned by rich men, the coolies and others who were forgotten by society); and actively helping bring about social and political changes (e.g., joining the revolutionary movement to overturn the emperor and to establish the Republic of China). To me, her life story answers in part the following questions: "What does it mean to care?" "How is care manifested and focused in human life?" (Noddings, 1992, p. 14)

Being an immigrant, the seductiveness of the notion of democratic government in the United States was a constant part of my growing up years. I listened to the tales of my parents and other Chinese elders who dreamed the American Dream and nicknamed the United States of America "Hwa-Chi" because of its freedom and opportunity, the "Country with the Flamboyant/Flowery Flag."

I was a student in Greensboro, North Carolina, during the "Woolworth" sit-ins that started the civil rights movement in the 1960s; the struggle for democracy was at its height. I heard both my black and white friends passionately express opposing positions about civil rights. Both groups told me that I could not understand their feelings, because I had not walked in their shoes. I tried to understand their positions by listening to their stories. Through their stories I began to better understand the strengths and challenges of a democracy. I also began to appreciate that if diverse people will tell, listen, and try to make sense of each others' stories, the struggles of democracy could be brought to a new level.

These and other stories have colored my views on democracy, freedom, equality, and social justice. I have learned, through the years in telling and listening to stories, the importance of examining one's standpoint from sociocultural and sociohistorical perspectives. Inevitably, I am going to share with you ideas that have influenced my construction of the notion of democracy. They reflect my sentiments of the ideals of freedom, equality, tolerance, and human rights in the continuous struggles of a democracy. I am reminded of what Greene (1988) wrote in *The Dialectic of Freedom:* that I am one of those "persons who could never take freedom for granted in this country: Women, members of minority groups, immigrants, newcomers" (p. 55). I also recall what Ling (1990) wrote in *Between Worlds:* There will always be those who are "between-worlds" (p. 177).

Regardless of who we are, there are always times when we are between worlds, outsiders or insiders in different situations. As Ling (1990) said, "The very condition of being between-worlds on the one hand . . . can be interpreted to mean occupying the space or gulf between two banks; one is thus in a state of suspension, accepted by neither side and therefore truly belonging nowhere. . . . On the other hand, viewed from a different perspective, being between-worlds may be considered as having footholds on both banks and therefore belonging to two worlds at once . . . " (p. 177). Permitting ourselves to tell our stories and listen to other people's stories will facilitate our construction of a democracy. Edelman (1992) reminds us to "remember and help Americans remember that the fellowship of human beings is more important than the fellowship of race and class and gender in a democratic society" (p. 54). To me, fellowship is built on trust, good faith, caring, and a desire to share ourselves in conversations. Otherwise, conversations on diversity can be blocked in part by "the suspicion that we have often defined ourselves against some unknown, some darkness, some 'otherness' we chose to thrust away, to master, not to understand" (Greene, 1993, p. 15).

In good conversations we try to engage listeners in the context of the story while not imposing our views on them. If we impose our values on others "we risk losing those values that are most needed in a dynamic society—that encourage reflective criticism, revision, creation, and renewal" (Noddings, 1992, p. 165). A crucial aspect of caring conversation is the belief that it is a process of social construction of knowledge of ourselves and others. It is an educative process:

> . . . of trying things out with the valued help of experts, of evaluating, revising, comparing, sharing, communicating, constructing, choosing. Strictly speaking there is no end product—no ideally educated person—but a diverse host of persons showing signs of increasing growth. There will be commonalities, of course, but these will have been achieved in the process and not necessarily through exactly similar experiences. Even when common values are achieved by one group, they cannot be simply transmitted to another. The new group can be guided; we can share what we have learned. (p. 165)

The experts in democratic conversations are We the People. The art of good conversation relies on speaking and listening with respect to voices that represent different histories and views about the world and believing that, in so doing, we can make sense of diverse perspectives on democracy.

WHAT IS DEMOCRACY?

As mentioned, the metaphors of the United States reflect multiple perspectives on democracy. Listen to the voices of politicians and the media, who provide a range of definitions of democracy and interpretations of its characteristics (or moral values). The voices of the so-called liberals, conservatives, and ultraconservatives have very different interpretations of democracy, the role of the government, and individual rights. Changing political power structures often leads to redefining democracy based on the voices of the elite in power. These voices often ignore or silence those with opposing views, thereby challenging the essence of democracy. Democracy does not so much mean that the majority rules, but that the rights and privileges of minorities as citizens are guaranteed.

Competing, changing, and dynamic conceptions of democracy may contribute to a sense of discomfort among those who see democracy as static. Those who believe that democratic principles should be narrowly defined and remain the same through time may not be permitting themselves and others to create a space for conversation. This belief that democracy is "divinely ordained" works against the core of democracy itself. History informs us that for democracy to survive and thrive it has to build on moral values such as equality; tolerance; justice; loyalty; free speech; and, I would like to add, caring. All these values work to promote, if not guarantee, human dignity and human rights through conversation. As Noddings (1992) has pointed out:

> Democracy is not the outcome of a common set of words and customs. Rather, it is an achievement—one that depends on the desire to communicate and the goodwill to persist in collaborative inquiry. Common language, customs, and values are the marks of achievement in the effort at building a democracy, not its prerequisites. To achieve a democracy we must try things out, evaluate them without personal prejudice, revise them if they are found wanting, and decide what to do next through a process of reasoned consensus or compromise in which the authority of expertise is consulted but not allowed to impose its views with no discussion of how, why, and on what ground. (pp. 164–165)

Democracy has been conceived as a way of life, "a life of social progress and reform" (Dewey, 1940). It is a social practice that is informed by competing ideological concepts of power, politics, and community (Giroux, 1988). From this perspective, I see the struggles of democracy as a life that is filled with contradictions and tensions among contrasting principles: "freedom vs. control, security vs. risk, self vs. other, right vs. wrong, real vs. ideal, the interest of the person vs. the interest of society, and so on" (Van Manen, 1991, p. 61). These are the principles that affect our daily living in various social contexts in the ecology of human development. "Democracy works on behalf of human dignity and human worth . . . that allows and cultivates human dignity," (Cecil, 1990, p. 25) and it unravels in the people in a free society a sense of self-worth, self-discipline, freedom to choose, "and the duty to preserve social order that makes such choices possible" (Cecil, 1990, p. 25).

Democracy is also a "public space" or "community" of struggle. Greene (1988) talks about "the making and remaking of a public space, a space of dialogue and possibility . . . a continuing effort to attend to many voices, many languages, often ones submerged in cultures of silence. . . . The aim is to find (or create) a public space, that is, one in which diverse human beings can appear before one another . . . the best they know how to be" (p. xi). In this space, those who are submerged in cultures of silence can participate, regardless of race, ethnicity, religion, socioeconomic status, age, gender, sexual orientation, and functional status. It is to search for a way for voices to be set free and to be heard. Conversation enhances the possibility of moving toward what might be or ought to be. W. E. B. DuBois (1903–1982) said that "questions of social equality" should be addressed directly and should not be silenced. In a democratic society, we have the right and opportunity to evaluate, decide, and compare competing cultural ideologies in terms of what is in the best interest of human development. This cannot be achieved through instant telephone polls or catchy sound bites that fail to provide thorough information for discussion and decisions based on thoughtful reflection and evaluation of various topics.

Central to the notion of democracy is free speech. I add that it is not only free speech, but also actively listening to what people with different voices are saying. The role of speech in democracy reminds me of the Simon and Garfunkel song *The*

Sounds of Silence; if we listen, we might learn from each other. Silencing voices that we do not share can be a symptom with conflicting meanings that reflects various conditions of life. Silence can be a symptom of power. Those in power who exercise silence may, in their silence, silence those who have limited or no power. Silence, on the other hand, can be a symptom among those without power. Silence for members of this group may be reflective of an inability to make their voices heard, or it may reflect a learned silence, a belief that their voices are not important and will not make a difference. Collectively, those in power create institutions of silence that control or prevent open conversation. This dichotomous relationship exemplifies one of the most basic and obvious conflicts in any social system: The tension between freedom and control. This conflict is found between people everywhere—in families, in classrooms, in neighborhoods, and in society at large. "Associated with freedom are notions such as autonomy, independence, choice, license, liberty, room, latitude. In contrast, the language of control is associated with ideas such as order, system, discipline, rule, regulation, precept, organization" (Van Manen, 1991, p. 61). Are not these competing ideas underlying the notion of democracy? Are these also not the same ideas that exercise the right to have one's voice be heard or silenced?

WHAT IS TOLERANCE?

Tolerance is another fundamental principle of democracy that must be practiced in the public space. When we tolerate those with whom we disagree, we listen to their stories hermeneutically, searching for truth. Continuous search for truth is the legacy of freedom of the mind (Cecil, 1990; Dewey, 1940a, 1940b). Dewey stated the following:

> The democratic idea of freedom is not the right of each individual to do as he pleases, even if it be qualified by adding "provided he does not interfere with the same freedom on the part of others." While the idea is not always, not often enough, expressed in words, the basic freedom is that of freedom of mind and of whatever degree of freedom of action and experience is necessary to produce freedom of intelligence. (Dewey, 1940a, 1940b, p. 341)

The media-created notion of "political correctness" provides a context in which the notion of tolerance is challenged. Should tolerance be extended to those who are determined to destroy others' efforts to find truth? (Cecil, 1990). Should some "truths" be silenced because they are outside the limits of tolerance? Are there limits to tolerance?

Yes, I believe there are limits to tolerance. Cecil (1990) asserts that, "As paradoxical as it may sound, intolerance of intolerance defends tolerance, while tolerance of intolerance defeats the principles of tolerance and with it one of the essential prerequisites of democracy" (p. 21). However, there is also a fine line between the constructive power of tolerance and the destructive outcome of preventing other people's views from being expressed in the public space. Intolerance of diverse perspectives through silencing should not be tolerated.

People often perceive freedom from an individualistic perspective that "signifies a self-dependence rather than relationship; self-regarding and self-regulated behavior rather than involvement with others" (Greene, 1988, p. 7). This perspective could undermine the principle that with freedom, come certain duties and responsibilities to others; that is, duty to make responsible decisions that protect the rights of others to be free and equal. In protecting the rights of others, we find the most effective means of securing our own freedom (Cecil, 1990, p. 20). The danger of viewing the democratic principles of freedom as self-dependence, individual choice, or autonomy, from an individualistic perspective, is the possibility that we will neglect the welfare of our fellow human beings, or create indifference.

Gilligan (1982) noted that there is a difference in the construction of morality from the perspectives of morality of human rights and responsibility. I see in this distinction different notions of democracy. The former is the "rugged individualist," free, autonomous, and self-serving, believing in the right to do as one pleases without interfering with someone else's rights; the latter represents a different value system that subscribes to the belief of "choices being made in a fabric of mutuality and concern, of ongoing dialogue and conversation, of cooperation rather than competition" (Greene, 1988, p. 84).

Wuthnow (1991), argued that we need to pay attention to the sociological side to compassion. That is, compassion as a "social good . . . a commitment to those who may not be able to reciprocate, an acknowledgement of our essential identities as human beings, and a devotion to the value of caring itself" (p. 13). Freedom, success, and self-interest are perhaps the most prized legacy of our national ideology of democracy and goals to be pursued, that is what is popularly referred to as "American individualism." However, from an ecological standpoint, the reality is that the pursuit of these goals is influenced by certain social, political, and moral constraints and opportunities. For some, they seemingly are given in life; whereas for others, they are out of their reach.

Compassion and caring should also be aspects of the ethos of democracy. "Caring preserves both the group and the individual and . . . it limits our obligation so that it may realistically be met. It will not allow us to be distracted by vision of universal love, perfect justice, or a world unified under principle" (Noddings, 1984, p. 101).

Wuthnow (1991) raised a question that warrants further reflection and conversation: How do we reconcile the paradoxical elements of our ethos of democracy: to be a "rugged individualist" and be compassionate and caring at the same time? An answer may be found in Greene's (1988) proposition that we shall look for "freedom developed by human beings who have acted to make a space for themselves in the presence of others, human beings become 'challengers' ready for alternatives, alternatives that include caring and community" (p. 56). Thus, to discover these answers, it pays for us to listen and reflect on the stories of those who have succeeded.

CREATING A PUBLIC SPACE

How do we create a public space that promotes democratic conversation? I recommend that we adopt some child development principles: the zone of proximal development (ZPD), intersubjectivity, and the concept of caring. The *zone of proximal development* is a social system or a hospitable and accommodating space for learning (Moll, 1990). Within this zone, whether it is between adult and child or between peers, is the possibility for change. First, according to Vygotsky (1978), this zone has the capacity for play and imagination. For us to grow, we need to be able to think of ourselves in ways that are different from the ways they are now. Second, according to Bruner (1962) this zone has "the capacity to make use of help of others, the capacity to benefit from give-and-take in experiences and conversations with others" (p. 288). This space offers opportunities to talk, listen, ask questions, seek help to understand, and engage in problem solving. Collectively, possibility exists for growth and development, for change. Interactions with the ZPD can be enhanced by adopting the concept of *intersubjectivity,* a sharing of purpose or focus in the coordination of perspectives (Rommetveit, 1985; Trevarthen, 1980). Intersubjectivity is of crucial importance in the interactions within the ZPD. Being able to engage in meaningful activity or conversation with others will help us determine a common ground for communication for us to understand the interests, values, and goals that we expect of each other (Fu, Stremmel, & Stone, 1992). Also crucial to "connected teaching" and connected conversation is caring. Caring involves establishing and maintaining intersubjectivity between partners to apprehend the other person's reality, feeling what he or she feels as nearly as possible. This is essential from the view of the one doing the caring.

This theoretical conceptualization needs to be put into action where people with different voices and ideologies can create a public space or community for conversation. In this space everyone is empowered to struggle for the rights and privileges of a democracy.

CONCLUSION

In becoming more multicultural, we need to create spaces where the Stories of We the People can be told. Participants in these conversations are tolerant of and listen to diverse voices; and, they are prepared to learn and change. The essence of democracy, I propose, is a constructive achievement of people with different voices who have adopted a multicultural stance; that is, they are open to learning about new things and new beliefs and to finding meaning in reference to one's own history.

It is a time for America to come together, to empower each other to tell the Stories of We the People, and to join in the struggles of our democracy. The metaphor of "connected teaching," where teachers and students share teaching–learning responsibilities, informs us of a way that promotes democracy as a way of life. We can all be teachers and learners in our journey to affirm diversity through conversations by adopting the stance of a reflective teacher, one who attempts to

> . . . look through students' eyes, to struggle with them as subjects in search of their own projects, their own ways of (knowing) making sense of the world. It is to interpret from as many vantage points as possible lived experience, the ways there are of being in the world. (Greene, 1988, p.120)

As reflective and caring participants in democratic conversations, we can find similar ways to engage and connect with diverse people. Together we can move democracy to another level that mirrors the multiple, ever-changing sociopolitical and sociohistorical realities of Stories of We the People.

The stories of my childhood and those I am living in adulthood provide the ingredients for me to join in any democratic conversation. They are the lenses through which I make sense of my ideas of democracy in the company of others. I invite all of you to join in these conversations with anybody, anywhere, so that all our voices can be heard above the noise of media sound bites and political rhetoric. After all, the Stories of We the People *are* the voices of democracy. Permission to continuously reconstruct the notion of democracy that reflects the beliefs of We the People is an inalienable right of the past, current, and future generations of U.S. citizens.

REFERENCES

Bruner, J. (1962). Introduction. In L. Vygotsky, *Thought and language*. Cambridge, MA: MIT Press.

Bruner, J. (1985). Narrative and paradigmatic modes of thought. In E. Eisner (Ed.), *Learning and teaching in ways of knowing* (pp. 97–115). Chicago: National Society for the Study of Education.

Bruner, J. (1990). *Acts of meaning*. Cambridge, MA: Harvard University Press.

Cecil, A. R. (1990). *Equality, tolerance, and loyalty: Virtues serving the common purpose of democracy*. Austin, TX: The University of Texas Press.

Dewey, J. (1940a). Democracy and educational administration. In *Education Today* (pp. 337–347). New York: G. P. Putnam's Sons. (Original work published 1937)

Dewey, J. (1940b). *Education today*. New York: G. P. Putnam's Sons.

Edelman, M. W. (1992). *The measure of our success: A letter to my children and yours*. Boston: Beacon Press.

Fu, V. R., Stremmel, A., & Stone, T. J. (1992). Role of intersubjectivity in teaching culturally diverse preschoolers. *Conference Proceedings of New Directions in Child and Family Research: Shaping Head Start in the '90s*. Washington, DC: Administration on Children, Youth and Families.

Gilligan, C. (1982). *In a different voice*. Cambridge: Harvard University Press.

Giroux, H. A. (1988). *Schooling and the struggle for public life: Critical pedagogy in the modern age*. Minneapolis: University of Minnesota Press.

Greene, M. (1988). *The dialectic of freedom*. New York: Teachers College Press.

Greene, M. (1993). The passion of pluralism: Multiculturalism and the expanding community. *Education Researcher*, *22*(1), 13-18.

Ling, A. (1990). *Between worlds: Women writers of Chinese ancestry*. New York: Pergamon Press.

Miller, A. (1953). *The crucible*. New York: Penguin.

Moll, L. C. (Ed.). (1990). *Vygotsky and education: Instructional implications and applications of sociohistorical psychology*. Cambridge, MA: Cambridge University Press.

Noddings, N. (1984). *Caring: A feminine approach to ethics and moral education*. Berkeley, CA: University of California Press.

Noddings, N. (1992). *The challenge to care in schools*. New York: Teachers College Press.

Rommetveit, R. (1985). Language acquisition as increasing linguistic structuring of experience and symbolic behavior control. In J. V. Wertsch (Ed.), *Culture, communication, and cognition: Vygotskian perspectives*. Cambridge, MA: Cambridge University Press.

Trevarthan, C. (1980). The foundations of intersubjectivity: Development of interpersonal and cooperative understanding in infants. In D. R. Olson (Ed.), *Social foundations of language and thought* (pp. 316–342). New York: Norton.

Van Manen, M. (1991). *The tact of teaching: The meaning of pedagogical thoughtfulness*. Albany, NY: State University of New York Press.

Vygotsky, L. (1978). *Mind in society*. Cambridge, MA: Harvard University Press.

Witherell, C., & Noddings, N. (1991). *Stories lives tell: Narrative and dialogue in education*. New York: Teachers College Press.

Wuthnow, R. (1991). *Acts of compassion: Caring for others and helping ourselves*. Princeton: Princeton University Press.

CHAPTER 2

Hermeneutic Listening in Multicultural Conversations

STEPHANIE L. KIMBALL AND JIM GARRISON

All of us engage in conversations every day: in school, at home, in the checkout line at the grocery store, with our neighbors, and at work. We seek to communicate our ideas, needs, and intentions to friends and strangers who inevitably differ from us in some fundamental way—by gender, age, nationality, language, political interests, race, and so on. In fact, we often notice these differences only when we find ourselves in the midst of misunderstandings. Interaction with others, regardless of our differences, is vital to establishing and maintaining democratic community; however, lack of understanding often jeopardizes our chances of continuing the conversation. Most people expect to disagree with others often on one point or another, but to feel misunderstood, or incapable of understanding another, often leads to confusion, anger, fear, and paralysis. But is it really feasible, or desirable, to try to understand a person? Surprisingly, we want to suggest that the answer is "no." This does not

We would like to acknowledge the helpful comments of four Social Foundations of Education students: Greg Abel, Bruce Carter, Natasha Bhalla, and Hugo Harrison. We would also like to thank Katherine Allen and T. J. Stone for their thoughtful responses to previous drafts of this manuscript.

mean it is impossible to produce interpersonal understanding; rather, we believe it is important to distinguish between understanding people and understanding their ideas and values. In this chapter we will look at something called *hermeneutics*, the art of interpretation.

Gadamer (1993), a German philosopher, wrote the following:

> Conversation is a process of coming to an understanding. Thus it belongs to every true conversation that each person opens himself to the other, truly accepts his point of view as valid and transposes himself into the other to such an extent that he understands not the particular individual but what he says. (p. 385)

To engage in conversation, then, is to undergo change. Through the creation of a mutual understanding, a person not only considers another's point of view, but also examines her own position in light of new questions. The clarification or refinement of her own views may then help her understand someone else's positions differently, which in turn casts new light on herself. As long as the conversation continues, this cycle does too.

By definition, a *multicultural conversation* involves participants with differences in language, beliefs, values, habits, tastes, or cultural traditions. *Multiculturalism* could be defined as the belief that there is no single right way to live; no set of cultural practices is predetermined as the superior or "right" way to be. Thus, respect for other people's experiences, and their interpretations of those experiences, is fundamental to multiculturalism. To participate in a multicultural conversation is to be committed to creating new understandings among people, and this implies a willingness to change one's own point of view in the face of new challenges and insights.

We propose that listening is crucial to reaching understandings. However, we do not mean passively receiving another's views—that is dangerous, especially for the less powerful participants in a conversation. Children are often told to listen to adults this way; they are expected to accept what is said because of the speaker's authority. Obviously this can be necessary at times. But what if the authority figure constantly tells the child that he is stupid, or that his race, gender, or religion is inferior? Shouldn't the child resist these messages and refuse to be defined according to that "authority"? We believe that there are times in everyone's life when this sort of passive listening would be likely to reinforce inequality and domination rather than promote understanding.

The extreme opposite of passive listening is empathetic listening and it too can be dangerous. The goal of empathetic listening is to "see through the eyes of another." In other words, it encourages listeners to set aside or ignore their own experiences, characteristics, beliefs, and so on that make them different from the speaker and therefore block understanding. The problem is that we can never really know what it is like to be another person. If we assume that we understand someone that intimately, we are probably trivializing that person's life and, even worse, imposing our interpretations on the other person. So, whereas passive listening gives the speaker all the power to define and interpret a situation, empathetic listening reserves all that power for the listener. In each case, a subtle form of domination occurs. The passive listener is left open to the dangers of being theorized or colonized, while being "assimilated" by some dominant cultural standard, or defined in someone else's terms. Meanwhile, the empathetic listener may be an unconscious colonist.

As an alternative, we propose a concept of listening that is compatible with the idea of hermeneutics. Originally, the hermeneutic process was developed as a way to find out the "truth" of religious texts written in historically distant times. However, hermeneutics can also be applied to the task of achieving interpersonal understanding, where spoken conversation is the "text" to be interpreted. In our opinion, the hermeneutic approach is particularly applicable to multicultural settings, primarily because it diminishes the likelihood of domination.

A common conception of *interpretation* is that the goal is to discover the "truth" of a statement and reproduce it for oneself. In contrast, hermeneutics assumes that understanding meaning is a productive process that occurs within a particular context, among particular participants. Thus, instead of trying to figure out a person, or looking to some central core of her being, the task of hermeneutics is to produce new understandings or interpretations for both conversants. As Gadamer (1993) stated, the "miracle of understanding . . . is not a mysterious communion of souls, but sharing in a common meaning" (p. 292).

What does it mean to "open oneself to another," especially in a multicultural setting where beliefs, traditions, values, habits, languages, and tastes may differ widely? How can people come to understandings through conversation, without dominating others or allowing themselves to be dominated? And why is it important to focus on understanding what a person says, rather than understanding the person? Furthermore, why should we want to make ourselves vulnerable by opening ourselves to others? These are some of the questions we will address in the following discussion of hermeneutic listening and multicultural conversations. We will begin with an overview of how hermeneutics works, further distinguishing this approach from empathy in the process. We use the term *ontological hermeneutics* to emphasize our view that fully participating in true conversations has consequences for our ontologies, or identities. Next, we will discuss how Gadamer's notions of "openness" and "fusion of horizons," two qualities of hermeneutics, apply to multicultural conversations. Finally, we will address the importance of listening in democratic dialogue.

FROM EMPATHY TO ONTOLOGICAL HERMENEUTICS

One fundamental difference between empathy and hermeneutics concerns how each approach views the role of prejudices in the task of understanding. As we have already mentioned, the empathetic listener acknowledges the existence of prejudices, but claims to be able to put them aside to understand others as they really are. However, despite good intentions, from the standpoint of hermeneutics such a listener actually limits her ability to understand by refusing to acknowledge her inevitable prejudices, or prejudgments. If a person believes he has no prejudices, he is claiming to be neutral or objective. But in fact, we are all conditioned by the circumstances of the time and place where we live. In other words, one's values, beliefs, interests, perceptions, and so on, are at least partially determined by the social context of a given historical moment (Gadamer, 1993). We cannot eliminate this conditioning or the prejudices that result; we can only deceive ourselves into believing we have.

Part of the problem here is that prejudice today is generally assumed to be a harmful quality, something that people should strive to get rid of to create more harmonious and understanding communities. However, Gadamer (1993) pointed out that this assumption is erroneous:

> The history of ideas shows that not until the Enlightenment does the *concept of prejudice* acquire the negative connotation familiar today. Actually "prejudice" means a judgment that is rendered before all the elements that determine a situation have been finally examined. . . . Thus, "prejudice" certainly does not necessarily mean a false judgment, but part of the idea is that it can have either a positive or a negative value. (p. 270)

Prejudices are just the "prejudgments" necessary to make our way in everyday conversation, thought, and action. Think what it would be like if we had to judge every situation as if it were a totally new experience, without any preconceptions to guide us. For instance, if you were cooking a meal and had no prejudgments about what ingredients, utensils, or procedures to use, food preparation would not only be tedious and frustrating, but also potentially dangerous! In other words, the existence of prejudice is necessary for learning, because any assumption, theory, or belief on which a person bases a decision could be considered a prejudice. Furthermore, prejudices are not necessarily cognitive in nature; in fact, it may be helpful to speak more broadly of a person's beliefs, habits, and values.

As we mentioned, people are conditioned by historical circumstances: Through participation in our communities, we learn the prejudices (beliefs, habits, and values) of our culture. These prejudices constitute our identities. Of course, each of us is actually part of a number of cultures. For example, family, peers, school, state, nation, race, and religion may each exist for us as separate but overlapping communities, possibly with different sets of beliefs, habits, and values. Gadamer (1993) pointed out that we come to know who we are within these social contexts long before we try to understand ourselves through self-examination. In other words, participating in various overlapping communities shapes the way we see the world and our places within it—and these prejudices are what make us who we are.

The point, then, cannot be to free ourselves of all prejudice, but to examine our historically inherited and unreflectively held prejudices and free ourselves of those that hinder our efforts to understand others. However, it is not possible to know beforehand which prejudices are "positive" and enable understanding, and which are "negative" (see Gadamer, 1993, p. 295). Even in social and historical contexts where prejudices like racist and sexist attitudes are generally recognized as impediments to understanding, it is quite common to be oblivious to the way such prejudices operate in one's own life. Some women who have grown up in a sexist society, for instance, may find that they have certain habitual ways of interacting with others or representing themselves that contradict their commitments to feminist ideas and perpetuate their own oppression. In fact, while under the influence of a prejudice, it is impossible for us to fully recognize it as one; and if we cannot identify the prejudices that constitute our identities, then in some sense we cannot know ourselves, much less understand somebody else.

This is precisely why differences are essential to achieving new understandings. It is not until a person encounters the differences of another's point of view that she can recognize her own prejudices and question them. For instance, a prejudice that affects many of us in the United States is the belief that hard work will be rewarded with status, recognition, and material wealth. Many people are not even aware that they live according to this underlying assumption, and if it were pointed out, they would likely argue that this belief is "normal" or "natural" rather than socially conditioned. For them, this tacit belief would seem to be a universal way of thinking, until they encounter someone who has been conditioned differently—and then only if they avoid judging the other long enough to listen! Therefore, interacting with someone who is different might provoke us to become aware of ourselves in new ways, especially if we are willing to question our own prejudices, assumptions, and understandings. Gadamer (1993) highlighted the importance of the question, writing that "the essence of the question is to open up possibilities and keep them open" (p. 299). Questioning our prejudices (beliefs, habits, and values) does not mean that we simply accept the other person's perspective in place of our own. A hermeneutic conversation might not necessarily result in a person taking the other's views, but it will result in change of some sort. Whether this change consists of clarifying one's own views, entertaining new doubts about them, or actually coming to an agreement with other conversants, the result is the production of some new understanding.

The hermeneutic process is generally described in terms of a circle. An example of this is the idea that one cannot know the whole without understanding its parts, but one cannot understand the parts without the context of knowing the whole. This is not a "vicious circle" that leads nowhere; however, it is more like an expanding spiral of understanding. By coming into contact with different beliefs, habits, and values, we become aware of our own prejudices. If we are willing to question those prejudices in light of the alternatives we now perceive, then new understandings of self and other are made possible. This in turn allows us to be more open to other aspects of difference, which leads to greater understanding, and so the cycle continues.

Therefore, prejudices and difference, which are both usually assumed to be stumbling blocks to understanding, are actually crucial to the hermeneutic process of interpretation. From this perspective, tensions between ideas are actually opportunities to produce new understandings and make new meanings. Encounters with different beliefs, habits, and values also make us more aware of our own prejudices, therefore increasing our self-knowledge and enabling personal growth.

The *hermeneutic process,* then, is compatible with the goals and concerns of multiculturalism. On the other hand, the notion of *empathy* is problematic for multiculturalism for at least three reasons. First, empathy assumes that differences among people are barriers to understanding which must be overcome. It seems self-evident that if difference is not valued, then those farthest from the dominant cultural standard are most often excluded from the conversation.

Second, insisting that prejudices can be set aside simply invites people to inter-pret others in their own terms, without reflecting on their own prejudgments in the process. The idea, for example, that an able-bodied, white, upper-class male raised in urban North America can empathetically know what it is to be a disabled, unem-ployed Mexican immigrant in rural Texas is not only unbelievable, it may also be domination in disguise. Gadamer (1993) wrote, "The claim to understand the other person in advance functions to keep the other person's claim at a distance" (p. 360). After all, if we are confident that we already understand a person, we are not likely to listen to him tell his own story. What Gadamer describes here is the epitome of self-righteous, self-assured do-gooders who believe they know all they need to know about themselves and others. Such people are likely to come to conclusions about other people and their situations based on their own very different experiences.

Third, the aim of empathy is to reproduce the speaker's original meaning. If conversations are limited to reproducing participants' knowledge, there is not much chance of reaching new understandings. The wonder of hermeneutics, however, is that it produces new, multicultural understandings.

Openness

A familiar conception of *openness* refers to the willingness to learn something new or listen to different people; for instance, we may say we are "open to new ideas" or have an "open mind" when it comes to accepting others' points of view. Gadamer's use of the term *openness* is similar but refers more directly to the idea that "under-standing is not static or closed; it is open to continuing development and change" (Stewart, 1983, p. 383). Thus, there is a dual meaning to the concept of openness, which Stewart (1983) summarized effectively:

> The listener is not simply "open to what the other means" so that he or she can repro-duce it; instead, the listener is open to the meanings that are being developed between oneself and one's partner. These meanings, moreover, are also open—fluid, and continu-ously context-dependent. Rather than simply being brought to the conversation, they are, to a significant degree, a product of the persons' meeting. (p. 384)

Again, the idea emerges that meanings are produced rather than reproduced. Of course, this does not suggest that there are no constraints on meaning, nor does it imply that each person can arbitrarily or haphazardly assign meanings. Rather, the production of meaning or understanding is a joint process involving more than one person within a specific sociohistorical context. To ignore this point is to risk falling into cultural relativism. For instance, to claim that there are no absolute moral stan-dards is not to suggest that murderers or rapists should be free to live by their own personal codes of behavior but to emphasize that it is a social process that deter-mines which behaviors are morally acceptable and under what circumstances the rules apply. It is also important to remember that if the goal is to reach understand-ing, then personal, idiosyncratic meanings are not very helpful. Think how you would react if someone were to tell you that a particular word or object or event had a "special meaning" for her. Most likely, you would ask her to explain what that meaning was, in which case you would be pursuing a common understanding. If she insisted on keeping her "meaning" private, there would simply be no new understanding between the two of you. Therefore, it is important to keep in mind that the concept of *openness* does not imply that "anything goes."

One way to think of openness in the context of multicultural conversations involves openness to alternative interpretations, including interpretations of self and culture. We all have stories about ourselves, which are really stories about our experiences within our various cultures. Interestingly, our stories may not mean the same thing to us at the time of our experiences as they do later, after we have encountered new people and situations and reflected on these new experiences. A simple scenario may exemplify this concept of openness of meaning: Liz and John are high school sweethearts, who, like many teen-agers, believe they are destined to be together always. But several years later they have parted, gone to different colleges, initiated new relationships, and lost contact with each other. At this point, each of them may think of their former relationship as relatively insignificant, compared with what it meant to them years ago. However, even this interpretation is open to change: The circumstances of their lives may lead Liz and John to cross paths again, in which case their earlier acquaintance takes on great significance, whether as a foreshadowing of great joy or impending doom. Even if they do not meet again, their relationship will continue to have effects their lives, no matter how subtle, involuntary, or unconscious those effects may be. For example, feelings that may have been cultivated within the relationship, such as care, confidence, rejection, or confusion, may influence their perceptions of themselves, the ways they interact with others in the future, and so on. In a sense, then, the meaning of something is determined as much by the events that follow it as by those that precede it, and therefore, unless all events stop, no meaning is ever final.

In the same way that the passage of time may allow reinterpretation of the stories of our lives, conversing with others can also expose us to alternate interpretations. First, simply by telling our stories we may unwittingly discover (or create) new meanings in them. For instance, what you choose to say and what to omit, as well as other aspects of your narrative such as the tone and pitch of your voice, your gestures and cadence—all of these reflect your prejudices; so if you can listen to yourself as you try to tell "your story" to someone different from you, you may become more aware of your own beliefs, habits, and values, and how they have been influenced by your experiences. Second, by listening to others' stories and how they tell them, we may be able to understand our own experiences differently in contrast. We may realize, for instance, that we have taken something for granted that someone else describes with great reverence, or vice versa. Third, participants in multicultural conversations may be able to offer each other alternative interpretations to consider. These three features are the basis for the possibility of creating new understandings and meanings through multicultural conversations.

What is the difference between this kind of understanding and the effort to "get inside another's head"? Again, the main distinction is that a person committed to hermeneutic understanding acknowledges that every conversant (including oneself) is conditioned by different historical circumstances—that is, even among people of the same race or nationality, there are bound to be differences in gender, age, religion, socioeconomic class, education, and so on that have influenced the experiences each person has had and the meanings assigned to those experiences. Instead of trying to eradicate these differences, one must use one's own culturally conditioned prejudices to imagine another person's experience. In other words, a listener might respond to a story saying, "I know I haven't been there, but is what you are describing like when I . . . ?" The analogy the listener generates is inevitably an imperfect comparison, but once again, it is by exploring the differences between people's experiences that new meanings can be made.

One cultural prejudice of the West that we believe often disables understanding is the emphasis on *doubting* in critical thinking. Typically, ideas are considered rigorous only if they can stand up to a barrage of methodological doubt. In everyday conversations, this leads us to question other people's stories ("That didn't really happen—you're exaggerating") or their interpretations of their experiences ("You're being paranoid—he didn't mean anything by that comment/look/touch"). This is not to say that doubting is never appropriate; rather, it is overemphasized in Western thinking.[1] Doubting can convey suspicion, mistrust, and a lack of respect for another person; thus, when a person doubts before attempting to understand, what often results is an argument or a refusal to continue the conversation, neither of which is conducive to building understanding. Elbow (1986) described a method for reaching understandings that he calls the "believing game." This involves assuming that a speaker's perspective is valid, at least for that speaker, and attempting to understand for what experience the speaker's interpretation holds. Elbow (1986) explained:

> By methodological belief . . . I mean the disciplined procedure of not just listening but actually trying to believe any view or hypothesis that a participant seriously wants to advance. Imagine five or twenty-five of us sitting around a text. One person has an odd view. We must not just refrain from quarreling with it, we must try to believe it. If we have trouble, we ask for help from the few who do better. We ask them to explain—not defend. For example, if someone proposes that "Tyger, tyger, burning bright" with its glowing eye is really a strange new nineteenth-century steam engine with its bright headlight in the night, we must not ask, "What are your arguments for such a silly view as that" but rather, "What do you see when you see the text so? Give me the vision in your head. You are having an experience I don't have: Help me to have it." (pp. 260–261)

In the same way that the people in Elbow's example must attempt to believe another's interpretation of a text, participants in multicultural conversations must attempt to believe each other's interpretations of their own narratives, at least temporarily. Without this fundamental respect for other people's accounts of their lives, we are simply judging their stories by our own culturally conditioned standards, and therefore disabling understanding. On the other hand, commitment to the concept of openness of meaning can enable listeners to imagine new possibilities and develop new understandings.

---

[1]Belenky, Clincy, Goldberger, and Tarule (1985) argue that such overemphasis on doubting is gender-biased against women as well. Also see Garrison and Kimball (1993).

FUSION OF HORIZONS IN MULTICULTURAL CONVERSATIONS

So far we have characterized hermeneutic listening as a continuous, cyclical process by which we become more aware of ourselves as well as the unfamiliar "other," resulting in the mutual creation of new understandings and meanings. The point in the hermeneutic circle where new understandings are reached is what Gadamer called "fusion of horizons." A person's horizon is "the range of vision that includes everything that can be seen from a particular vantage point" (Gadamer, 1993, p. 302). This "range of vision" is determined by the prejudices (prejudgments) that we hold (or hold us) at a given moment. It is the set of possibilities that we can imagine within our framework of beliefs, habits, and values. Gadamer (1993) pointed out that "Applying this to the thinking mind, we speak of narrowness of horizon, of the possible expansion of horizon, of the opening up of new horizons, and so forth" (p. 302). Intuitively, it seems plausible that people's horizons are determined by their experiences, and that those who have encountered many different situations, beliefs, habits, values, will probably have a wider range of vision in imagining experiences and interpretations different from their own.

Given the openness of meaning discussed in the previous section and the fact that we continuously engage in new experiences, horizons are not static. "The horizon is, rather, something into which we move and that moves with us. Horizons change for a person who is moving" (Gadamer, 1993, p. 304). Any time we encounter situations that test our prejudices, our horizons are likely to be redefined.

The act of understanding involves the fusion of horizons. Gadamer (1993) explained that "to acquire a horizon means that one learns to look beyond what is close at hand—not in order to look away from it but to see it better, within a larger whole and in truer proportion" (p. 305). We broaden our horizons by looking at the landscapes of other people's lives, so to speak. It is important to distinguish this idea from the notion that one person's view must "win out" over another's. There is bound to be tension between two sets of prejudices, but "the hermeneutic task consists in not covering up this tension by attempting a naive assimilation of the two but in consciously bringing it out" (Gadamer, 1993, p. 306). Common understanding is something we create together, and the result is not something that is possessed by either party but rather a social construction shared by all.

So instead of dominating or being dominated, listening hermeneutically involves "rising to a higher universality that overcomes not only our own particularity but also that of the other" (Gadamer, 1993, p. 305). But this does not mean that fusing horizons erases all differences. As we have said, it is only through contact with another horizon that one's own becomes definable, but horizons are not necessarily reconcilable. Rather, to fuse horizons is to see one's own prejudices in a broader scope. In Gadamer's (1993) words, to "'have a horizon' means not being limited to what is nearby but being able to see beyond it. A person who has a horizon knows the relative significance of everything within this horizon, whether it is near or far, great or small" (p. 302).

Although we are talking about more than a physical horizon, a concrete analogy may help clarify the concept of fusion of horizons. Imagine standing on a mountainside on a clear day with another person, gazing at the view. In the distance there are several other mountain ridges, which eventually seem indistinguishable from the sky. After a moment, your companion exclaims, "I think that's the rock face that I climbed last month." Seeing your confusion, she points in the direction she is looking, but it seems to you that she could be referring to any number of rock formations in the distance. How do you respond? If you are not interested, you may just nod, or ignore her comment altogether. But if it is important to you to understand what she is saying, you will probably begin asking questions: "Do you mean that flat gray rock on the next ridge?" And as long as she remains interested in communicating, she will probably continue to refine her information: "No; see that road? Look to the left of it ...." Interestingly, neither of you will ever be absolutely certain that you are looking at the same point, but if you continue to converse cooperatively, at some point you will probably feel comfortable that you have reached a common understanding. In the process of describing what you are seeing and comparing your view with the other person's descriptions, both of you are most likely noticing details that you had not seen before, and learning to describe them more clearly. For that matter, in looking carefully at the landscape your companion may find that she was mistaken, and recognize a different rock face as the one she had climbed. Notice also that if your companion were to refuse to listen to your questions and descriptions, and instead only emphasized her own view by simply repeating it ("No! That rock, over there!"), reaching an understanding would be difficult and frustrating, and maybe even impossible. One final observation is that if the two of you are successful in reaching a common understanding, your new common focal point can provide an opportunity for further dialogue; for instance, your astonishment at the apparent difficulty of the climb may lead you to ask more questions, and through the answers you may learn as much about your companion (and yourself) as you do about rock climbing.

The connection between coming to an understanding regarding a literal vision and reaching understandings between different points of view should be quite clear. Both involve describing how we see things, listening to the other, and revising (or the re-vision of) our thoughts according to the new information we encounter. Neither situation requires denying our own points of view, or the prior knowledge and experiences that determine those points of view. As Stewart (1983) put it, "To conceptualize the event of interpretive listening as a 'fusion of horizons' is to emphasize the global breadth of prejudices that always affect one's interpreting, to highlight the open, fluid nature of those prejudices, and to underscore the fact that understanding is not a static state but a tensional event, a stasis defined by the contact of two lifeworlds" (p. 388). Fusion of horizons is the building of a common ground from which to create and sustain the dialogue. Once again, it is a mutual process that does not require the erasure of differences, and does not require one person to submit to the interpretations of the other(s). Thus, there is a major difference between this sort of hermeneutic listening and the conversation that seeks to colonize by imposing categories of understanding on others.

Throughout this text, readers will probably find many opportunities to produce new understandings through fusion of horizons. For instance, within the horizon of the dominant ("traditional") viewpoint, the "normal" family is defined as a father, a mother, and their biological offspring. The horizon, or range of vision, of someone whose vantage point is taken from within this traditional interpretation of the "normal" family may not be able to see any sense in what T. J. Stone and Katherine Allen have to say about feminism and alternative lifestyles in Chapters 3 and 12. They simply will not understand it, and perhaps they will reject it. But there are possibilities for expanding the horizon of the traditional vantage point, except where traditionalists will not listen, to preserve their advantage.

In a typical college classroom, many could speak of being "practically adopted" when they were young, perhaps by the parents of a good friend. Others were actually legally adopted. Several may have been cared for, at least for a time, by an aunt, uncle, grandparent, or older sibling. Still others may come from a single-parent family. A conversation in a college classroom about the "families" that the students came from would likely turn up many nontraditional family bonds. Because of the oppressive power of the norm, though, many would not want to talk about their nontraditional families. These variations are abnormal according to the traditional interpretation of *the family*. Yet all of them can, it is hoped, have at least one thing in common: The children were cared for by somebody. For those of you who tend toward the traditional definition of family, your ability to understand those with different experiences depends on whether you can stretch your concept of the meaning of family to include all of those who love and care for children with all their hearts. Notice, we are not asking you to affirm the "truth" of T. J. and Katherine's story (or anybody else's), but we believe you can begin to understand it. At the very least, your own prejudices, positive or negative, come into sharper focus through this process of fusing horizons.

LISTENING AND DEMOCRATIC DIALOGUE

Early in this chapter we stated that our identities are constituted by our prejudices. In our discussions of openness and fusion of horizons we have emphasized that if we are to engage in the process of understanding, these prejudices are continuously questioned in light of other people's beliefs, habits, and values. Our horizons shift as we encounter new ideas and see our own experiences in perspective with them. In short, to engage in hermeneutic listening is to challenge our views of ourselves, our culture, and other people—thereby risking our identities. Why should we put ourselves in such a position? Most especially, why should we listen in multicultural conversations where we are likely to encounter significant differences that challenge our worlds proportionally?

Sometimes, we seem to have little choice. It is as if we get "whacked in the head" by some unexpected encounter that we might have chosen to avoid if we could have seen it coming. For instance, in a recent television documentary, World War II veterans described what it was like to suddenly be literally face to face with the mythical enemy—close enough to see the other man's eyes. They described how this forced them to acknowledge for the first time that the opposing army was made up of young men similar to themselves, not the demented or savage creatures they had been encouraged to imagine. As soldiers, they were not seeking this new understanding at that time; in fact, for many it became difficult to continue fighting, haunted by new images of enemy soldiers as human beings with dreams of their own and families who would mourn their deaths.

In most cases, however, one's commitment to seeking understanding is a conscious choice. So the question remains, why would a person wish to listen, when to do so could potentially disrupt his or her life so drastically? We can think of at least three reasons that make such a risk worthwhile. First, education is all about challenging the comforts of familiarity to reach new understandings. The word *educate* comes from the Latin *educare*, to bring out. One cannot bring oneself out, one must be brought out through encounters with other people and events. So, if one is committed to being educated, then the phenomenon of change should be a familiar event.

Second, we have seen that we can only know ourselves insofar as we encounter those who are different. For instance, one who speaks only English is not likely to realize how his thoughts are constrained by the vocabulary and sentence structure of this language; however, once he encounters an untranslatable Spanish phrase, the limits of his own understanding may become more obvious. When our prejudices are tested by those who interpret their experiences differently, we become conscious of our own interpretive frameworks. In other words, we come to know ourselves through our encounters with others. Gilligan (1982) expressed this point: "These disparate visions in their tension reflect the paradoxical truths of human experience—that we know ourselves as separate only insofar as we live in connection with others, and that we experience relationship only insofar as we differentiate other from self" (p. 63).

Third, there are times when we find our narratives of self inadequate for the lives we wish to live. Anybody who has attempted to overcome shyness or some other characteristic is probably aware that such change in identity takes more than simply willing oneself to be different. It is through interactions with others that people can learn the new vocabulary they need to tell the stories of their lives differently—in other words, to become different people. Such change is social process, not an internal, individualistic event whereby some "central information processor" decides which aspects of one's personality to keep and which to discard.

So although there is some degree of risk involved in initiating and sustaining conversation with those who are ontologically different from us, achieving new understandings can also be exceedingly beneficial in terms of personal growth and development. Personally, for us, there is yet another way in which a productive (versus reproductive) view of understanding is appealing: It is compatible with the principles of democracy. The ideal on which democratic theory rests is that all people, rather than some elite group, should significantly contribute to the construction of their worlds; in other words, in a democracy meanings are co-produced. For example, according to the democratic ideal, one person (or culture) does not have the privilege of determining for all what is the one "right" way to live, or which experiences are to be valued over others. What distinguishes democracy from other forms of association is not that people vote—oppressive societies can hold elections, too— but that democracy values differences and resists the urge to measure people against some arbitrary cultural standard and, thus, enables people to create themselves through encounters with others.

CONCLUSION

Finally, we would like to point out a few of the ironies and paradoxes of writing this chapter. First, throughout this chapter we have referred favorably to concepts of multiculturalism, democracy, difference, and the desire to grow—all of which are our own cultural prejudices. Even the desire to understand others is a prejudice, and by no means is it universal. Furthermore, what we define as differences or sameness are also culturally conditioned prejudices. Is gender a significant "difference"? What about age or nationality? Some may consider differences in height or Zodiac sign or earned income to be significant in achieving understandings. What determines which "differences make a difference"? Finally, like all attempts at communication, we have invoked countless conventions to clarify our points, all of which reflect more of our prejudgments. For instance, our references to the works of other authors indicate our expectations of a primarily academic audience. Even the fact that we are writing in English and referring to ideas that are likely to be familiar to other English speakers, such as the Western Enlightenment, reflects our historically conditioned consciousness.

Obviously, we believe that these are enabling rather than disabling prejudices: They seem to enhance understanding rather than impede it. Nevertheless, to claim that these are universal or timeless ideas and ideals would be to contradict all that we have said so far. Rather, we view our position as built on historically situated concepts, and expect that in time they, too, will need to be reconstructed. It is our hope that readers will come to question some of their own prejudices through their encounter with these ideas, and create new understandings in the process.

REFERENCES

Belenky, M. F., Clinchy, B. M., Goldberger, N. R., & Tarule, J. M. (1985). *Women's ways of knowing*. New York: Basic Books.

Elbow, P. (1986). *Embracing contraries: Explorations in learning and teaching*. New York: Oxford University Press.

Gadamer, H. G. (1993). *Truth and method* (2nd ed.). New York: Continuum Publishing Company.

Garrison, J., & Kimball, S. (1993). Dialoguing across differences: Three hidden barriers. *Philosophy of Education 1993: Proceedings of the Forty-Ninth Annual Meeting of the Philosophy of Education Society*. Urbana, IL: Philosophy of Education Society.

Gilligan, C. (1982). *In a different voice*. Cambridge, MA: Harvard University Press.

Stewart, J. (1983). Interpretive listening: An alternative to empathy. *Communication Education, 32*(4), 379–391.

CHAPTER 3

A Feminist Perspective on Diversity

Taking Women's Voices Seriously

KATHERINE R. ALLEN

Noah's Wife Addresses the Department of Interior

Birds, though they sing
sweetly, can be hell
when cramped in cages.

Cats of all kinds
do not take well to boats.

All primates stink
albeit they are clever.
Giraffes are a pain
in the neck to feed.
Try it once, you'll see.

Chickens are dumb
and geese are mean.
Swans are not always graceful.

Bears are loners. Wolves
stick with their kind,
though elephants warm up
to strangers rather fast.

The snakes weren't half
as bad as I'd imagined.
Rats—though they, too, have
their place—most decidedly were.

The insects, I got used to,
though at first I forgot
and swatted a few. Lizards
are more temperamental
than turtles. Pigs make better
housemates than gazelles.

Now that we just have
a dog and a couple of goldfish,
the place seems kind of empty.
There's nothing to pet.

Of the whole menagerie,
I'd say I miss the zebras most.
One dove still visits
twice a year, though
considering the state
of affairs these days,
he is often a bit depressed.

When I think of what we
went through trying to keep
that whole damned zoo afloat—
the times I sat up all night
with a homesick horse, the time
all the deer and elk came
down with the croup

Of course, when the rainbow
arced new hope on the horizon,
I realized it had all been worthwhile.

But now, when I see
what we managed to save *progress*

Well, if I wasn't a God-fearing
woman, I swear, some days
I'd start praying for rain.

(Grace Bauer, 1992,
Noah's wife addresses the Department of Interior,
Frontiers: A Journal of Women's Studies, XIII(1), 167-168.)

Although women and family are viewed as synonymous in many of the stories we tell about our society, the reality of women's lives rarely matches the mystification of marriage and motherhood that serves as a standard against which real women and their families are judged (Baber & Allen, 1992). The everyday experiences of women and their families have been appropriated by the media, politicians, and scholars to benefit their professional interests. Inappropriate assumptions are made about marginalized groups of women by more powerful others who do not share any of the social characteristics or life circumstances of those whom they are investigating. Compare the biographies and opportunities of poor teen-age mothers with the researchers who are conducting studies *about* them (Burton, 1993). Feminists ask whose interests are served by research that is not explicitly *for* women (Acker, Barry, & Esseveld, 1983).

What do families look and feel like when described by women? In the poem "Noah's Wife Addresses the Department of Interior," Bauer (1992) illustrates how the silencing of women's voices in families is taken for granted. Although the story of Noah is well-known, how many of us have ever thought about his mate? How did she feel? What did she endure? What did she contribute to the world? Who was she as a person? What does it mean to be an essential player in family life but to have no recognized public voice apart from an androcentric view that women's place is in the home? To tell women's stories as distinct from stories about "THE family" (Scanzoni, Polonko, Teachman, & Thompson, 1989) requires us to suspend judgment about what "should be" to hear what "is." In this chapter, I will apply a feminist perspective to the subject of diversity in postmodern society by placing women and their experiences in the center of analysis.

TOWARD A GENDERED UNDERSTANDING

Given the lack of attention to women's perspectives on the family, we need to participate in an intellectual affirmative action by taking women's voices seriously (Bernard, 1987). The perspective that guides this analysis, postmodern feminism, holds in tension the differences and similarities among women, their partners, their children, and their closest affiliations (Baber & Allen, 1992). Although women as a group are devalued, which means they share a standpoint of gender oppression, each woman's life is mediated by other experiences such as age, socioeconomic status, race, and sexuality. By addressing women's perspectives, my aim is not to exclude male voices. The mystique of masculinity in our culture also oppresses and challenges men. Rather, my point is to begin with women—something that is rarely done—and to examine family life from the perspective of women as social actors in their own right, not just in terms of their prescribed roles as wives and mothers.

Men, as a group, may experience advantages related to their gender privilege, but feminist analyses by male scholars reveal that men suffer oppression under patriarchy and its accompanying masculine mystique (Kimmel & Messner, 1992). *Patriarchy* refers to the fact that men are dominant in social institutions and that male authority is protected and reinforced, but the precedent of institutionalized male power offers most men little control over their daily lives. Consider Goffman's account of the stigma of being less than the perfect man:

> There is only one complete unblushing male in America: a young, married, white, urban, northern, heterosexual Protestant father of college education, fully employed, of good complexion, weight, and height, and a recent record in sports. Every American male tends to look out upon the world from this perspective, this constituting one sense in which we can speak of a common value system in America. Any male who fails to qualify in any one of these ways is likely to view himself—during moments at least—as unworthy, incomplete, and inferior. (cited in Kimmel & Messner, 1992, p. 18)

A postmodern feminist perspective offers a way of seeing the complexity of gender in people's lives. Simplistic dichotomies between women and men are abandoned and replaced with ways of thinking about families that are sensitive to people's life experiences. A postmodern feminist perspective on family diversity suggests that knowledge about families must be reconstructed because certain voices have been excluded, historically and systematically. U.S. families are constantly changing; trends include the rise in single-parent households, the increase in the proportion of the population remaining single over the life course, delayed marriage, contracted childbearing years, relational careers in place of long-term marriage, the growing visibility of gay men and lesbians and their families, and the increased rates of divorce, cohabitation, and remarried families (Allen & Baber, 1992; Thornton, 1989). Yet the story of family life has been told from mythic sources that focus on an ever-narrowing but idealized version of what Goode (1956) termed "the classic family of Western nostalgia," reflecting little of the ethnic, racial, and gendered diversity of our population.

I define families by beginning with the perspectives of women; their experiences have been misrepresented and relegated to the empirical categories of "wife" and "mother." The distortions about women's lives do a disservice to the diversity of ways women connect with men, children, and other women in and out of family relationships over the life course. By reconstructing family experiences in the late 20th century from women's perspectives, a more realistic view of family diversity is possible. Families are a tangle of love and domination; the ways in which emotional and structural aspects of parenthood and other caring relations are experienced vary by gender (Baber & Allen, 1992; Ferree, 1990; LaRossa, 1988; Thompson & Walker, 1989). Although parenthood as an ideology is enshrined in sentiment, real mothers and fathers are expected to manage on their own without much societal support. Mothers are charged with the task of producing children who are acceptable to society, but they are given few tangible supports or rewards to carry out this invisible labor, and they are blamed when problems inevitably arise (Ruddick, 1989).

Family life is full of contradictions, such as the competing demands of paid and unpaid labor at work and at home; the complexity of choices involved in meeting individual, partner, and family needs; and the changing nature of caring relationships, in which women can now expect to spend more time caring for elderly parents than for young children. In contrast to positivist accounts of social organization, a postmodern feminist perspective does not treat race and gender merely as variables.

Rather, the interlocking systems of oppression and opportunity that structure individual and family lives according to race, class, gender, sexual orientation, physical capacity, and family status are recognized using this perspective.

As the next century approaches, families are adapting to far-reaching economic and social changes (Allen & Baber, 1992). Critical social issues, especially children's future well-being, are linked to the changing status of women and the changing priorities and opportunities of men. Antimodern social critics (Cheal, 1991) warn that the country should return to traditional gender roles to "save" the family from the selfish pursuits of individual members. They advocate for women's function in society to be mediated solely through their families, under the supervision of a husband, and in service to others. Feminist analyses, on the other hand, reveal the detrimental and often devastating effects that strict, traditional gender roles have on women's health and well-being. Traditional gender roles exploit women's labor by requiring a double burden of work at home and by limiting women's access to paid employment and the power that comes from earning a significant wage (Hochschild, 1989; Okin, 1989).

To begin a conversation about diversity with women's voices de-centers the assumed natural order of family life and exposes the alleged gender symmetry of "the family." In the prevailing or so-called traditional ideology of the family, men and women are presumed separate but equal. But, a gendered understanding of the family reveals how power affects intimate relationships in systematic ways and challenges "the symmetrical pseudomutuality of male and female," as Hare-Mustin (1989) observed: "What do we observe in opposition to man? Man or mouse? Man or beast? Man or superman? Man or child? Man or mountain? Man or machine? Man or woman? Which is the opposite?" (p. 69). Hare-Mustin's observation about the illogical equation of male and female as an essential dualism upsets the mystification that occurs in conversations about families. Even among the well-informed, assumptions about how men and women are supposed to function in families, at work, and in society are often rooted in stereotypes and myths and are resistant to change (Goode, 1982).

By deconstructing "the family" as a monolithic entity (Thorne, 1982), a feminist perspective breaks from this dualistic thinking that pits male against female. Paradoxically, because male experience is *the* standard for adulthood, men are seen as more "whole" than women, thus obscuring their dependence on women (Baber & Allen, 1992). Deconstruction is a method of analysis that involves taking apart "concepts and constructions of reality that are accepted as natural and unchangeable" (Baber & Allen, 1992, p. 13).

DECONSTRUCTING THE STANDARD OF MARITAL PERMANENCE

Individuals have different needs and expectations regarding intimate relationships, caregiving, and work. They construct widely diverse family relationships and connections with intimate partners. They make a multiplicity of choices about work and parenting. Family history reveals that there is no unitary experience in families (Coontz,

1992). No one standard exists against which all other families should be compared. Yet prevailing beliefs about family life—rooted in ideology, sentimentality, and myth—prescribe that intimate life should proceed in lock-step fashion. The concept of the family life cycle suggests that you are born, grow up, meet someone of the other gender, fall in love, get married, have children, one of you dies, and the other becomes widowed. This is the script or story we tell ourselves and each other, that our personal lives should reflect: one size fits all, one firm foundation for all families. Political rhetoric and public policies too often parrot this sentimentalized belief in one pathway to family survival, mental health, and social approval.

Even people who depart from this script may still measure themselves and others against its singular standard of marital permanence. But the paradox of permanence is that so very few of us are able or want to live up to this standard. Real life, compared with the "nostalgia myth" (Coontz, 1992), is complex and dynamic. Throughout history, a plurality of lifestyles and structures has been normative (Duberman, Vicinus, & Chauncey, 1989; Mintz & Kellogg, 1988); no one standard of family life exists.

The contemporary debate about the family, so tied to the changing lives of women, sets up a false dualism in which women's individual well-being is pitted against family survival. Family survival is measured by the permanence of marriage—particularly first marriage. Yet, looking at the lives of women and men who have lost jobs, partners, and children during the demographic, cultural, and economic shifts of the late 20th century (Stacey, 1990), it is clear that new standards are needed to evaluate our success in families. For example, divorce is not necessarily a personal failure or a rupture in the kin network. Divorce has the potential to extend kin relations, as Stacey (1990) found among the working class women she interviewed in California. Like the black women in Stack's (1974) urban ethnography 20 years before, these women turned former partners into new friends and extended family members to the benefit of their mutual children.

It is time to abandon the value-laden notion of "intact family" and take a more contextual approach to family configurations. Households have always had a malleable or accordion-like structure (Hareven, 1987), tied to the changing economic circumstances of family members. Families, in turn, are not passive recipients of change but shape the economy and the nature of employment by sending out mothers, fathers, youth, and other members to work in the paid labor force (Hareven, 1987).

POSTINDUSTRIAL SOCIETY AND POSTMODERN FAMILIES

The modern ideal of the family—nuclear and intact—is the form against which all families are compared, but it was only very popular for one decade, at least among white, middle-class Americans. During the postwar period from 1948 to 1958, about 60% of U.S. households corresponded to the corporate, political, and media-created ideal of a working husband, his stay-at-home wife, and their dependent children. The rise of the suburbs, the proliferation and subsequent downsizing of corporations, and the ideology of the nuclear, intact family reached its zenith during that period—and has been unraveling ever since (Cheal, 1991; Stacey, 1990).

Although most Americans do not live in the families that appear in magazines and textbooks, many cling to the romance of "till death do us part," in which first-time partners form commitments and rear children with each other for the rest of their lives. This romantic myth about lifelong family stability falsely equates stability with family harmony and resists the competing reality that a variety of intimate behaviors and lifestyles has always been practiced throughout history. Perhaps the only thing that changes over the years is the ease, willingness, and openness people feel in discussing and disclosing the diversity they live (Rubin, 1990).

At mid-century, the economy was shifting from the industrial era, which began about 150 years ago in the 19th century, to the current postindustrial era, which started in the 1950s. The economy went from heavy industries to nonunionized clerical and service industries, and new sectors, such as the computer industry (Stacey, 1990). Corporate employers sought and found cheap labor in the newly emerging suburbs among married women and mothers.

Widespread changing economic, social, legal, and political structures had great effect on families (Cheal, 1991; Stacey, 1990). The divorce rate, already on the rise since the turn of the 20th century, and in remission during the 1950s, picked up again. Divorce law reform permitted greater personal choice in adult intimate lifestyles. Women, following the anomalous demographic bulge of the 20-year baby boom of the postwar era, gained control of their fertility once more, after 1964, when the boom declined. Now mothers of young children, who were also mothers with few children, were working for wages in great numbers outside the home. They went back to school and entered the job force in record numbers, picking up where they left off after World War II. Of course, working class women and women of color never had the chance to leave the work force; they have always had a double day of family work and market work (Dill, 1988).

Marginalized groups, forming as autonomous social movements, experienced renewed activism borne out of frustration with the status quo (Ferguson, 1991). The demand for basic civil rights escalated, rooted in the anger, betrayal, and impatience felt by many African-Americans who had been promised real improvements for too long and who were mobilized for change. Women were alerted to the feminine mystique (Friedan, 1963), realizing that they had little authority in their families and society, yet were held responsible for nearly all of the problems. New terms were invented for what mothers were doing wrong, and the blaming of women for social ills (as in the concepts "codependence" and "broken home") continues today.

In the late 20th century, society is characterized by unanticipated changes in the broader social structure. Most Americans can no longer expect to surpass their parents in terms of education, income, and occupation, the three traditional ways in which socioeconomic achievement has been measured. The changes include escalating inflation, a shrinking middle class, the prohibitive cost of home ownership for all but the wealthy in most urban and suburban areas, and job insecurity due to layoffs, plant shutdowns, and the ever-changing nature of work life, with new occupations arising and established ones made obsolete overnight (Ehrenreich, 1989; Stacey, 1990).

In spite of these complex changes, women continued to hold their families together, sometimes with the support of their male partners and sometimes without it. Some women escaped the tyranny of the unitary standard of marriage, leaving empty-shell marriages and living singly or sharing a lesbian partnership with another woman. Some men really listened and found that they, too, desired an egalitarian relationship. They adopted the label "feminist" for themselves and worked to end the gender oppression that limited women's opportunities (Blaisure & Allen, 1995).

FAMILIES AND DIVERSITY

Diversity is the real permanent feature of family life in U.S. history. If there is any one standard that Americans have followed throughout history, it is the inevitability of change. The "textbook family" (Mancini & Orthner, 1988) reflects the myth of the "good old days," and stands in sharp contrast to the reality of diverse family structures and processes.

Regarding family structure, diversity includes dual-career families, single-parent families, teen-age parent families, and blended families (Coleman, 1991). Specific examples include a young black mother whose nonresidential male partner co-parents her child, an interracial couple with an adopted child, lesbian mothers with a child conceived through donor insemination, four generations of female kin under one roof, a divorced–extended family in which a child interacts regularly with two sets of parents and multiple sets of grandparents, and a lifelong single woman caring for her aging mother.

New descriptions are needed to define family structures that do not necessarily link marriage and parenthood. It is often assumed that there are uniform rates of father absence in the homes established by teen-age mothers, particularly those of African-American origin. Yet, Mott (1990) has conducted an analysis of the National Longitudinal Survey of Youth to examine family transitions in terms of paternal presence or absence in homes without a biological father. The data, drawn from women ages 14 to 21, showed that for all races, 60% of children of unmarried mothers are likely to have at least weekly contact with their nonresident fathers or other father figures, such as their mother's new partner. Although the biological father may not reside with the mother, many children still have contact and support from fathers and father figures. By considering demographics other than marital status, these analyses are more sensitive to the realistic, complex, and diverse ways in which women and men join in parenting their children.

Turning to family process can shed light on the high divorce and migration rate among families. Individuals have high expectations for the therapeutic aspect of family life and can become impatient or demand change if emotional needs are not met. Psychological pressures in family life contribute to a desire to change one's relationships if those relationships are perceived to be unhappy (Demo, 1992; Glenn, 1990). It is not that marriage is no longer valued. Rather, therapeutic relationships are so important that individuals are willing to discard partners in which relationships are not emotionally fulfilling, even if they are working economically (Ehrenreich, Hess, & Jacobs, 1986).

During the 1980s and '90s, as many people have been getting comfortable with diverse ways of living, working, and caring for children, a political backlash has emerged, trying to curtail the acceptance of family diversity. This backlash has launched a shameless attack on U.S. women, playing unfairly with the facts (Faludi, 1991). Its political supporters seek to deny family diversity and thus dismantle special programs for families. However, the backlash cannot stop certain realities that contemporary families live with daily: Women's lives are characterized by intricate patterns of family relationships and responsibilities; family life is tension-filled; although families are a source of satisfaction, growth, and fulfillment for many, they can also be an arena of domination, abuse, and pain; and women and their families need real resources, not sentimentality and lip-service to quaint family values and empty promises (Baber & Allen, 1992). Ferguson (1991) suggested that women, blacks, lesbians and gays, and members of many other autonomous social movements join across their differences and form coalitions of support to empower themselves and work for social change.

A Feminist Vision for Families

Feminism interweaves theory and practice to facilitate social change. Like other groups who envision a safer, more equitable society, feminists are committed to practical solutions to improve the life chances and well-being of all members of society (Baber & Allen, 1992). A goal that most feminists can agree with is improving life for all people by redistributing the power and rewards of society more equitably. At the same time, feminists attend to gender oppression, working first to name and recognize women's subordination as well as to define and revise visions for a more inclusive world. Baber and Allen (1992) proposed four themes that provide pragmatic strategies to broaden women's options. These strategies constitute a plan of action to empower women and their families in ways that strengthen women's voices and enhance their opportunities to be heard in conversations about diversity.

First, women—like men—require economic autonomy. Having one's own income helps a woman have a voice in her intimate relationships, resist abuse and domination, leave an oppressive relationship, and achieve positions from which to influence policies and programs that can help others (Okin, 1989). Although working has always been a necessity for women, economic autonomy cannot be achieved unless social supports are available for more than just elite women. At a minimum, government-subsidized, high-quality, affordable child care must be available to families with young children so that women are as free as men to pursue paid work.

Second, relational choice and equality are necessary so that women and men can make authentic choices about the intimate relationships that best fit their own needs and orientations. Traditional patriarchal marriage, in which the wife is a "junior partner," has been considered the bedrock of stable family relationships, but traditional marriage, in which women lack power, is not in women's best interest. Women are vulnerable by marriage, and their vulnerability increases when they have young children, when they are not employed full-time or long-term, and when they divorce (Okin, 1989). Relationships modeled on the equality and mutuality of a best friendship, such as feminist marriages and the cohabiting unions of heterosexual and same-sex couples, hold more promise for growth and stability than traditional, gender-structured marriage.

Third, women's equality is linked to their reproductive freedom, and their ability to achieve economic autonomy is limited by their lack of reproductive control. If women are to have the same educational and occupational opportunities as men, they must be able to plan the timing and number of the children they bear.

Fourth, all individuals deserve the right to lifelong education for a critical consciousness. Education from birth is needed to prepare all people for the realities of postindustrial society. Young people need valid and practical information, counteracting the myth that ignorance will keep them safe. Society cannot afford to teach a traditional view of the family that presumes that sexuality, marriage, and parenthood automatically go together. Diverse families need acknowledgment and social support, not condemnation or mere tolerance.

Surprisingly, these modest proposals are considered controversial. Yet, the values underlying these proposals—equality, choice, and education—are necessary for wise decision-making and empowerment (Baber & Allen, 1992). Women are sprouting some odd branches in the family tree (Stacey, 1990), often relinquishing traditional marriage and creating relationships based on mutual respect and personal freedom. They are integrating the needs of self and others in a society where social and behavioral scripts are in flux.

Diverse families face an uphill climb in terms of gaining acceptance and their fair share of societal resources. What are practical ways that educators can respond? Family practitioners should avoid the extreme assessments of Pollyannas or doomsayers in considering new proposals for policy, advocacy, and change (Mancini & Orthner, 1988). Bronfenbrenner and Weiss (1983) suggested several proposals for change to help parents and thus support child development and growth. One proposal is a curriculum of caring in the schools so that every child begins early in life to know how to care for and about other living beings. One gender or one race should not have the unique experience of having their needs met by some other subordinated group.

CONCLUSION

When we focus on families from the perspectives of women, feminist concerns are evident. What do women want? I cannot speak for every woman, but I can share my own wish list: a safe home, a cooperative workplace free from harassment, a full voice in my own governance, healthy children in my life, the peace of knowing my loved ones are secure, and an end to oppression. In thinking about the future, we must not forget the past. Historical amnesia about the legacy of institutionalized oppression limits the life chances and choices of contemporary individuals (Lorde, 1984). We need to look back on history and face the painful experience of recognizing that we, as a diverse people, have discriminated against and constrained the lives of others who may not be or look like ourselves (Ferguson, 1991). Even as women have made great strides in this century, an incredible backlash has surfaced to blame them for their own struggles, all the while ignoring culprits much more formidable than women's quest for full personhood. These culprits include economic injustices, archaic ideas about women's proper place, a culture that is repressive and exploitive about sexuality, the condoning of violence against children in families and social institutions, and the stain of racial and class prejudice and exploitation that is woven into the fabric of our society and culture.

Acknowledging these injustices and in taking responsibility for resolving them requires wisdom and courage. Moral action involves making decisions that "do no violence to self or other" (Gilligan, 1982). As we approach the 21st century, we confront the tension between our own needs for well-being and those who have fewer resources to draw on in the struggle for survival. Women have been leading the way toward the postmodern revolution of families, creating unusual structures and arrangements that defy neat description (Stacey, 1990). Perhaps we can take a page from the book of those educated black women who, 100 years ago, founded the National Association of Colored Women's Clubs. "Lifting as we climb" was their model for racial uplift and social change (Collins, 1990, p. 149).

As more of us learn to attend to the diversity in families that women have been responsible for dealing with all along, let us wonder aloud about things we do not understand, ask each other about the realities of our own lives, and really care enough to listen to the responses. Perhaps then we will feel comfortable with the inevitability of change that goes on around us, sometimes at a terrifying and unprecedented rate. Most of all, let us be careful with our own and each other's lives. Thinking about families from women's perspectives is a way to open up new conversations about diversity and propose more effective strategies for social change.

REFERENCES

Acker, J., Barry, K., & Esseveld, J. (1983). Objectivity and truth: Problems in doing feminist research. *Women's Studies International Forum, 6,* 423–435.

Allen, K. R., & Baber, K. M. (1992). Starting a revolution in family life education: A feminist vision. *Family Relations, 41,* 378–384.

Baber, K. M., & Allen, K. R. (1992). *Women and families: Feminist reconstructions.* New York: Guilford.

Bauer, G. (1992). Noah's wife addresses the Department of Interior. *Frontiers: A Journal of Women's Studies, XIII*(1), 167–168.

Bernard, J. (1987). Re-viewing the impact of women's studies on sociology. In C. Farnham (Ed.), *The impact of feminist research in the academy* (pp. 193–216). Bloomington: Indiana University Press.

Blaisure, K. R., & Allen, K. R. (1995). Feminists and the ideology and practice of marital equality. *Journal of Marriage and the Family, 57,* 5–19.

Bronfenbrenner, U., & Weiss, H. B. (1983). Beyond policies without people: An ecological perspective on child and family policy. In E. F. Zigler, S. L. Kagan, & E. Klugman (Eds.), *Children, families and government: Perspectives on American social policy* (pp. 393–414). London: Cambridge.

Burton, L. M. (1993). Teenage childbearing as an alternative life-course strategy in multigenerational black families. In R. A. Pierce & M. A. Black (Eds.), *Life-span development: A diversity reader* (pp. 163–176). Dubuque, IA: Kendall/Hunt.

Cheal, D. (1991). *Family and the state of theory.* Toronto: University of Toronto Press.

Coleman, M. (1991). Planning for the changing nature of family life in schools for young children. *Young Children, 46*(4), 15–20.

Collins, P. H. (1990). *Black feminist thought: Knowledge, consciousness, and the politics of empowerment*. Boston: Unwin Hyman.

Coontz, S. (1992). *The way we never were: American families and the nostalgia trap*. New York: Basic.

Demo, D. H. (1992). Parent–child relations: Assessing recent changes. *Journal of Marriage and the Family, 54*, 104–117.

Dill, B. T. (1988). Our mothers' grief: Racial ethnic women and the maintenance of families. *Journal of Family History, 13*, 415–431.

Duberman, M., B., Vicinus, M., & Chauncey, G. (Eds.). (1989). *Hidden from history: Reclaiming the gay & lesbian past*. New York: NAL Books.

Ehrenreich, B. (1989). *Fear of falling: The inner life of the middle class*. New York: Pantheon.

Ehrenreich, B., Hess, E., & Jacobs, G. (1986). *Re-making love: The feminization of sex*. Garden City, NY: Anchor.

Faludi, S. (1991). *Backlash: The undeclared war against American women*. New York: Crown.

Ferguson, A. (1991). *Sexual democracy: Women, oppression, and revolution*. Boulder, CO: Westview.

Ferree, M. M. (1990). Beyond separate spheres: Feminism and family research. *Journal of Marriage and the Family, 52*, 866–884.

Friedan, B. (1963). *The feminine mystique*. New York: Dell.

Gilligan, C. (1982). *In a different voice*. Cambridge, MA: Harvard University.

Glenn, N. D. (1990). Quantitative research on marital quality in the 1980s: A critical review. *Journal of Marriage and the Family, 52*, 818–831.

Goode, W. J. (1956). *Women in divorce*. New York: Free Press.

Goode, W. J. (1982). Why men resist. In B. Thorne & M. Yalom (Eds.), *Rethinking the family: Some feminist questions* (pp. 131–150). New York: Longman.

Hareven, T. K. (1987). Historical analysis of the family. In M. B. Sussman & S. K. Steinmetz (Eds.), *Handbook of marriage and the family* (pp. 37–57). New York: Plenum.

Hare-Mustin, R. T. (1989). The problem of gender in family therapy theory. In M. McGoldrick, C. M. Anderson, & F. Walsh (Eds.), *Women in families: A framework for family therapy* (pp. 61–77). New York: W. W. Norton.

Hochschild, A. R. (1989). *The second shift*. New York: Viking.

Kimmel, M. S., & Messner, M. A. (Eds.). (1992). *Men's lives* (2nd ed.). New York: Macmillan.

LaRossa, R. (1988). Fatherhood and social change. *Family Relations, 37*, 451–457.

Lorde, A. (1984). *Sister outsider*. Freedom, CA: Crossing Press.

Mancini, J. A., & Orthner, D. K. (1988). The context and consequences of family change. *Family Relations, 37*, 363–366.

Mintz, S., & Kellogg, S. (1988). *Domestic revolutions: A social history of American family life*. New York: Free Press.

Mott, F. L. (1990). When is a father really gone? Paternal-child contact in father-absent homes. *Demography, 27*, 499–517.

Okin, S. M. (1989). *Justice, gender and the family*. New York: Basic.

Rubin, L. B. (1990). *Erotic wars: What happened to the sexual revolution*. New York: Farrar, Straus & Giroux.

Ruddick, S. (1989). *Maternal thinking*. Boston: Beacon.

Scanzoni, J., Polonko, K., Teachman, J., & Thompson, L. (1989). *The sexual bond: Rethinking families and close relationships*. Newbury Park, CA: Sage.

Stacey, J. (1990). *Brave new families: Stories of domestic upheaval in late twentieth century America*. New York: Basic.

Stack, C. B. (1974). *All our kin: Strategies for survival in a black community*. New York: Harper Colophon.

Thompson, L., & Walker, A. J. (1989). Gender and families. *Journal of Marriage and the Family, 51*, 845–871.

Thorne, B. (1982). Feminist rethinking of the family: An overview. In B. Thorne & M. Yalom (Eds.), *Rethinking the family: Some feminist questions* (pp. 1–24). New York: Longman.

Thornton, A. (1989). Changing attitudes toward family issues. *Journal of Marriage and the Family, 51*, 873–893.

CHAPTER 4

Weaving Multiculturalism into the Fabric of the Community

KAREN DEBORD

As an extension home economist in rural southwest Virginia in the early 1980s, my mission was to help families improve their quality of life. I worked with other extension home economists, social service personnel, and family members who were representative of the people living in the community. We kept a file that the Cooperative Extension Service called the "all reasonable efforts" file. In this file, we documented audiences that we worked with each week, month, and year. We kept a running tally of head counts by gender and race.

Extension was probably one of the first service agencies to actually try planning with ALL people in mind. The affirmative action law mandated that extension personnel develop specific inclusive planning strategies. What happened, it seems to me, is that a plan was put in place, but reality did not fit the plan. As I reflect on the combined educational mission of Extension and the dual government requirement of documenting "all reasonable efforts" to include more males in a traditionally female program (homemaking at that time) and to include more minorities from a community with a 3.8% minority population, I question some of my actions.

I was well aware that there was a black church in the community. I had been advised that contacting the leadership of this church was a way to help determine community and family needs and to plan educational programs to meet the needs of the black community. I had been advised that planning publicly advertised programs that were "open to all people" and scheduling events and educational programs in handicapped-accessible community centers and public buildings met the specifications of "all reasonable efforts."

However, the phone calls I made to the black preacher went unreturned, and the educational meetings that I planned for family members were attended only by the white majority. I now wonder why my contacts with the black church were unsuccessful? Was I really relieved when the preacher did not call back? Why didn't I seek out community members in a different way? Did my shyness around new people get in the way of making these contacts or was there something more? Was I really prepared if minority leadership showed up at a planning meeting? Would it have made "regular" participants uncomfortable and decrease the participation of the established audience?

Despite the lack of minority involvement, I continued documenting all my "all reasonable efforts" as valid. I realize now that I may indeed have been apprehensive and ill-prepared to open the dialogue and devote time to conversation that could have moved the community into a different realm. I was not aware of the ecological makeup of intertwined systems that created a domino effect in the community. Until we take the risk to open the conversation, communities will continue to function in a disconnected fashion with well-intentioned elected, appointed, and employed community leaders simply meeting the demands of all their "all reasonable efforts" file. In this chapter, I compare what I know now about prejudice, racism, and multiculturalism, with the model for community work and empowerment.

COMMUNITY INVOLVEMENT

With growing interest, and in the name of multicultural education, communities are devoting special attention and resources to spotlighting various cultures. In reality, multicultural education is not just a topic taught in school, an equal-rights file kept by a social agency, a sexual harassment policy, or an international festival organized by a community. Multicultural education involves a sense of shared respect and community understanding that can open the door for enriching conversations among groups and individuals. For a true understanding and acceptance of multiculturalism, the concept of multiculturalism must be woven into the fabric of the community.

Hooks (1989) wrote that we should undertake social actions that celebrate, acknowledge, and affirm differences and variety. According to the community leaders we will hear from in this chapter, these social actions are crystallized through multiple discussions between and among community members. Plans are then made to design practices that demonstrate acceptance of individuals in families, classrooms, workplaces, and larger communities. As with any conversation, this construction of community understanding and acceptance begins with individuals who possess unique perspectives and who hold respected community roles as educators, parents, business leaders, or decision makers.

In this chapter I address inclusive strategies for developing communities with a focus on diversity. These strategies have been expressed by community leaders who share their experiences developing connectedness in contexts in which a sense of community is lacking. Bronfenbrenner's (1979) ecological systems model provided a basic thread that was woven throughout the community-building strategies.

Defining Community

A *social ecological framework* is an operative, community-based approach that lends understanding and appreciation to human behavior in various contexts (Bronfenbrenner, 1979). This approach forms the basis for broadening understanding and acceptance of the interrelatedness of various individuals, cultures, and lifestyles, while providing a constructive path for designing community education programs. If a clear understanding of the fluid linkages within a community exists, then issues of concern to individuals and families are woven into all individual life stages, family types, and economic, social, and political ideologies associated with each structure in U.S. society.

A total community comprises individuals connected by some common thread of interest, proximity, or characteristic. Communities vary in a range of individual factors: age, ethnicity, and family size. They also vary by the services available, economic conditions, job opportunities, health, and child-care options. Bronfenbrenner, Moen, & Garbarino (1984) suggested that within communities a feeling of common identity exists, a "spirit of interdependence and interconnectedness; a safe diverse space where individuals and groups are allowed to unconditionally invest in a process to explore differences, needs, and interests" (p. 286).

THE ECOLOGICAL PERSPECTIVE

Bronfenbrenner (1979) visually depicted multiple societal systems as concentric circles. The innermost circle of the ecological environment, the *microsystem,* represents the most direct day-to-day reality for children and families, such as their home, school, or neighborhood settings. Individuals within this systems are dynamic and in continual development. Linkages or interrelationships between settings (i.e., home, school, workplace, neighborhood) are called *mesosystems*. Although depicted as a separate circle, mesosystems represent reciprocity and interaction between individuals and their multiple environments.

In a separate circle, *exosystems* refer to one or more settings that do not directly involve a person, but do have an effect. Examples include a parent's workplace and its indirect effect on a child, or a community network of friends who support one another. The outermost circle or system is referred to as the *macrosystem*. The macrosystem represents broad interconnected beliefs, attitudes, and social systems such as economics, media, immigration, or public policy decisions. Within any culture or subculture, settings of a given kind (homes, schools, churches) tend to be similar; however, between cultures, settings are distinctively different. These complicated systems, referred to as *cultural blueprints,* underlie institutional organizations, people's attitudes and assumptions, and the workings of political and economic systems (Bronfenbrenner, 1979). These blueprints, however, can be modified. Garbarino (1982) contended that it is possible to "socially engineer" systems to cope with differences and developmental problems. This possibility for change is the door that many communities are trying to open to maximize the development of children and families.

Some community leaders are making strides to engineer public attitude relative to multicultural understanding, although it is a lengthy and sensitive process. The key to successful negotiation between settings is to first recognize the co-existence of subsystems and linkages between mesosystems that are already woven together in many integrated ways (Bronfenbrenner et al., 1984).

MAXIMIZING COMMUNITY SYSTEMS DEVELOPMENT

The following set of assumptions taken from Bronfenbrenner's (1979) work support what community leaders indicate are major factors in creating a sense of community. Bronfenbrenner hypothesized that to maximize the developmental potential between systems, we must assure that the demands on individuals in different settings are compatible. This echoes Hawkesworth (1989), who asserted that what we know and how we know depends on our role or position in the social hierarchy. When changes occur in settings, changes also occur in the individuals positions or roles in that new setting. For example, transition in roles occur when new parents are presented with their newborn child. A change in role for a working individual occurs when there is a change in jobs or after retirement. Roles must be in agreement with what the individual can manage.

According to Bronfenbrenner, another component to maximizing developmental potential between individuals is assuring that supportive linkages between settings and that an individual's entry into a new setting is made in the company of one or more persons with whom she or he has participated in other settings. The link with an unfamiliar group or individual can be eased through others. Locating someone who is at ease in both settings and knowledgeable about both environments can build bridges between settings and between people. Such a person is a *primary link,* one who can help provide entry for newcomers into new settings and also help in translating the dialogue between people with different languages, beliefs, communication styles, and cultures.

The most productive mode of communication between settings is personal or face-to-face. To build multicultural communities, open communication between settings must be evident with as much inclusion of family members in the communications network as possible. Entry into new settings without two-way communication and supportive linkages can lead to imbalances between systems and, perhaps, to misplaced decisions. Misunderstanding at decision points is another point at which dialogue is obviously critical. An example of a supported transition is when a person in a position of authority or power, before making a decision, consults with others who can lend understanding of and insight into the issue at hand. Greene (1993) stated that to understand the problem, we must hear from the people who are critically involved in the process, rather than the so-called experts. Individuals who have experienced multiple ecological transitions among settings can provide valuable input but be ignored for their unique and privileged vantage point (Baber & Allen, 1992).

Positive changes between individuals and systems are secure when changes produced in an individual carry over into other settings. Teachers report examples of transitions between settings when adolescents who learn about conflict resolution at school attempt to assuage flaring tempers at home. Additional evidence of transpiring changes include linkages between settings that encourage growth, trust, goal consensus, and a continual appraisal of new information. An example would include policy makers seeking the opinions of those affected by the policy.

Further evidence of developmental change is a shift in the balance of power. For a shift in power to occur, individuals and groups must yield personal power and begin trusting emerging power structures. Any parent who has paused to question a childrearing decision in light of the child's opinion has struggled with feelings of power and control over valid arguments for alternative solutions.

PERSONAL EXAMPLES OF COMMUNITY CONTEXTS

Stories and testimonials are actually teaching and learning techniques. Stories are a way to reflect on individual life episodes and to provide a rich accounting of human experience. They are quickly evolving as central elements in research (Carter, 1993). In storytelling, the object is not only to share, but also to reconstruct new personal meanings. Through this process, self-awareness can increase while individuals build new contexts of understanding (Allen & Farnsworth, 1993). Sharing personal accounts also can build bridges between functional systems and move individuals toward a broadened understanding of others. We can view events from various angles, view ourselves in varying roles, and analyze the influence of multiple environments. The following section details stories from two community leaders who were asked to reflect on community building processes. These stories demonstrate a ways to increase potential for multicultural experiences in communities.

One of the two interviews was with L. Jones, an African American female who directs a Youth Alliance in St. Joseph, Missouri, the major city in a county with a population of 84,000. The second interview was with B. Gines, an African American male who works as an assistant school superintendent in a large urban school district in Missouri. Both were asked to respond to the following:

1. What is the meaning of "community"?
2. How do community leaders create respect for diversity?
3. Please share a story that illustrates how you have arrived at this understanding.

The Story of L. Jones

"Community" is people working together, communication, trust, honesty, and a willingness to share. Being connected to each other can inspire and create an atmosphere of separate but equal.

Community leaders can create respect for diversity through their unconditional acceptance and willingness to invest in the process of developing an understanding of the many aspects of culture and differences. We don't have to always change things. We get caught up in personal perceptions of others. People can't all have the same values. Having different beliefs and values doesn't mean that people who are different from us are hateful or disgusting. They are just different. My grandmother taught me the golden rule. Treat people the way you want to be treated. But instead, we treat people the way we think they should be treated.

In relationships I have had, there's an element of caring and "letting people be." To care, we have to work on it every day. There are constant challenges in how we relate. "Letting people be" and valuing them even if we can't agree with them is what I want to see in our leaders.

Bias is another element that must be approached. I thought our group was progressing until I kept getting complaints about group members. They had not fully understood one another nor disclosed their personal feelings. I noticed it when we were planning the cultural diversity event at the park. There was some grumbling about others' attitudes and the event was not well attended. So we went back and talked through our personal beliefs some more and worked through some things. We decided we needed broader representation, to identify and focus on a specific goal of the event, and to increase our visibility through community awareness.

Collaboration is a process, not a goal. It may take three to four years to communicate and coordinate before you can collaborate—don't give up. Community partnerships are more empowering. There must be a shared vision with all partners.

Reflecting on how she arrived at her personal understanding, Jones shared this story:

My mother and my grandmother both graduated from college. Two generations of black women with degrees was fairly unheard of back then. After my mother graduated from University of Nebraska in 1954 with her degree in interior design, she applied for a job with a prominent interior decorating company. When she went to talk to them, they indicated they had filled the position, but that they needed someone to clean on the premises three days a week. She let them know she hadn't gone to school and graduated to become a "cleaning lady!" Mom became bitter towards them. Then this bitterness spread to others. My sisters seemed to have taken on my mother's values, but it has been more of an inner struggle for me.

Although she didn't preach to me, she implied the need to be "on guard," to "be better and to protect myself." But I grew up and developed a different awareness. I found that all people were not bitter like my mother. I became drawn to people different from me. I found that even folks from within your "own people" can be hurtful. I had to develop my own definition and awareness of folks in general.

I aspired to be like both of my grandmothers. One grandmother taught me the "finer" things—art, enunciation, and so on. And she taught me about people. She taught me to be cautious because I didn't have power, but that everyone is not the same. My other grandmother taught me wisdom through her common sense. She taught me to "believe in me and everything else would fall into place." She taught me to accept folks, but to accept me first. She instilled in me the value of giving of oneself to others and enriching others' lives.

I am trying to be sensitive to my children's needs as they develop into adults and to be able to accept them and their values. My children have gained some of this, but they also have some of the bitterness of the '90s. Some of the bitterness can go back to the old saying, "When the river is low, the horses bite each other." It's true. Consider the Los Angeles riots. When times are bad—no jobs, poor economy—people lash out and burn their own stuff and hurt their own people.

In the year 20,000, maybe we will have it right!

In this story, Jones' mother provides an example of an ecological imbalance between mesosystems: the potential employer and her personal belief system. The outcome of the workplace bias was, in turn, passed on to another generation. Bronfenbrenner (1979) indicated that mesosystems must be mutually supportive and individuals must be compatible in the demands of their roles. Clearly, mutual support and compatibility of roles was absent.

In time, Jones found support from extended family that allowed her to freely reach out into new settings. The partnering and support of the grandmothers raised her level of personal comfort, allowing her entry into new settings leading to greater human exchange and social potential. This has empowered her today and is reflected in her own leadership style, which is filtered with a sense of caring and mutual understanding and support between systems.

The definition of *community* Jones provides has commonalities with that of Bronfenbrenner et al. (1984), particularly in the elements of common identity and fate. The experiences shared from the community process focused on a need to directly deal with personal bias of the leadership team, to assure community inclusion and broad community awareness. These are critical steps. Jones might not have had the insight into or personal motivation to invest in the community process without her personal and privileged vantage point.

B. Gines is an assistant superintendent of schools in urban Missouri. He proudly indicated that theirs is one of very few school districts to have adopted a district diversity plan. Ninety-eight recommendations made by a now-disbanded committee were approved. Currently an ad hoc committee oversees the implementation of the plan. During a telephone interview, Gines shared the following thoughts:

The Story of B. Gines

Community is a distinct identity of people interdependently involved in meaningful interaction. To build a sense of community, an exploration of the community's distinct identity is necessary. This takes time. My one piece of advice is to go slow, take your time, don't go too fast or people will be resentful. Be patient. The most difficult thing about our community is that it is transient. Last year there were 200 new kids out of 550 in one year. This degree of transience does not lend itself to building a sense of community.

Community leaders can create respect for diversity by assuring that they communicate what they stand for to others. If this does not happen, then people form their own conclusions, often incorrect. Leaders are exemplified by their sincerity and their willingness to sacrifice time and be proactive, giving more than just lip service to the effort. Every teacher, as a key player in a child's life, should develop a sensitivity for others. There is no way that teachers can be effective without recognizing different needs of students. Some groups merely communicate. Communication leads to learning and problem solving. A higher level of group processing is cooperation. Cooperation leads to coordination of people and resources to achieve individual objectives. The group interaction level at which most community programs are most successful and more fully institutionalized is when efforts are collaborative. Collaboration leads to integration and a systems change. There is shared vision, shared resources and shared accountability among all players.

Having a plan gives focus and direction. The working group focuses on the goals of the group instead of obstacles. Another element is to assure that students experience various relationships outside the school setting with others who are different from them. We have strategically planned some of these events (school swap programs and teen lock-ins).

At first, we viewed each school as an island. There was no collaboration. We recognized that the image portrayed by one school reflected on the whole school district. Collaboration plays a significant role in developing a sense of community. Building a sense of community means we are interdependent. We sink together or we swim together. We try to deliver and sell a sound message of interdependence.

Reflecting on how he arrived at his personal understanding, Gines shared this story:

My parents taught me to work hard and always give my best. That is almost an extinct attitude these days. In high school, I was on the wrestling team. I had always been a team member and supported the team. I was the only black kid on the team. The rest of the team was friendly. We hung out together, we'd laugh and joke around. I found out that when I was with them, they were nice, but when I wasn't they would talk to me behind my back. When I was the only one on the team to win the state championship, the rest of the guys shunned me. They stopped associating with me.

I wonder if what happened then is what seems to happen now with older students. It seems that the elementary school kids get along no matter the class, race, or ethnicity. But as kids get older, they polarize. When a white kid is hanging out with black kids, the other white kids say, "Are you trying to be black?" And when the black kid is hanging out with the white kids, the black kids say, "Are you trying to be white?" So kids then get caught in the middle of their peers, are forced to decide, and choose those most like themselves.

Gines' experiences as a teen-ager carried over into his adult life. Being accepted among the wrestling friends was comfortable, but in winning the state championship, Gines experienced what Bronfenbrenner (1979) refers to as role transition. *Role transition* is a "shift in a person's position in the ecological environment as a result of a change in role, setting, or both" (p. 103). Additionally, the question Gines poses about teens choosing between associating with one racial group or another may be expanded with Bronfenbrenner's hypothesis that transitions of people between settings depends on the reasons for leaving old settings, coupled with the challenges involved in remaining in the new setting and the support found in that setting.

Gines' interpretation of transience is an interesting concept that truly may affect the entire issue of diversity. Bronfenbrenner hypothesizes that the developmental potential of a setting is a function of the extent to which roles and relations offered by a setting can sustain momentum. Gines' advice to take time and "go slow" may be valid; however, with the level of transience in the community, the developmental potential continues to backslide as new groups of people move into the community system. The element of time and the investment in dialogue and conversation may be a strategy that can strengthen the community and decrease transience as well.

Gines' definition of *community,* like Bronfenbrenner et al. (1984), included common identity and fate or, as Gines calls it, "distinct identity with meaningful interaction." The points he makes about what works are crucial to the community-building process. His advice to be patient and "go slow" eludes to the fact that community building is a long-term process in which listening and learning collectively plays a critical role.

COMMUNITY PROCESS TO AFFECT MULTICULTURAL SENSITIZATION

Community development efforts require a series of interrelated processes. In community development, practitioners recognize that the outcomes are not as important as the process (Cochran, 1993). When community leaders discuss common strategies that have worked to build community and affect multiculturalism, people involvement is apparent.

In a study by DeBord and Thompson (1994), interview data were collected using a cross-sectional approach to select community leaders. Leaders were located through personal and professional networks by asking who had been active in affecting community understanding of multiculturalism or diversity. A nonrandom selection process was used to develop the sample. Contacts were made by phone or U.S. mail. Eleven community leaders were contacted by telephone and agreed to be interviewed. Telephone or face-to-face interviews lasted an average of 45 minutes to one hour. Three community leaders were school district administrators, four were college faculty, and four were Extension community development youth project leaders. Seven were males and four were females; four were African American, six were white, one was from India, and one was from China.

For both telephone and face-to-face interviews, community leaders posed open-ended questions about community factors and actions that they perceived as critical in cultivating community acceptance of diversity. In general, the questions focused on changes in human development as framed by Bronfenbrenner (1979). The questioning framework included (1) factors that created linkages between settings, (2) factors that encouraged growth, trust, and goal consensus, (3) how community leaders continued to appraise new information, and (4) how the balance of power is managed.

The format of the interviews generally began with a question about the community and their activities in regard to multiculturalism. Following this discussion, the interviewer probed for the sort of multicultural activity that had been accepted within the community. Questions about the community leaders' personal involvement in affecting community attitude were followed by questions about their perceptions of the community climate and receptivity.

Global community-building strategies surfaced from these interviews. The strategies exemplify what Phillips (1988) described when referring to culture as a "process." This further demonstrates the extensiveness of the process involved in engineering community respect.

In addition to the interviews, 16 participants who had enrolled in a continuing education course on multiculturalism were asked to complete a questionnaire nearly three months after an educational session. Respondents represented 11 states and had occupations such as Head Start teachers, child care center directors, and school administrators.

The open-ended questionnaire asked respondents to explain how they had approached the topic of community acceptance of multiculturalism in their community and what important components that could be learned from their experiences. Other than their state and position, no other demographic information is available on the respondents.

These experiences provide evidence of supportive community partnerships that bridge systems while creating awareness and sensitizing citizens about individual lifestyle, ethnic origination, race, belief, family structure, and other differences. Communities can incorporate many of the strategies suggested by the "experts" interviewed, while building community and understanding cohesion. These strategies—assessment, awareness, action, and adaptation—are offered here as a guide with the understanding that implementation will not unfold in the same way in each community. They provide a road map for new communities initiating multicultural community-building strategies. This process, as depicted in Figure 4.1, is a community development process. Melaville and Blank (1993) stressed that community groups will find themselves repeating stages within community development processes as new peo-

Figure 4.1
Framework for Community
Action

Assessment
- Assess coalition members' values and beliefs
- Assess community values and beliefs

Awareness
- Increase public education, awareness, sensitivity about multiculturalism
- Build community support for diversity

Action
- Organize a representative coalition
- Identify dynamic leadership
- Design a plan (mission, goals, objectives, priorities)
- Involve citizens

Adaptation
- Track progress
- Adjust and evaluate
- Reflect on work
- Monitor roadblocks and barriers

ple become engaged in the work of the community and as the group continues to clarify its purpose and intent.

Assessment

An assessment should be made of community readiness to receive and digest new insights and information. This step parallels Bronfenbrenner's (1979) reference to assuring compatibility of roles between community leaders and communication between systems.

There is a primary level of leadership assessment and a secondary level of assessment of community readiness. The primary assessment involves a recognition of personal bias from those who make up the core leadership group or coalition, which sets the stage for the entire educational process. One experienced multicultural coalition leader warned that "if you don't set the stage properly, you will only get a slight extrapolation for what you ARE" as opposed to what you should strive to be (DeBord & Thompson, 1994).

This level of assessment resoundingly surfaced during interviews as a key component to community action. This sort of self-analysis can be risky and tense but demonstrates commitment from the leadership. Often the fear lies in "giving up a self-protected aura complete with privileges, guilt, and self-hatred" before one can personally move into positive action (Markowitz, 1993).

Personal assessment requires being able to reflect on one's personal past. Within the community coalition, members should plan to participate in what one community leader called a "storming stage" where they discuss barriers, question personal biases, and collectively view multiculturalism. Chen (cited in Grimes, 1992) stated that culturally competent people must first become aware of their own cultural values and beliefs and recognize how these beliefs influence their personal attitudes and behaviors. This step of leadership assessment was resounded in the interviews with Jones, Gines, and others. Senge (1990) noted that exceptional organizations are characterized by visible conflict in which all members feel secure in speaking out and are deeply entrenched in doing so. The desired outcome is development of the view that differences are equivalent to strengths. This stage is sometimes painful, often tense, and generally uncomfortable; however, the conscious penetration of ingrained ideas is a vital step. By taking time to attend to this step, it is reported that organizations and communities move from the current comfort zone to transcend status quo (DeBord & Thompson, 1994). This process may also require revision.

L. Jones said her community group thought they had thoroughly become aware of one another's beliefs and constructed a comfortable place for conversation, dialogue, and action. However, there were many roadblocks and they had to step back and further explore personal feelings before they could overcome these barriers. Revisiting this step and re-storming allowed them to continue their work. A secondary assessment is a more formal community assessment that appraises the resources, skills, knowledge, and level of commitment from within the community. One way to conduct an assessment is to ask key individuals representative of the community the same open-ended question to determine their baseline attitudes about differences among people and their suggestions for creating a sense of community. Other methods may include formal mail or telephone surveys or focus group interviews.

Awareness

Awareness is a general community sensitization toward understanding multiculturalism. Not only should there be a plan to begin educating the public about differences between people, but there should be a campaign to inform community citizens about the efforts of leaders to affect understanding. Individual and community awareness assures support between systems and builds a foundation of community support.

For collective awareness to occur, individual awareness must develop. To create sensitive awareness and facilitate the process, movement from a comfortable setting into a less comfortable setting may be necessary. This movement from one's primary setting, which Bronfenbrenner (1979) calls "ecological trajectory," can enhance community understanding. An example of this movement is evident in the story shared in the introduction of this chapter by questioning where meetings that welcome *all* participants are planned, and by having leadership take steps to move from comfortable, traditional settings to build bridges to new settings. Under the leadership of L. Jones, the Youth Alliance reorganized the importance of community awareness when free community functions only drew limited attendance. Jones realized that efforts to transcend traditional methods of reaching people were necessary to expand individual and community awareness and broaden between group awareness.

The creation of individual and public awareness may take any variety of forms. Using creative methods by which to get information to the grassroots public is essential. Two creative and effective methods shared by other communities are the following:

1. *Walk for Harmony.* 300 people divided the neighborhood and went door-to-door handing out window signs that read: "We support harmony." On the reverse side of the sign was the mission of the multicultural coalition. Also included were invitations to a "Celebration of Diversity" featuring an array of art, music, food, and exhibits.

2. *Voices.* Two representatives from each elementary school serve on this subcommittee that meets regularly. If there are concerns or problems, inequities, or misrepresentations in neighborhoods, the concerned people may contact the community coalition representatives with the problem. The problem is then shared with the total coalition who then responds or refers. The representatives of Voices then return to the originator of the concern with the action taken. This active grassroots effort has successfully created awareness and enabled many citizens to become a part of the multicultural effort.

Individual awareness among the leadership can expand into the community as the conversation continues and people make connections to build collective awareness. Collective awareness is critical in building a foundation of support. This lengthy process will prepare the community to develop an action plan.

Action

Community leaders (DeBord & Thompson, 1994) advise communities to organize a "cadre of diverse, respected people" to serve on a representative coalition. One community leader said, "Following awareness, add questioning. Questions are like planting seeds. Then comes intervention. That means talk and move on. Then add action" (DeBord & Thompson, 1994).

To act, a coalition is essential to build broad community support and understanding between systems. By forming a coalition, responsibility, accountability, and respect can be shared by the group. The empirical nature of this step is echoed by Bronfenbrenner (1979) who recommended partnering between organizations and agencies to build interconnectedness between various systems.

The action step can be the most exciting step but also the most time- and resource-intensive. Community leaders advise developing a coalition of leaders to develop an extensive plan driven by specific objectives. Along the way, sensitivity in addressing issues of power and privilege, and a cross-system collaboration that includes the family, should be threads woven throughout the plan (DeBord & Thompson, 1994).

As a first action step, an initial group of concerned citizens and key leaders should be identified to form a council or task force. If the community is defined as a geographic region, planners should not forget to include formal community structures. Bronfenbrenner et al. (1984) specifically noted that schools, as a hub to communities, can influence what happens in immediate settings where community development takes place—such as in the family or workplace.

Representatives on a local coalition should include local school and government leaders, media, law enforcement, and other diverse and interested organizations, as well as key delegates from informal social networks. Bott (1957) defines social networks as all or some of the social units with whom an individual or group is in contact. Assuring representation of various family forms, lifestyles, religions, and ethnicities from within the community is imperative. Particular efforts to target minority leadership, to gain geographic representation, to include a wide range of ages and statuses while assuring gender balance, is critical. Personal referrals are suggested as one way to build this web of leaders. Bronfenbrenner et al. (1984) stated that networks can be a conduit to power and a means of exerting influence.

A coalition, however, needs leadership itself. Successful coalitions stress the importance of the quality of the leadership. Their experience indicates that dynamic leaders can carry the process through many critical phases. Dynamic Leadership is necessary to create and communicate excitement, enthusiasm, and understanding about efforts. Leadership can be elected, assumed, or appointed.

Although Bronfenbrenner does not refer overtly to leadership, there are applications in his ecological hypothesis to the balance of power. Bronfenbrenner (1979) indicated that shared leadership may be one way to balance power, but optimal situations for development are ones in which the balance of power gradually shifts in favor of the developing person or group and there is a joint opportunity to control situations. This aspect is described by community leaders as the necessity to have good leadership with shared responsibility through collaboration.

Development of awareness, like most endeavors in life, requires planning. A plan includes the development of a mission, setting goals, defining objectives, and setting priorities. Activities create momentum and develop a continuing process towards an end. But plans are not an end in and of themselves. Success and expanded involvement occur when people serving on the coalition divide the work of the plan. Additional people can connect to the effort by working on subcommittees that report back to the overall coalition. To activate the plan, delegation of planned actions must be placed on a time line. Time lines also serve as methods against which to evaluate. The entire action step is a lengthy process that should be developmental and be adapted when necessary.

Adaptation

Great action plans are interwoven with opportunities to modify, adjust, revise, and evaluate. An evaluation plan should be designed from the initial phases of a project. By monitoring actions, requests, changes, and suggestions, progress can be tracked. This information is used to show progress of the work of the coalition and can be used to reshape plans. Planning for adaptation and evaluation is the step most likely to be omitted from the total effort, but it is a step that assures smooth transitions between systems.

Some methods of tracking progress used by community groups include keeping a record of inquiries, charting inquiries against time lines and outcomes, following families as case studies, and comparing baseline attitudinal data of citizens to attitudes after actions across time. Cochran (1993) said that a particularly important step is to employ critical reflection. By reviewing the records, the actions taken, and feedback received, members of the coalition may reflect critically on where they have been, how they are doing, and where they want to go. Reflection involves the whole group. Mere evaluation of records are useless without questioning and then making adaptations in the environment, in the systems, and between the multiple dimensions of the community.

To continue building community energy, visible changes must be evident. For school systems in particular, evidence of change is most visible in hiring practices. Minority students and families who visibly see that there are more minority teachers and administrators in the schools report positive feelings associated with overall programs (DeBord & Thompson, 1994). This visible and diverse representation should be evident in all efforts including leadership councils, media releases, and family events.

Weaving the Steps Together

These strategies are simply a framework to begin community building. No one solution exists that can be constructed, only actions that can catalyze changes in attitude and community interactions. Along with strategies, community leaders provide the following advice when faced with barriers:

"It (the process) is not a recipe, it has glitches."

"Change is often painful."

"This is social reform and social reform is not easy."

"It is necessary to rebuild the paradigm of communities as segmented and specialized. We do not yet operate in a holistic manner."

There are multiple barriers in this process. Stories of lessons learned from roadblocks also provide valuable information. Several community leaders listed precautions:

■ Resist the temptation to simply focus on the dominant minority and broaden definitions of diversity to include all ethnicities, classes, and oppressions.

■ Be cautious of some groups who may act counter productively to the mission of the coalition. Fold these persuasions into the overall operation of the coalition.

■ If the defined community is a school, involve all teachers from the beginning. Teachers should take part in the same intense bias deconstruction process as the leadership coalition. Trying to "fit the teacher training into a short period of time was a mistake." Processing time to co-construct meaning is critical. When time limitations allow for only a brief guest lecturer presentation, intimidation and alienation occurs.

■ Programs must be financially pragmatic. Soliciting funds to support efforts is a valid strategy.

CONCLUSION

In conclusion, I invite readers to return to the theme of the opening story—exhausting all reasonable efforts. On reflection, my personal definition of *all reasonable efforts* has changed. It is obvious to me that for an understanding of multiculturalism to be woven into the community, we as educators, decision makers, and community leaders cannot assume that understanding will unfold over time without strategically creating heightened sensitivity with all groups with whom we come in contact. This is not the sole responsibility of any one educational system or organization. As citizens together, we must intensify efforts for community awareness that will lead to actions to complete this intricate community tapestry. Through conversations with community representatives, we can continue to learn about what works to build a supportive framework of strategies for multicultural communities. As further empirical research unfolds and the sociocultural framework continues negotiated within communities, practitioners should begin to realize the implications for local programs and services. The suggested strategies for being should be incorporated according to the community needs, but the common thread for beginning the process is created through conversation.

REFERENCES

Allen, K., & Farnsworth, E. (1993). Reflexivity in teaching about families. *Family Relations, 42*(3), 351–356.

Baber, K., & Allen, K. (1992). *Women and families: Feminist reconstructions*. New York: Guilford.

Bott, E. (1957). *Family and social network: Roles, norms and external relationships in ordinary urban families* (2nd ed.). London: Tavistock.

Bronfenbrenner, U. (1979). *The ecology of human development: Experiments by nature and design*. Cambridge, MA: Harvard University Press.

Bronfenbrenner, U., Moen, P., & Garbarino, J. (1984). Children, family, and community. In R. Parke (Ed.), *The family: Review of child development research* (Vol. 7) (pp. 283–328). New York: Sage.

Carter, K. (1993). The place of story in the study of teaching and teacher education. *Educational Researcher, 22*(1), 5–12, 18.

Cochran, M. (1993). [Interview by M. Powers with Moncrieff Cochran, professor of human development and family studies at Cornell, Jennifer Greene, associate professor of human service studies at Cornell, Josephine Allen, associate professor of human services, and Donald Barr, professor of human service studies at Cornell]. *Human Ecology Forum*, 6–9.

DeBord, K., & Thompson, A. (1994). *Community diversity issues: Strategies for a comprehensive multicultural framework*. Unpublished manuscript.

Garbarino, J. (1982). *Children and families in the social environment*. New York: Aldine.

Greene, M. (1993). The passion of pluralism: Multiculturalism and the expanding community. *Educational Researcher, 22*(1), 13–18.

Grimes, M. (1993). Cultural competence. *Missouri 4-H Youth Connections*, 5.

Hawkesworth, M. E. (1989). Knowers, knowing, known: Feminist theory and claims of truth. *Signs, 14*, 533–557.

Hooks, B. (1989). *Talking back: Thinking feminist, thinking Black*. Boston: South End Press.

Markowitz, L. (1993). Walking the walk. *Family Networker, 17*(4).

Melaville, A., & Blank, M. (1993). *Together we can: A guide for crafting a pro-family system of education and human services* (Contract No. RP912060001). Washington, DC: U.S. Department of Education and U.S. Department of Health and Human Services.

Phillips, C. B. (1988). Nurturing diversity for today's children and tomorrow's leaders. *Young Children, 43*(2), 42–47.

Senge, P. (1990). *Fifth discipline*. New York: Currency Doubleday.

PART Two

Practices in Diversity

CHAPTER 5

Use-of-Self in Social Constructionist Therapy

Some Guidelines for a Multicultural Practice

WILLIAM R. SCOTT

The field of family and systems therapy continues to evolve from its roots in the 1950s communication projects of Gregory Bateson (Hoffman, 1981). This early work was a reaction to the dominant therapy models of the day: psychoanalysis and behaviorism. The family and systems therapy field has shown that change is constant. New models and methods of family and systems therapy come from the influx of new ideas and theoretical perspectives, as well as examination and replication of what takes place in the treatment context that is believed to account for change (de Shazer, 1991). Feminist, constructivist, and social constructionist theories sensitize us to the co-constructions of clients, therapists, supervisors, trainers, researchers, educators, and writers.

In this chapter, I will outline the theoretical background for a social constructionist and multicultural model of therapy and offer a summary of the shift in focus from *structure* to *meaning* in the multicultural model of therapy. The multicultural model looks at the social construction of meaning and includes the focus on the "self" of the therapist. In this model, it is important for therapists to remain aware (as observers of themselves) of the "self" they bring to the therapeutic dialogue with the client and the role of use-of-self themes in the joining process. In addition, I will outline what I consider to be five guidelines for a social constructionist and multicultural practice of therapy. The proposed guidelines lead to therapy being more culturally, socially, and politically sensitive as the co-construction of meaning in the therapy context stresses the evolving therapeutic conversation.

THEORETICAL BACKGROUND

The theoretical background of this approach is influenced by constructivist writers (e.g., Bateson, 1972; Maturana & Varela, 1987; Segal, 1986), and social constructionist philosophy (De Man, 1979; Derrida, 1978, 1981; Foucault, 1965, 1972, 1980). In constructivism, realities (what we perceive as "out there") are individually invented rather than discovered (i.e., meaning is attributed to what is sensed "out there" by the individual). In social constructionism, the "out there" is determined by consensual linguistic process, conversation, and dialogue. For both constructivists and social constructionists, we, as observers, participate in the construction of our realities.

For example, growing up and playing rough in a family of brothers led to quite a few mishaps and accidents. It was fortunate that my mother, a pediatric nurse, kept her cool during those times. I remember incidents of feeling pain but withholding judgment about it until I could look into my mother's eyes to determine how "bad" she thought it was. Her communication about the seriousness of an injury would affect my assessment of the injury and invariably how much more it would hurt. I was always "okay" in her eyes, no matter how hurt I was. In fact, I have never not been okay. I silently thank my mother for this gift now.

Feminist writers and family therapists have critiqued the family therapy field and have begun to question its "normalizing truths" (Gilligan, 1982; Goldner, 1985, 1988; Hoffman, 1990; Luepnitz, 1988; McGoldrick, Anderson, & Walsh, 1989; Roberts, 1991; Sheinberg & Penn, 1991; Walters, Carter, Papp, & Silverstein, 1988; Wheeler, Avis, Miller, & Chaney, 1989) and to "deconstruct" the basic assumptions underlying the family therapy field (Erickson, 1988). It is clear that theories are influenced by gender.

Additionally, the ideas of Milton Erickson have been important to the evolution of language based approaches. The notion that every client requires a different model is commonly ascribed to Erickson. Therapy involves learning how others need to help themselves and creating the conditions for that work to take place. Erickson believed in the ability of clients to find their own solutions within their own unconscious resources (Havens, 1985).

In summary, therapeutic focus has shifted from structures to individual belief systems and shared meaning systems. Cognitive maps or belief systems are altered through changes in shared meanings that make up the belief systems. Others (e.g., Anderson, Goolishian, & Winderman, 1986; Goolishian and Anderson, 1988) would argue that there are only shared meanings and no individual belief systems existing outside of the shared meaning systems. Fruggeri (1992) wrote of the hermeneutic circle of interpretation–action: "Beliefs held by individuals construct realities, and realities are maintained through social interaction which, in turn, confirm the beliefs that are then socially originated" (p. 43).

Like Fruggeri, I believe individual belief systems or cognitive maps exist independent of interaction and are brought to communicational events where meaning is co-created and shared. The meanings that are shared contribute to the validation and construction of the beliefs we hold.

Meaning is altered through the influx of new information. New information is brought into the system through the introduction of *news of difference*, a difference that makes a difference (Bateson, 1972), which is determined by each member of a "communicating system." Restricted ideas can be expanded through the introduction of news of a difference, thus opening up the system to the evolution of new meaning. Also, exceptions and fluctuations from a pattern can be punctuated, magnified, and built on to bring about new meaning and change (de Shazer, 1988; O'Hanlon & Weiner-Davis, 1989).

Focus has shifted from structures to the co-creation of meaning systems. Each person engaged in communication is involved in the creation of shared meaning. The therapist can no longer be the interventionist working outside of the client system as the expert but is part of a new system, the therapy system, which includes the client(s), the therapist, and their shared meanings. There is renewed interest in the contribution of the therapist to this system.

Therapists and supervisors have cognitive maps or belief systems they bring to therapy and supervision. Their cognitive maps and belief systems, lenses for perceiving and interpreting their worlds, are made up of use-of-self themes.

USE-OF-SELF

Use-of-self depends on the notion of *self* that is being used. My definition of *self* and *use-of-self* allows certain possibilities and at the same time places restrictions on the self that is being constructed. As Gergen (1991) noted, any discussion of self is bound by culture, that is, the self is located in the culture at a period in time. The notion of self changes throughout time and culture. The notion of self used in this section is influenced by the current culture and authors who have come before me. I will present my conception of use-of-self below. Like de Shazer (1991), I believe the evaluation of any construction is based on its usefulness and practicality. I hope and believe that the construction of self, use-of-self, and use-of-self themes outlined below are useful in therapy and supervision. Ultimately, you and others will have to judge the utility of these notions. The constructions outlined here will remain as long as they are useful or until more useful notions are constructed. In this section, I will provide a social constructionist description of use-of-self themes.

Use-of-Self Description and Theory

Our lives are storied lives or narratives (White & Epson, 1990). To translate our sensory experience we use language to assign meaning. The memories of our past may be stored as sensory information (visual, auditory, kinesthetic). When these memories are communicated to another, we use language, which then shapes those memories.

Our language can restrict and predispose us to experience the world in ways that fit with our language (Gergen, 1991; Whorf, 1956). Our memories are communicated in a narrative form. We internalize these stories or narratives about ourselves (White & Epston, 1990). These internalized stories become filters for our sensory experience as they draw certain distinctions out of the mass of sensations bombarding us at any one moment (Bateson, 1972; Maturana & Varela, 1987).

Early narratives about one's life tend to form themes by which one lives one's life. Every story involves a selection of certain elements at the exclusion of others (Parry, 1991; White & Epston, 1990). Other individuals may help us select and interpret the elements of our stories. Use-of-self themes consist of the beliefs, in the form of narratives, the individual brings to communication. Unlike Gergen (1991), I do not believe that relationships "create" the sense of "I" but rather that relationships bring forth a sense of "I." One's beliefs or narratives predispose one to perceive experience and construct meanings in ready-made ways (i.e., ways that fit with previous narratives) (Fruggeri, 1992). Use-of-self themes include predisposition to construct meanings about race, culture, gender, class, and age. These narratives may change over time as our present may also influence the past we choose to remember (Boscolo & Bertrando, 1992). The use-of-self themes do not have to be longstanding but can be connected to current issues with which one is struggling. For example, when my wife and I were refinancing our home and struggling with the bank and lawyer over paper work and contracts, I saw and was interested in contracts in my personal and professional lives.

Current Use-of-Self Themes

I attempt to stay aware of the use-of-self themes that operate in my life. These themes are the lenses through which I experience and make meaning of my world. I have visual images from the past that help me recall experiences and construct these themes, but when I share these memories, I put these experiences into words. The memories become narratives, and the words I use and have accessible to me help shape these narratives.

Several major use-of-self themes continue to operate in my life. The themes of power, gender sensitivity, and individual responsibility are correlated and circular. The sharing of power can lead to the assumption of individual responsibility and the appreciation of differences. To punctuate this interaction differently, the assumption of individual responsibility over victimization leads to the taking of personal agency and the assumption of personal power and the appreciation of differences.

The themes related to power, gender, and individual responsibility and overfunctioning affect my work as a therapist, supervisor, husband, and parent. As a supervisor, I am sensitive to abuses of power and am more willing to share power with my staff and adopt a model of empowerment. In my therapy, I share power with my clients, and feel more comfortable using a social constructionist model of therapy rather than the previously adopted structural/strategic model. I struggle with clients with certain presentations: men who abuse power (I want to take them on); constantly depressed women (I want to tell them to stand up); and clients who are not willing to work hard (I initially work too hard, harder than they, become frustrated, and then want to tell them to go home and come back later). As a husband, I communicate more with my wife about decisions and about our communication. As a father, I strive to be fair with my daughters, respect their special constructions of meaning and internalized stories, and continue to be amazed by their construction of meaning.

I am sensitive to the social construction of gender. I believe that gender differences exist and that differences are not all a matter of perspective. Until power and equality are shared along gender lines, gender will continue to be dichotomized socially and differences will be experienced as less than or greater than, rather than as differences that create and lead to our diversity. I have similar views concerning inequality and differences related to race and culture. I am open to dynamic versus static expressions of gender (i.e., gender does not have to be expressed in any particular way). For me, the dichotomy between male and female ways of thinking and behaving break down. While sensitive to feminist causes, I cannot wholly embrace this movement, just as I could not get too close to my mother. I find comfort in and am influenced by the men's movement, which I defend, like my father, against feminist critiques.

My tendency to work hard and take individual responsibility has led me to overfunction and be very productive at home and work. I can get a lot done. As I have become more differentiated from my family of origin (Bowen, 1978), I have become more the author of my own story (Keen & Valley-Fox, 1989) and am more aware of the motivation behind my overfunctioning. I can overfunction for different reasons.

USE-OF-SELF AS POINTS OF CONNECTION

In this section, I propose that use-of-self themes become points of connection for individuals engaged in conversation. These themes affect the evolution of shared meaning and contribute to parallel process in other contexts.

Points of Connection

We all have use-of-self themes through which we filter experience to construct meaning. When two or more individuals enter into a conversation, they search for a way to join. This joining is usually around some common interest or theme. Without the joining in conversation the individuals engage in separate monologues while in the presence of others. The joining in conversation, rather than monologue, punctuates the points of connection between the conversants. They co-create a dialogue between them. Social constructionists refer to this as *the creation of meaning through consensual linguistic process.*

Points of Connection in Therapy

When the therapist and client begin to form a therapeutic relationship, they search for and establish points of connection that are connected to use-of-self themes. Elkaim (1990) called these points of connection between the client and therapist *systems resonances:*

> More recently, the concept of resonance has allowed me to see that these different systems can be joined by a link that is more than the quasi-mechanical replication of the same rule from one level to the next. (p. 141)

The therapist and client create shared meaning in their conversations. Use-of-self themes are evident when the numerous ways that a particular situation could be experienced and described are compared with the particular description chosen by a client, and the possible comments made by a therapist are compared with the chosen punctuation. The shared meaning co-created by the therapist and client may be replicated thematically in other contexts for both the therapist and the client due to the involvement of use-of-self themes.

For therapy to be effective and to start the dialogue process, I believe there have to be points of connection, similar to Elkaim's resonances. The points of connection allow for the introduction of "newness" or the introduction of a difference that makes a difference. If the therapist simply joins with the client and that is the extent of the therapy, the therapist has established points of connection that do not necessarily introduce differences, unless joining with someone is a different experience. Differences are not typically points of connection, though. To be a source of difference, therapists must maintain maneuverability within the therapy system; therapists need to be able to have moments of awareness where they experience themselves in relation to the client. Therapists manage their use-of-self to introduce differences.

An Example

Before moving on with the discussion about the stance of the social constructionist therapist, I would like to share an example that may illuminate the previous discussion. Recently I worked with a woman, Betty, who was about five months pregnant with her second child. Her husband was emotionally and psychologically abusive, and he left her just before Christmas while having an affair with another woman. She had attempted suicide, was hospitalized briefly, and was referred to me for follow-up work in January.

Betty was ready to work. She had to take care of a 4-year-old son and an unborn baby, with little or no family or social support. She had many decisions to make. The husband, while living with his new girlfriend, continued to be abusive to Betty. Betty was making progress in therapy. The husband would say to her, "I will undo in 5 minutes what you and your counselor have taken a month to do." Needless to say, based on old use-of-self themes, I was joined to the client.

I was not aware of other unconscious connections I was making to her and her situation. I knew something was going on when I felt myself wanting to offer to be Betty's Lamaze coach. Betty had not asked for a Lamaze coach, but I felt like offering. I took this case to supervision, where I became aware of the connection between this situation and a recent loss I had experienced. My wife and I lost our second child in a miscarriage at about 10 weeks. The due date for my second child would have been about the same as that of my client's. I was trying to save and protect Betty and her child as I would have liked to have done in my own situation. I needed to grieve the loss of my child. Betty did not know all of this, but I am sure she could feel the presence of something other than what we were discussing. I had tried to help my wife through this period and had neglected myself, trying to hold it together for everyone else. I shared with Betty this personal story, as well as my earlier desire to help myself by being her coach. I did this without asking her for anything. She did not need to take care of me. I allowed myself to grieve the loss of my child. My client went on to find a coach, and I can recount this story without tears. I had connected with Betty over old themes but also too closely over an unresolved issue I was still carrying around.

STANCE OF THE SOCIAL CONSTRUCTIONIST THERAPIST

Based on the theoretical notions presented earlier, and therapy literature, I would like to present five guidelines for a stance of a social constructionist and multicultural therapist. I will state these in terms of guidelines for therapy, although they may certainly apply to other disciplines and professions.

Therapy as Conversation

Conversation and *dialogue* have similar implications and are increasingly being used as a descriptive metaphor in therapy (Goolishian & Anderson, 1992; Hoffman, 1991; de Shazer, 1991; de Shazer & Kim Berg, 1992). Therapy is a circular process, or conversational "dance" between the client and the therapist, where information is constantly exchanged. Therapists receive information about the clients (perceptual), filter this information through their perceptual systems, arrive at some meaning (conceptual), and then respond in some fashion (executive) (Tomm & Wright, 1979). Clients repeat a similar process outside of the therapist's awareness. Therapy is a matter of alternating, in a respectful way, between following and leading, receiving and responding. The therapist learns the client's dance and language. A new language and dance is created and shared by the therapist and the client. The change in language is often subtle and difficult to detect by an observer, and simply appears as a conversation rather than a therapeutic intervention. The therapy is respectful of the client and involves a doing "with" rather than a doing "to."

Therapist use-of-self becomes important because the therapist is no longer an objective observer but a participant observer (Fine & Turner, 1991; Hoffman, 1986). Problems no longer rest within an "it," a person or the family structure, but within the "meaning system" or understanding reached between the therapist and client (Hoffman, 1986, 1990; de Shazer, 1991).

Therapists must examine their part of the interaction with their clients, explore family-of-origin issues (Adler, 1929; Bowen, 1978; Hoopes & Harper, 1987; Kramer, 1985; Toman, 1988), and issues related to training and theoretical assumptions (Havens, 1985; Hoffman, 1990; Liddle, Breunlin, & Schwartz, 1988; Liddle, Breunlin, Schwartz, & Constantine, 1984; Liddle & Saba, 1983), including lenses that filter experience based on gender and ethnicity. It is crucial that therapists be trained to be aware of and manage use-of-self issues they bring to the therapeutic system (Aponte, 1992; Keller & Protinsky, 1984; McDaniel & Landau-Stanton, 1991).

It is important for therapists to avoid prepared language or monologue, which shuts down dialogue. Therapists can have notions about what they would like to explore and be ready to introduce them into the dialogue when the opportunities present themselves (Seikkula & Haaradangas, 1991), but they should also be ready to "dance" and enter into a dialogue with the client.

Therapy as Intentional

A distinction exists between *willfulness* and *intentionality* (Friedman, 1987; Atkinson & Heath, 1990). *Willfulness* is a state in which therapists are invested in the goals for the therapy and instrumentally pursue those ends, while *intentional* therapists are aware and purposeful in their actions without the attachment to the outcome. I believe that when therapists are being willful they are inducted by a use-of-self issue into the emotional process with the client. Friedman (1986) believes that a position of willfulness and induction into their clients' emotional processes leads to a feeling of ineffectiveness on the part of therapists. In these cases, therapists often seek more professional information and knowledge, which Freidman believes is focusing on the "wrong stuff." Intentional therapists avoid positions of willfulness (i.e., trying to change the client) but, instead, attempt to become aware of and manage their part of the interactions.

Therapy is full of decisions made by therapists. They need to be aware of the decisions that are made. Therapists take responsibility for these decisions, and make overt what is covert. Just as strategizing (Tomm, 1987a) between the therapist and the therapeutic team was brought into the open by Andersen's (1991) reflecting team, therapists, similarly, introduce their intentions into the session and make them open for dialogue. Therapists remain curious (Cecchin, 1987) as to the clients' reactions to their introduction of intentions and difference.

Therapy as Creating New Possibilities

Our clients have internalized stories about themselves or ways in which they define or understand themselves in the world. What is the client's story that has become internalized? It is helpful to deconstruct the meaning generated in the conversation with the client to identify underlying and basic assumptions held by both client and therapist.

Also, and possibly more important, what is not being said? Solutions to problems often lie outside of our immediate awareness in what is not, or cannot be, said (Andersen, 1991; Goolishian & Anderson, 1992). Maintaining "curiosity" and "freedom" (Cecchin, 1987; Fine & Turner, 1991), that is, not knowing too soon, allows for the consideration of alternative perspectives. The use of questions, especially questions that ask for differences (Penn, 1982, 1985; Tomm, 1987b, 1988), often opens "therapeutic space" by introducing new ways of looking at and experiencing situations (Goolishian & Anderson, 1992). It is also important to listen for and explore beliefs and assumptions regarding gender and culture by asking questions about the operation of these influences (Roberts, 1991; Sheinberg & Penn, 1991).

Taking a step back, into a reflecting position, leads to a different perspective (Andersen, 1991). Being able to experience oneself may lead to a difference. Giving up a stance of "either/or" and adopting a stance of "both/and" entertain the possibility of understanding the situation in more than one way. The solution may lie in what we are not allowed to access, that is, what has been restricted from us by culture, family, and the socialization process (Bly, 1988).

Therapy as the Introduction of Difference in the Present

It is not helpful to go on exploratory missions or archeological digs into the client's past. We will go there with our clients if this is where they lead us, and once there, we will be curious about the meaning and significance of this experience. "Problems do not exist outside of the present, or rather, if it is outside of the present it is no longer a problem but the memory of a problem or the possibility of a problem" (Boscolo & Bertrando, 1992, p. 121). We can choose a different future. Therapy needs to help the client disconnect from the past and project a different future (Boscolo & Bertrando, 1992). We do not have to look back for cause-and-effect explanations and suggest, "This is why you are like this."

The client's problem has evolved as a result of sameness and absence of new information. The attempted solutions have become part of the problem (Watzlawick, Weakland, & Fisch, 1974). The family therapy system has used an old paradigm that does not allow for the possibility of solution but rather for more of the same. Therapists become a source of newness and difference, and intend to introduce a "difference that makes a difference" to their clients (Bateson, 1972). Therapists look for exceptions to the problem—which are the presence of something other than the problem—and magnify them (de Shazer, 1988; O'Hanlon & Weiner-Davis, 1989). By focusing on these exceptions and spending less time in problem talk, the exceptions can grow and become solutions.

Therapy as Narrative

We ascribe meaning to our experience through language. The ways we talk about experience affect that experience. The metaphors of *narrative* and *story* are increasingly being used in therapy (Hoffman, 1991; Goolishian & Anderson, 1992; Laird, 1989). Talking differently can lead to change (Anderson, Goolishian, & Winderman, 1986; Goolishian & Anderson, 1988). Our lives are storied lives (Laird, 1989; Parry, 1991; White & Epston, 1990). Problems are situated within stories. We need to examine the stories we have internalized about ourselves, externalize them to become aware of them, and determine whether they are the stories we want to direct our lives (Tomm, 1989; White & Epston, 1990). We can become the authors of our own stories. The use of therapeutic stories can counter the problem stories and lead to change (Keen & Valley-Fox, 1989). Goolishian and Anderson (1992) believed change comes from the creation of new meaning through the co-construction of new stories in therapy (i.e., like Andersen [1991] the co-construction of stories which have yet to be told).

CONCLUSION

Goolishian and Anderson (1992) summed up the practical application of the stance and guidelines of the therapeutic approach described earlier:

> The process of therapy based on this hermeneutic stance involves what we call a therapeutic conversation. Therapeutic conversation refers to an endeavor in which there is a mutual search for understanding and exploration through dialogue around the always changing "problems." Therapy, and hence the therapeutic conversation, entails an "in there together" process. People talk "with" each other as opposed to talking "to" each other. Therapeutic conversation is the process through which the therapist and the client participate in the co-development of new meanings, new realities, and new narratives. (p. 12)

In the co-construction of meaning that takes place in therapy, we need to remain aware of the self that we bring to these conversations. When we find ourselves moving into a position of willfulness, we need to step back from the conversation, into a reflecting position, to try to become aware of what issue or theme is guiding our actions. By doing this we can remain focused on the clients, remain sensitive to differences in our stories and our clients' stories, and refrain from writing their story for them, thereby robbing them of the opportunity to become their own author, thus their own authority. By keeping these guidelines in mind, we can become better multicultural therapists.

REFERENCES

Adler, A. (1929). Position in family influences life-style. *International Journal of Individual Psychology, 3*, 211–227.

Andersen, T. (Ed.). (1991). *The reflecting team: Dialogues and dialogues about the dialogues.* New York: W. W. Norton & Company.

Anderson, H., Goolishian, H., & Winderman, L. (1986). Problem determined systems: Towards transformation in family therapy. *Journal of Strategic and Systemic Therapies, 5*(4), 1–11.

Aponte, H. J. (1992). Training the person of the therapist in structural family therapy. *Journal of Marital and Family Therapy, 18*, 269–281.

Atkinson, B. J., & Heath, A. W. (1990). Further thoughts on second-order family therapy—This time it's personal. *Family Process, 29*, 145–156.

Bateson, G. (1972). *Steps to an ecology of mind.* New York: Ballantine Press.

Bly, R. (1988). *A little book on the human shadow.* San Francisco: Harper & Row.

Boscolo, L., & Bertrando, P. (1992). The reflexive loop of past, present, and future in systemic therapy and consultation. *Family Process, 31*, 119–130.

Bowen, M. (1978). *Family therapy in clinical practice.* New York: Jason Aaronson.

Cecchin, G. (1987). Hypothesizing, circularity, and neutrality revisited: An invitation to curiosity. *Family Process, 26*, 405–413.

De Man, P. (1979). *Allegories of reading*. New Haven: Yale University Press.

Derrida, J. (1978). *Writing and difference* (A. Bass, Trans.). Chicago: University of Chicago Press.

Derrida, J. (1981). *Positions* (A. Bass, Trans.). Chicago: University of Chicago Press.

de Shazer, S. (1988). *Clues: Investigating solutions in brief therapy*. New York: W. W. Norton & Company.

de Shazer, S. (1991). *Putting difference to work*. New York: W. W. Norton & Company.

de Shazer, S., & Kim Berg, I. (1992). Doing therapy: A post-structural re-vision. *Journal of Marital and Family Therapy, 18*, 71–81.

Elkaim, M. (1990). *If you love me, don't love me: Constructions of reality and change in family therapy*. New York: Basic Books.

Erickson, G. (1988). Against the grain: Decentering family therapy. *Journal of Marital and Family Therapy, 14*, 225–236.

Fine, M., & Turner, J. (1991). Tyranny and freedom: Looking at ideas in the practice of family therapy. *Family Process, 30*, 307–320.

Foucault, M. (1965). *Madness and civilization: A history of insanity in the age of reason*. New York: Random House Press.

Foucault, M. (1972). History, discourse and discontinuity (A. Nazzaro, Trans.). *Salmagundi, 20*, 229–233.

Foucault, M. (1980). *Power/knowledge: Selected interviews and other writings*. New York: Pantheon Press.

Friedman, E. (1986). *The responsibility triangle: Stress in the helping professions*. Paper presented at the meeting of the American Association for Marriage and Family Therapy's 44th Annual Conference. Orlando, Florida.

Friedman, E. (1987). How to succeed in therapy without really trying. *The Family Therapy Networker, 11*(3), 26–31, 68.

Fruggeri, L. (1992). Therapeutic process as the social construction of change. In S. McNamee & K. Gergen (Eds.), *Therapy as social construction* (pp. 40–53). Newbury Park, CA: Sage.

Gergen, K. J. (1991). *The saturated self: Dilemma of identity in contemporary life*. New York: Basic Books.

Gilligan, C. (1982). *In a different voice*. Cambridge, MA: Harvard University Press.

Goldner, V. (1985). Feminism and family therapy. *Family Process, 24*, 31–47.

Goldner, V. (1988). Generation and gender: Normative and covert hierarchies. *Family Process, 27*, 17–32.

Goolishian, H., & Anderson, H. (1988). Human systems as linguistic systems: Preliminary and evolving ideas about the implication for clinical theory. *Family Process, 27*, 371–393.

Goolishian, H. A., & Anderson, H. (1992). Strategy and intervention versus nonintervention: A matter of theory? *Journal of Marital and Family Therapy, 18*, 5–15.

Havens, R. A. (1985). Erickson vs. the establishment: Which won? In J. L. Zeig (Ed.), *Ericksonian psychotherapy. Volume I: Structures* (pp. 52–59). New York: Brunner/Mazel.

Hoffman, L. (1981). *Foundations of family therapy: A conceptual framework for systems change*. New York: Basic Books.

Hoffman, L. (1986). Beyond power and control. *Family systems medicine, 3*, 381–396.

Hoffman, L. (1990). Constructing realities: An art of lenses. *Family Process, 29*, 1–12.

Hoffman, L. (1991). A reflexive stance for family therapy. *Journal of Strategic and Systemic Therapies, 10*(3 & 4), 4–17.

Hoopes, M. H., & Harper, J. M. (1987). *Birth order roles and sibling patterns in individual and family therapy*. Rockville, MD: Aspen Publishers.

Keen, S., & Valley-Fox, A. (1989). *Your mythic journey: Finding meaning in your life through writing and storytelling*. Los Angeles: Jeremy P. Tarcher.

Keller, J. F., & Protinsky, H. (1984). A self management model for supervision. *Journal of Marital and Family Therapy, 10*, 281–288.

Kramer, J. R. (1985). *Family interfaces: Transgenerational patterns*. New York: Brunner/Mazel.

Laird, J. (1989). Women and stories: Restorying women's self-constructions. In M. McGoldrick, C. M. Anderson, & F. Walsh (Eds.), *Women in families: A framework for family therapy* (pp. 427–450). New York: W. W. Norton & Company.

Liddle, H. A., Breunlin, D. C., & Schwartz, R. C. (Eds.). (1988). *Handbook of family therapy training and supervision*. New York: The Guilford Press.

Liddle, H. A., Breunlin, D. C., Schwartz, R. C., & Constantine, J. A. (1984). Training family therapy supervisors: Issues of content, form and context. *Journal of Marital and Family Therapy, 10*, 139–150.

Liddle, H. A., & Saba, G. W. (1983). On context replication: The isomorphic relationship of training and therapy. *Journal of Strategic and Systemic Therapies, 2*(2), 3–11.

Luepnitz, D. A. (1988). *The family interpreted: Feminist theory in clinical practice*. New York: Basic Books.

Maturana, H. R., & Varela, F. J. (1987). *The tree of knowledge: The biological roots of human understanding*. Boston: New Science Library, Shambhala.

McDaniel, S. H., & Landau-Stanton, J. (1991). Family-of-origin work and family therapy skills training: Both–and. *Family Process, 30*, 459–471.

McGoldrick, M., Anderson, C., & Walsh, F. (Eds.). (1989). *Women in families: A framework for family therapy*. New York: W. W. Norton & Company.

O'Hanlon, W. H., & Weiner–Davis, M. (1989). *In search of solutions: A new direction in psychotherapy*. New York: W. W. Norton & Company.

Parry, A. (1991). A universe of stories. *Family Process, 30*, 37–54.

Penn, P. (1982). Circular questioning. *Family Process, 21*, 267–280.

Penn, P. (1985). Feed-forward: Future questions, future maps. *Family Process, 24*, 299–311.

Roberts, J. M. (1991). Sugar and spice, toads and mice: Gender issues in family therapy training. *Journal of Marital and Family Therapy, 17*, 121–132.

Segal, L. (1986). *The dream of reality: Heinz von Foerster's constructivism*. New York: W. W. Norton & Company.

Seikkula, J., & Haaradangas, K. (1991, June). *The co-evolution of meaning in polyfonic dialogue: The system of boundary*. Paper presented at the meeting of the Third World Family Therapy Congress, Jyvaskyla, Finland.

Sheinberg, M., & Penn, P. (1991). Gender dilemmas, gender questions, and the gender mantra. *Journal of Marital and Family Therapy, 17*, 33–44.

Toman, W. (1988). *Family therapy and sibling position*. Northvale, NJ: Jason Aronson.

Tomm, K. (1987a). Interventive interviewing: Part I. Strategizing as a fourth guideline for the therapist. *Family Process, 25*, 3–13.

Tomm, K. (1987b). Interventive interviewing: Part II. Reflexive questioning as a means to enable self-healing. *Family Process, 26*, 167–183.

Tomm, K. (1988). Interventive interviewing: Part III. Intending to ask lineal, circular, strategic, or reflexive questions?. *Family Process, 27*, 1–15.

Tomm, K. (1989). Externalizing the problem and internalizing personal agency. *Journal of Strategic and Systemic Therapies, 9*, 54–59.

Tomm, K. M., & Wright, L. M. (1979). Training in family therapy: Perceptual, conceptual and executive skills. *Family Process, 18*, 227–250.

Walters, M., Carter, B., Papp, P., & Silverstein, O. (1988). *The invisible web: Gender patterns in family relationships*. New York: Guilford Press.

Watzlawick, P., Weakland, J., & Fisch, R. (1974). *Change: The principles of problem formation and problem resolution*. New York: W. W. Norton & Company.

Wheeler, D., Avis, J. M., Miller, L. A., & Chaney, S. (1989). Rethinking family therapy training and supervision: A feminist model. In M. McGoldrick, C. M. Anderson, & F. Walsh (Eds.), *Women in families: A framework for family therapy* (pp. 135–151). New York: W. W. Norton & Company.

White, M., & Epston, D. (1990). *Narrative means to therapeutic ends*. New York: W. W. Norton & Company.

Whorf, B. L. (1956). *Language, thought, and reality*. Cambridge, MA: MIT Press.

CHAPTER 6

Developing Interpersonal Understanding in Teaching Culturally Diverse Children

ANDREW J. STREMMEL

In the fields of human development and education, consensus is growing about the need for (1) reforming teacher education, (2) improving teaching and learning, and (3) implementing multicultural education. Basically, these are interrelated notions inherent to decisions about *what*, *when*, and *how* to teach children. In teaching at the early childhood level, caregivers must be continually responsive to the interests, needs, and intentions, of children (Elkind, 1976; Lay-Dopyera & Dopyera, 1990). Because the children enrolled in early childhood programs will continue to come from more diverse backgrounds, teaching in the twenty-first century will become more challenging and complex (Spodek & Saracho, 1990). To meet these challenges, teaching practices must be relevant to and meaningful in the sociocultural context of the systems in which children live and develop (Rogoff & Morelli, 1989).

During the past twenty years, our thinking about the nature of learning and development has been heavily influenced by the ideas of Jean Piaget. Piaget's theory, though recognizing the importance of the social environment, hypothesized that the emergence of cognitive development and intellectual activity are largely intrapersonal. In recent years, understanding and appreciation have grown toward the social context that surrounds and influences development in general and learning in particular. This appreciation has been greatly influenced by the translation and interpretation of the theoretical work of Lev Vygotsky (e.g., Rogoff & Wertsch, 1984; Vygotsky, 1978; Wertsch, 1985a, 1985b). Extending Piaget's view that children are active participants in their development, the Vygotskian stance emphasizes that social interaction involving more capable others provides the context for a shared construction of knowledge and understanding.

Drawing on insights from Piagetian and Vygotskian perspectives, the primary aim of this chapter is to present a teaching approach that is both developmentally and culturally appropriate. Employing a social constructivist framework, I contend that development is facilitated in both the spontaneous and contrived interactions that occur between children and more mature members of their communities (Wood, 1988). That is, what children learn is a cultural curriculum, structured and orchestrated by the sociocultural activities and members of their communities (Rogoff, 1990). Furthermore, I propose that to effectively teach children from diverse cultural backgrounds, one must become increasingly able to recognize and appreciate the perspective and purpose of the learner. More specifically, it is argued that meaning and understanding are socially constructed by partners in communicative interaction. This requires teachers to examine their fundamental beliefs and practices in light of observations made of the beliefs and teaching–learning patterns of other cultures, and to include their own experiences and values explicitly in the analytic equation. Finally, I present some timely recommendations for early childhood instructional practice, teacher education, and research. Implications for policy also are addressed.

Although the synthesis presented in this chapter is not fully comprehensive, it does provide a basis for better understanding how early childhood teachers can teach young children within an increasingly pluralistic society. To date, few appropriate curriculum models exist for early childhood education that employ elements of Vygotsky's sociocultural theory (for an example, see Edwards, Gandini, & Forman, 1993). The theoretical assumptions and implications for teaching that are integrated here derive largely from the work of Rogoff (1990), Wood (1988), and Tharp and Gallimore (1988).

PERSPECTIVES ON DEVELOPMENT—PIAGET AND VYGOTSKY

Perhaps Piaget's greatest contribution to the understanding of children's cognitive development, at least in educational terms, is the view of children as active learners who are capable of constructing their own understandings. Piagetian theory, though largely an individualist orientation, suggests that social interactions among children may foster development by exposing them to other perspectives and to conflicting ideas that may encourage them to reformulate their ideas or ways of thinking (Piaget, 1932). However, the cognitive benefits of social interaction (i.e., interaction among peers of equal status) become evident only with the decline of egocentrism, when children are more capable of coordinating two differing perspectives (Tudge & Rogoff, 1989). Thus, the pre-operational child cannot think about what the world is like from another's point of view. To do so would require the ability to ignore one's own position and "construct" an event or situation from another's perspective. Mutual under-

standing is hypothesized to occur when children reach the stage of concre
tions (about ages 7 to 11).

A major implication of this perspective is that any attempts to teach (e.g., question, show, explain) before a child is mentally "ready" will do little to foster development. In fact, premature teaching may interfere with the child's own attempts at
exploration and discovery or may result in the acquisition of empty procedural knowledge (Wood, 1988). Therefore, teaching cannot foster understanding; this is achieved
largely through unassisted activity.

Although Vygotsky's theory of development is not as detailed and well-integrated
as Piaget's, a number of important concepts and ideas have influenced current thinking about the relationship of learning and development. Vygotsky's sociocultural theory suggests that social interaction influences development from the beginning of life.
Like Piaget, Vygotsky held the view that children are actively involved in constructing
an understanding of the world; but, departing from Piaget, he posited that social
interaction with more skilled partners (adults or peers) is the means by which children become enculturated in the use of the intellectual tools of their society (e.g., language and mathematical systems). Social encounters in a variety of contexts lead to
understanding and self-regulation.

Vygotsky (1978) hypothesized that the process by which cognitive processes—
occurring first at the social level—become psychological is called *internalization.*
According to Vygotsky, "every function in the child's development appears twice: first
on the social level, and later on the individual level; first, between people (interpsy-
chological) and then inside the child (intrapsychological)" (1978, p. 57). Tharp and
Gallimore (1988) stressed that this process is not merely the transferal of culturally
defined tools and activities to a preexisting internal plane of consciousness. Children
actively reorganize and reconstruct their experiences. In this regard, Vygotsky's
thought is similar to that of Piaget: As the tools of culture are internalized, transforma-
tions in structure and function occur.

Guided participation is the term used by Rogoff (1986, 1990) to describe the
process in which adults and children, or partners of unequal skill, collaborate in structuring the situations that provide children with access to observe and participate in
culturally valued skills and perspectives, thereby enabling them to extend their current skills and knowledge to a higher level of competence. Vygotsky referred to the
range between what children can do on their own and what they can achieve in
guided participation as the *zone of proximal development* (ZPD). Working within
this zone, children gain skills that allow them to assume increasing responsibility for
their own learning. They learn not only how to accomplish a given task, but also how
to structure their learning and reasoning in solving a problem. Thus, all uniquely
human learning occurs as a transfer of responsibility for reaching culturally defined
goals in mutually guided activity (Rogoff & Gardner, 1984).

It is important to emphasize that this transfer of responsibility is jointly achieved
in a context in which one of the partners is more skilled than the other in a particular
domain of knowledge. The ZPD is thus "shared" with an adult or more capable peer
and is a domain-specific measure of learning potential, or what the child can do with
sensitive assistance (Belmont, 1989). This dynamic conceptualization of the ZPD is in

stark contrast to Piaget's rather static and individualistic concept of "readiness," which implies that cognitive development involves advances in general capacity.

The notion that development is largely a social construction appears to offer much in the way of an instructional methodology for teachers who want to be responsive to individual differences in educability (Belmont, 1989; Wood, 1988). Before explicating the strategies and procedures involved in responsive teaching, it is essential to point out a major emphasis shared by Vygotsky and Piaget that provides the foundation for this chapter's primary focus: the notion of interpersonal understanding (intersubjectivity). Because these ideas have been presented elsewhere (see Rogoff, 1990, for a cogent analysis), they are briefly summarized in the following section.

THE ROLE OF INTERPERSONAL UNDERSTANDING

The theories of Piaget and Vygotsky appear to converge in the assumption that development is more likely in the context of social interaction when the participants (either peer-partners or child-adult partners) work toward achieving mutual understanding of a problem and collaborate to arrive at a solution (Rogoff, 1990; Tudge & Rogoff, 1989). *Intersubjectivity,* the linguistic concept denoting a sharing of purpose or focus in the coordination of perspectives (Rommetveit, 1985; Trevarthen, 1980), is key to the assumption that different types of learning may be differentially facilitated by equal versus more skilled partners in social interaction. Trevarthen (1980) argues that the foundations of intersubjectivity are evident in the interpersonal activity of early infancy, wherein both infant and mother make sensitive adjustments to the behaviors (e.g., expressions) of the other.

For Piaget, collaborative problem solving between peers of equal cognitive status advances the individual's development. According to this view, cooperation in cognitive activity enables the child to become aware of differing perspectives and to resolve conflicts; however, this view does not recognize the possibility that individual cognitive processes derive from joint activity in social contexts (Rogoff, 1990). Forman (1987) described intersubjectivity from a Piagetian perspective as an individual process of perspective-taking based on socially provided information.

In contrast, Vygotsky views *shared thinking* (intersubjectivity) as an opportunity for unequal partners to engage in and make use of joint activity to expand understanding and skill (Rogoff, 1990). In this case inequality refers to level of expertise in a specific domain of knowledge and not in power. Intersubjectivity is crucial in guided participation. It is important for collaborative partners to establish a joint meaning, a common ground for communicating the interests, intentions, and understandings of the other. Within this context, children actively participate in the construction of knowledge, and as a result, "appropriate" (Rogoff, 1990) an increasingly advanced understanding of the skills and perspectives of their culture. It should be noted that interaction with a skilled other may have no direct association with children's learning or their performance on a task. Studies consistently show that it is not the presence of a partner that matters but the nature of the interaction between partners, in particular the partner's ability to achieve a shared focus of attention, with social guidance building on the child's perspective. Research conducted from both Piagetian and Vygotskian perspectives suggests that shared understanding between partners is essential in developing sensitivity to the problems that children are attempting to solve (Rogoff, 1990; Tudge & Rogoff, 1989).

An understanding of the role of intersubjectivity in the process of guided participation can be useful—I believe essential—in the teaching of culturally diverse preschool children. First, however, early childhood settings must be seen as a context for teaching as well as learning. The emergent contextualist view of development provided by neo-Vygotskian theorists and researchers (e.g., Minick, 1987; Rogoff, 1982, 1986, 1990; Rogoff & Wertsch, 1984; Wertsch, 1985a, 1985b; Tharp, 1989; Tharp & Gallimore, 1988; Wood, 1988) may be an appropriate foundation to guide the practice of early childhood teaching.

THE PROCESS OF GUIDED PARTICIPATION

Guided participation (alternatively conceptualized or described as *contingent teaching, scaffolding, reciprocal teaching, proleptic instruction, assisted performance* and *responsive teaching*) refers to the "teaching–learning context," in which pupil and teacher collaborate in negotiating and constructing a desired learning activity through responsive instructional interactions (e.g., conversations or dialogue) (Rogoff, 1986, 1990; Stone, 1985; Tharp & Gallimore, 1988; Wood, Bruner, & Ross, 1976, among others). According to Rogoff (1990), guided participation involves (1) building bridges between what children know and new information to be learned, (2) structuring and supporting children's efforts, and (3) transferring to children responsibility for managing problem solving. The bridging between the "known" and the "knowable" in communicative interaction presumes intersubjectivity. In dealing with culturally diverse populations, for example, initial differences in perspective must be modified to reach a common ground for communication (and thus learning).

As I mentioned earlier, children are active in their own learning and in managing their social partners. Both child and adult work together in structuring the learning situation. For example, the adult may determine the problem to be solved, its goal, and how the goal may be made more manageable, while the child may assume increasingly greater responsibility in managing the task as he or she nears its completion. Also known as scaffolding (Wood et al., 1976), guided participation does not involve breaking down or simplifying the task; rather, the task difficulty remains constant, while the child's initial contribution to or responsibility for the task is simplified in the teaching–learning context (Greenfield, 1984). Thus, the child's self-directed attempts to learn are carefully balanced with the adult's adjusted support that provides challenge and sensitive assistance. In this way the transfer of responsibility for problem solving in guided participation is contingent on the success of the learner.

Contingent teaching is paced by moment-to-moment signs of understanding and subsequent success by the child. Where the child demonstrates success, ensuing teaching should offer more child control in the learning process and greater degrees of freedom for potential failure; as the child shows signs of misunderstanding or likelihood of failure, more assistance should be given. Consequently, adult control is increased and the degrees of freedom for error are reduced (Wood, 1988, 1989). This form of teaching is sensitive to the child's zone of proximal development.

According to Tharp and Gallimore (1988), the means of guided participation, or in their terms, "assisted performance," are observable in all natural teaching contexts (e.g., in parent–child interaction), and in most joint activity settings where partners have different levels of expertise. Studies of the strategies used by caregivers in teaching young children suggest that adults vary the type and amount of instructional support they provide according to the age and expertise of the learner (see Rogoff, Ellis, & Gardner, 1984; Wertsch, McNamee, McLane, & Budwig, 1980). For example, in a study by Rogoff et al. (1984), middle-class mothers were observed to tailor their amount and type of assistance with a cognitive task to the perceived needs of 6- and 8-year-old children in a particular problem context. More instruction in the form of directives and questions was provided to younger children in a school task. This study demonstrates that mothers are capable of flexibly tuning instruction to their children's needs within the zone of proximal development.

While evidence supports the ubiquity of social guidance and participation in a variety of contexts and cultures (Rogoff, 1986, 1990; Tharp, 1989; Tharp & Gallimore, 1988; Wertsch, 1985b), cultural differences exist in the knowledge, skills, and values to be learned, and in the interpersonal arrangements necessary for learning. Likewise, differences exist in the contexts available to children for the practice of skills and incorporation of values. For instance, Wertsch, Minick, and Arns (1984) documented that parents in a rural Brazilian community are more likely to explain or demonstrate how children are to carry out a problem-solving task than to engage the child in contingent teaching. On the other hand, middle-class parents in the United States appear to engage readily in contingent teaching techniques (Rogoff & Gardner, 1984; Stone, 1985).

Gardner (1989) describes the different views held by Chinese and Western cultures of the preferred behavior of children and the proper role of adults in their socialization. In describing contrasting approaches to fostering creativity, he relates how in Chinese society, the older and more skilled person has the role of showing the younger person how to do a given task, thus ensuring continuities with the past in terms of performance standards and knowledge. As children become competent in a given area, they are sanctioned to introduce increasing departures from approved methods. The reversal of this process is observed in Western societies, wherein children initially are free to be creative (in early childhood education), sometimes engaged in joint quests for understanding with an adult, before being gradually reintegrated (in formal schooling) into the cultural perspectives and basic skills needed to function in society. Gardner concludes that, in spite of different views of schooling, each society is able to successfully produce individuals who exhibit both disciplined skills and genuine creativity. He recommends that each culture learn to appreciate the advantages of each other's approach. This recommendation seems to fit well with the notion of achieving intersubjectivity through guided participation, wherein a sensitive blending of teaching methods is used in the attempt to appreciate the perspective and purpose of the learner.

Although researchers influenced by Vygotsky's theoretical ideas are now attempting to articulate strategies for teaching in schools (e.g., Tharp & Gallimore, 1988), guided participation in the zone of proximal development is rarely promoted as a legitimate form of instruction in early childhood classrooms in this country.

A PLEA FOR RESPONSIVE TEACHING IN EARLY CHILDHOOD EDUCATION

Many early childhood educators, incorporating the ideas of Piaget and the "progressive educators" (e.g., Froebel, Dewey, Pestalozzi, and Rousseau), emphasize that child-directed activity, particularly exploration and discovery through play, is essential to child-centered approaches to early childhood education. In keeping with this thinking, the early childhood teacher's role is viewed as a co-explorer or facilitator. However, Henry (1990) provided convincing evidence of the importance of adult–child collaborative activity in home settings for children's overall development and calls for a need to include mutually directed activities in early childhood classrooms. Rheingold (1982), for example, has shown that children are intrinsically satisfied in collaborative household pursuits, in which active adult involvement with children is important to their continued participation. Tizard and Hughes (1984), in contrasting home and nursery school as learning environments, pointed out that nursery schools, with their primary emphasis on play, are deficient in opportunities for children to observe and participate with adults in challenging pursuits.

A recurring theme in this chapter is that when a child and a more skilled partner work at achieving intersubjective understanding of a problem or task, and collaborate to arrive at a solution, development is more likely. Tudge (1990) noted, however, that the key feature of this interactive context is not the pairing of partners having unequal competence, but the process of interaction itself, which leads to the attainment of joint meaning and understanding. Acceptance of this critical aspect of social interaction has far-reaching implications. It means that the child's development of knowledge and understanding can be described only in relation to a partner (or partners) who, with the child, achieves joint meaning in activities that are mutually constructed in a culturally defined context (Uzgiris, 1992). It is no longer meaningful to focus on either the child or the partner's contribution to activity, because the activity emerges out of interaction, such that it is impossible to say "to whom" a collaborative idea or an object of joint understanding or focus belongs (Rogoff, 1990).

Reconceptualizing our understanding of informal learning activities in early childhood classrooms as mutually directed activity settings is not antithetical to notions of the child as active learner; rather, it emphasizes collaborative (adult–child) learning—and teaching—that should be a part of any discussion of developmentally appropriate instruction, especially involving children from diverse backgrounds. With this in mind, it would seem that the best way to ensure sensitivity to the diverse learning patterns of children is through responsive assisted teaching in a variety of contexts that are consistent with children's developmental and sociocultural needs (Linney & Seidman, 1989; Tharp, 1989).

EXAMPLES OF RESPONSIVE TEACHING
IN EARLY CHILDHOOD

Responsive teaching differs from conventionally defined means of instruction, such as explanation or demonstration, because it relies on the construction of shared meanings (Stone, 1985). Traditional or teacher-directed forms of instruction involve making known the presuppositions about the task before the child engages in the task. This minimizes the child's active role in constructing understanding of the task, while maximizing the teacher's role. It also precludes the opportunity for the learner to contribute to a mutually determined, goal-directed context for completing a task.

Developmentally appropriate, responsive teaching includes a delicate balance of strategy (e.g., both questioning and explanation), in both formal and informal learning settings. Responsive teaching requires the teacher to possess some knowledge of each child's level of functioning and a sense of when to intervene and when to hold back, allowing children to make self-discoveries when they are able but also providing the necessary cues when children are moving off target. Children meanwhile must be intrinsically motivated and interested in a meaningful activity that will allow for varying degrees of challenge.

In the teaching–learning context employing the zone of proximal development, an early childhood teacher presents an activity or task with multiple options for challenge and involvement, one of which may be just beyond the child's current level of independent functioning. In early childhood classrooms, activities often do not have a clear obvious structure and usually do not require a "correct" way of approaching and accomplishing them. Therefore, the teacher must effectively identify the child's own goal or intentions in relation to the activity to be able to achieve a measure of intersubjectivity that will enable the child to reach the intended outcome. The teacher may simply provide reminders or suggestions, give hints or ask questions, or it may be necessary at times to show or tell the child exactly what to do.

For example, consider a situation in which a 3-year-old child has approached a collage activity planned for the art area in a preschool classroom. Art is an activity engaged in by people all over the world to represent historical and cultural events, as well as personal experiences (Ramsey, 1987). Thus, like adults in their society, children use various tools and materials to represent their experiences and to express their ideas, thoughts, and feelings through art activities. The collage activity is an example of a semistructured creative activity that is fairly common in early childhood education. Even before interacting with the child, the teacher has responsively selected and arranged the tools and materials that are appropriate for a child of this age. In a nature collage, for example, leaves of various sizes, shapes, and colors, in addition to twigs, seeds, and other items that children may have gathered themselves outdoors, may be provided along with paper and glue. The teacher's goal may be to have the child glue the various items onto the paper. However, this may not be the child's intention in attempting the activity. The sensitive adult must accurately tailor assistance to the child by responding to the child's understanding of the activity. If the child has a limited understanding of what to do, the teacher may offer a suggestion or ask a question (e.g., "What could you do with these?") to help the child get started.

The child may proceed by gluing items together (e.g., seeds onto leaves), as opposed to onto the paper. As the interaction continues, different ideas about how to use the materials may evolve as the teacher and child work together toward achieving increasing intersubjectivity. When some mutual conception of an appropriate way to do the task has been acquired through dialogue, the child can be allowed to work creatively and unassisted within acceptable and mutually understood parameters (e.g., the child may not glue items onto another's paper or onto the table). At this point, descriptive feedback about the process (e.g., "You are using leaves of different colors") or questions to extend the activity (e.g., "Is there another anything else you would like to add to your collage?") are appropriate.

Such an art activity may require less initial adult responsibility or supervision than activities such as cooking. Nevertheless, it requires the attainment of joint meaning and understanding and involves both child and adult in joint performance of the activity. Like art, cooking or preparing food is an activity observable in many cultures and in home settings. Children take part the preparation of food through the process of guided participation, in which opportunities to observe through modeling are common in everyday experience (Rogoff, 1986, 1990). This kind of collaborative activity typically requires adults to take greater responsibility because of its importance to survival. However, children actively participate at points where their skill levels are congruent with the task demands. In early childhood settings, children may take part in stirring, cutting, and serving, while the teacher demonstrates certain procedures or describes what is happening as ingredients are mixed, measured, and cooked. Such opportunities for mutual involvement in culturally meaningful activity should be valued as an important teaching–learning context.

It is critical to emphasize that developmentally appropriate, responsive teaching is a co-participant conversational activity that leads to meaningful and reciprocal interchange. Problems may occur when a child is unable to benefit from adult questioning that is unnatural or does not sustain meaningful dialogue. For instance, when children are asked questions repeatedly, they have little chance to contribute their own ideas and understandings. In overquestioning, adults assume too much control for the learning and prevent opportunities to be led by the children's understanding of a particular task or situation. Children's questions, too, lead to understanding created through sustained dialogue. When used appropriately, questions help child and adult continually adjust their understandings to those of the other. They also serve as useful barometers of mental performance, which enable the teacher to assess the level appropriate to the next stage of learning.

Early childhood classrooms must be viewed as a context for teaching as well as learning. Indeed the Russian term *obuchenie*, translated as instruction, means both teaching and learning, and recognizes the teaching–learning process as a social enterprise (Rogoff & Wertsch, 1984). Responsive teaching, which draws on a variety of teaching methods in collaborative activity, is offered as the best means of recognizing and accommodating the perspectives, values, and experiences of diverse cultures. In endorsing this child-sensitive approach, however, I am far from suggesting that responsive instruction can be a panacea for eliminating the inequities in school achievement among different cultures.

CONCLUSION

Increasingly we will be dealing with a diverse population of children in early childhood settings. These environments, if they are to provide teaching–learning contexts that are compatible with diverse cultures, must provide children with demands and challenges that are both continuous with those encountered in everyday experiences (e.g., at home) and discontinuous with such experiences. In other words, while it is important to be sensitive to the learning patterns of various cultures, the child care center or preschool classroom must be seen as having a culture of its own, with demands that are unique to that "culture" (Wood, 1988).

Peters and Kontos (1987) described how the notion of early intervention assumes that change in the home environment is necessary for developmental change in economically disadvantaged children. That is, providing discontinuity between home and school environments will lead to discontinuity in intraindividual development. Classroom-based programs, where there is minimal parent involvement, maximize discontinuity between home and school settings; whereas home-based programs attempt to make the home a more optimal learning environment by teaching parents to have the attitudes and skills of teachers. However, if learning and development are viewed as a social enterprise, then continuity between home and school is desirable in some measure. Thus, early intervention programs should not only try to help parents teach their children to respond appropriately and successfully to "school-specific" activities, they also should attempt to incorporate to a greater degree the values, beliefs, and learning patterns of the families they serve. As I will discuss shortly, this means more actively involving parents in the classroom.

It has been my contention that to optimally meet the needs, interests, and abilities of culturally diverse children, teachers must engage in responsive assisted teaching. Responsive teaching presumes the notion of intersubjectivity, in which perspectives are coordinated in collaborative learning. Further, it is recognized along with Tharp (1989) that developmentally appropriate instruction must be contextualized—it must relate to personally meaningful experience, use culturally important materials and contexts (e.g., mutually directed activity), and involve parents. Therefore, it is recommended that early childhood educators make efforts to move toward a focus on developmentally appropriateness that emphasizes "cultural" as well as age and individual appropriateness.

Responsive teaching is predicated on the interactive patterns observed between adults and children in many cultures and in joint activity settings where participants have different skills and skill levels. If informal teaching commonplace in parent–child interactions is as important to development as Vygotsky's theory suggests, then we must make every attempt to incorporate parents at the preschool level.

Henry (1990) suggested that parents might find early childhood education more accessible and easier to support if they saw adults and children engaged in mutually directed everyday, family-like activities (e.g., cooking, woodworking, caring for plants, washing and folding clothes, and maintaining the classroom), in addition to child-centered, but mutually-directed play. The rationale for this assumption centers on the opportunity for more open and meaningful information exchange between parents and teachers about ways that teachers can support parent–child home activities. Such exchange would empower all participants in the development of children.

Moreover, the inclusion of more mutually directed or collaborative activity in early childhood classrooms would provide a context where both parents and teachers are viewed as acceptable partners in the learning process. Opportunities for parents and children from various ethnic and racial groups to participate in joint activity would help to provide children with a strong sense of cultural identity, frequent sharing of authentic cultural activity, and a merging of cultural and "school-specific" skills (Swadener, 1988).

How best can we prepare prospective early childhood teachers to be responsive to diverse children? In this paper I have argued for a responsive teaching approach, in which sensitive assistance enables children to proceed through the zone of proximal development. Unfortunately, few teachers know how to do this. Teachers must not only be equipped with the pedagogical skills considered important to teaching young children (and there is no consensus on these), they must also be trained to use the skills essential to teaching in the zone of proximal development. Among other things, this includes the ability to assess the needs, abilities, and interests of a diverse group of children, and to know how to meet these once discovered, drawing from a reper- toire of teaching strategies. Even in early childhood classrooms where individualized learning is enhanced through activity centers that provide multiple options and chal- lenges for child involvement, considerable time, knowledge, and skills are necessary. Tharp and Gallimore (1988) suggested that to develop such skills, teachers must be provided with opportunities to (1) observe competent practitioners of responsive teaching, (2) practice newly acquired skills, (3) receive audiotaped and videotaped feedback about their instruction, and (4) have their teaching practice assisted by a skilled mentor. If we are going to be able to provide these opportunities, early child- hood teacher education models are urgently needed that employ the theory of teach- ing articulated by Tharp and Gallimore (1988).

Critical to a responsive teaching practice is the ability of teachers to be reflective during their interactions with children. Early childhood teachers, according to Lay- Dopyera and Dopyera (1987), appear to rely on what Schon (1983) termed "knowing- in-action" rather than "reflection-in-action." That is, they use actions that are carried out almost automatically with little deliberation before or during teaching interac- tions. However, responsive teaching is never entirely automatic; it involves reflection and active decision making (Tharp & Gallimore, 1988). Teachers who teach respon- sively need to reflect on what they are doing in the midst of their activity, evaluate how well it is working, and change their teaching practices accordingly.

Self-reflection has been recognized as a useful technique for connecting personal experience to that of others (see Bowman, 1989). Thoughtful and careful examination of teachers' own prior experiences (i.e., as a teacher and learner) is necessary for achieving intersubjectivity in responsive teaching. In this way of thinking, a teacher cannot begin to understand the perspective of the learner without first considering one's own system of values and attitudes about teaching and children's learning. As Gomez (1992) nicely pointed out, cultural identity provides the lens through which teachers view others; left unexamined, cultural lenses become restraints, narrowing the possibilities of our under-standings of and interactions with those who hold different perspectives. Thus, both pre-service and in-service training must encourage teachers to use self-reflection to help them get in touch with their own personal experiences and how these experiences may influence their teaching practices so as to examine such practices against the experi-ences, values, and beliefs of others, especially those from diverse backgrounds. Clearly more research is needed that combines qualitative and quantitative methods for examin-ing teaching–learning contexts in early childhood settings. Particularly, careful ethno-graphic studies of collaborative activity between adults and children, and between peers in many different activity settings, are needed to better understand responsive teaching in the zone of proximal development. Evidence from existing research suggests that chil-dren from diverse backgrounds do not interact equally with adults in classroom activities (e.g., Ingham, 1982; Ogilvy, Boath, Cheyne, Jahoda, and Schaffer, submitted). For exam-ple, Ogilvy and associates found that nursery school teachers are less likely to respond contingently to minority children, adopting a controlling style, regardless of individual differences in ability. Further, Gomez (1992) indicated that numerous studies provide evidence that "the darker one's skin, the poorer one's family, the greater the distance of one's language from 'standard American English', and the lower one's perceived ability, the more likely that a child will pass his or her days in school working on decontextual-ized skills and drills and the less likely he or she will be offered opportunities to read and write meaningful texts" (pp. 166–167). Despite what we know to be true about the dis-parities in teacher–child interactions that occur in children's earliest group experiences, children on the margins of society continue to be taught in ways that limit their oppor-tunities to help create meaningful learning experiences.

Research also is needed to test instructional models based on contextualist and interactionist views of development, such as the one offered by Tharp and Gallimore (1988), in early childhood classrooms. In doing so, researchers other than model developers should be involved in evaluating the effectiveness of the approach to avoid bias and other methodological limitations that have been associated with research designed to compare the effectiveness of preschool curriculum models (e.g., see Schweinhart, Weikart, & Larner, 1986).

Much of what has been recommended thus far has policy implications. For exam-ple, funds are needed to develop and evaluate early education models that employ responsive teaching methods or to compare such models with current preschool pro-gram models. Head Start has been interested in funding research focusing on innova-tive programs and intervention strategies designed for children and families from diverse populations. Head Start may serve as a leader in providing research funds to adopt, develop, or test responsive teaching models that are developmentally and cul-turally relevant in different contexts. In a time when many new challenges and oppor-tunities exist in the area of early childhood education, it is important to examine the skills, values, and professional and practical knowledge which guide teachers in their practice to determine if this practice is responsive and relevant to the sociocultural contexts in which children develop. Although interactions with culturally diverse peers and adults may be one of the best ways for children to receive education that is multicultural, collaborative exchanges in which teacher and learner work together to achieve mutual understanding of purpose and perspective may be the best way to optimize learning that is both developmentally and culturally appropriate.

REFERENCES

Belmont, J. M. (1989). Cognitive strategies and strategic learning. American Psychologist, *44*, 142–148.

Bowman, B. (1989). Self-reflection as an element of professionalism. *Teachers College Record*, *90*, 434–451.

Edwards, C., Gandini, L., & Forman, G. (Eds.). (1993). *The hundred languages of children: The Reggio Emilia approach to early childhood education*. Norwood, NJ: Ablex.

Elkind, D. (1976). *Child development and education*. New York: Oxford University Press.

Forman, E. A. (1987). Learning through peer interaction: A Vygotskian perspective. *The Genetic Epistemologist*, *15*, 6–15.

Gardner, H. (1989). *To open minds: Clues to the dilemma of contemporary education*. New York: Basic Books.

Gomez, M. L. (1992). Breaking silences: Building new stories of classroom life through teacher transformation. In S. Kessler and B. Swadener (Eds.), *Reconceptualizing the early childhood curriculum: Beginning the dialogue*. New York: Teachers College Press.

Greenfield, P. M. (1984). A theory of the teacher in the learning activities of everyday life. In B. Rogoff and J. Lave (Eds.), *Everyday cognition: Its development in social context* (pp. 117–138). Cambridge, MA: Harvard University Press.

Henry, M. (1990). More than just play: The significance of mutually directed adult–child activity. *Early Child Development and Care*, *60*, 35–51.

Ingham, E. (1982). British and West Indian children in day nurseries: A comparative study. *New Community*, *9*, 423–430.

Lay-Dopyera, M., & Dopyera, J. E. (1987). Strategies for teaching. In C. Seefeldt (Ed.), *Early childhood curriculum: A review of current research* (pp. 13-33). New York: Teachers College Press.

Lay-Dopyera, M., & Dopyera, J. E. (1990). The child-centered curriculum. In C. Seefeldt (Ed.), *Continuing issues in early childhood education* (pp. 207–222). Upper Saddle River, NJ: Merrill/Prentice Hall.

Linney, J. A., & Seidman, E. (1989). The future of schooling. *American Psychologist, 44*, 336–340.

Minick, N. (1987). Implications of Vygotsky's theories for dynamic assessment. In C. S. Lidz (Ed.), *Dynamic assessment: An interactional approach to evaluating learning potential* (pp. 116–140). New York: Gilford Press.

Ogilvy, C. M., Boath, E. H., Cheyne, W. M., Jahoda, G., & Schaffer, H. R. (submitted). Staff–child interaction styles in multi-ethnic nursery schools. *British Journal of Developmental Psychology*.

Peters, D. L., & Kontos, S. (1987). Continuity and discontinuity of experience: An intervention perspective. In D. L. Peters and S. Kontos (Eds.), *Advances in applied developmental psychology* (Vol. 2) (pp. 1–16). Norwood, NJ: Ablex.

Piaget, J. (1932). *The moral judgement of the child.* New York: Harcourt Brace.

Ramsey, P. (1987). *Teaching and learning in a diverse world: Multicultural education for young children*. New York: Teachers College Press.

Rheingold, H. L. (1982). Little children's participation in the work of adults: A nascent prosocial behaviour. *Child Development, 53*, 114–125.

Rogoff, B. (1982). Integrating context and cognitive development. In M. E. & A. L. Brown (Eds.), *Advances in developmental psychology* (Vol. 2) (pp. 125–170). Hillsdale, NJ: Erlbaum.

Rogoff, B. (1986). Adult assistance of children's learning. In T. E. Raphael (Ed.), *The contexts of school-based literacy* (pp. 27–40). New York: Random House.

Rogoff, B. (1990). *Apprenticeship in thinking: Cognitive development in social context*. New York: Oxford University Press.

Rogoff, B., Ellis, S., & Gardner, W. (1984). Adjustment of adult–child instruction according to child's age and task. *Developmental Psychology, 20*, 193–199.

Rogoff, B., & Gardner, W. P. (1984). Adult guidance of cognitive development. In B. Rogoff & J. Lave (Eds.), *Everyday cognition: Its development in social contexts* (pp. 95–116). Cambridge, MA: Harvard University Press.

Rogoff, B., & Morelli, G. (1989). Perspectives on children's development from cultural psychology. *American Psychologist, 44*, 343–348.

Rogoff, B., & Wertsch, J. V. (Eds.). (1984). *Children's learning in the "zone of proximal development"*. San Francisco: Jossey-Bass.

Rommetveit, R. (1985). Language acquisition as increasing linguistic structuring of experience and symbolic behavior control. In J. V. Wertsch (Ed.), *Culture, communication, and cognition: Vygotskian perspectives*. Cambridge, MA: Cambridge University Press.

Schon, D. A. (1983). *The reflective practitioner: How professionals think in action*. New York: Basic Books.

Schweinhart, L. J., Weikart, D. P., & Larner, M. B. (1986). Consequences of three preschool curriculum models through age 15. *Early Childhood Research Quarterly, 1*, 15–45.

Spodek, B., & Saracho, O. N. (1990). Preparing early childhood teachers for the twenty-first century: A look to the future. In B. Spodek & O. N. Saracho (Eds.), *Yearbook in early childhood education (Vol. 1): Early childhood teacher preparation* (pp. 209–221). New York: Teachers College Press.

Stone, C. A. (1985). Vygotsky's developmental model and the concept of proleptic instruction: Some implications for theory and research in the field of learning disabilities. *Research Communications in Psychology, Psychiatry, and Behavior, 10*, 129–152.

Swadener, E. (1988). Implementation of education that is multicultural in early childhood settings: A case study of two day care programs. *The Urban Review, 20*, 8–27.

Tharp, R. G. (1989). Psychocultural variables and constants: Effects on teaching and learning in schools. *American Psychologist, 44*, 349–359.

Tharp, R. G., & Gallimore, R. (1988). *Rousing minds to life: Teaching, learning, and schooling in social context*. New York: Cambridge University Press.

Tizard, B., & Hughes, M. (1984). *Young children learning: Talking and thinking at home and at school*. London: Fontana.

Trevarthan, C. (1980). The foundations of intersubjectivity: Development of interpersonal and cooperative understanding in infants. In D. R. Olson (Ed.), *Social foundations of language and thought* (pp. 316-342). New York: Norton.

Tudge, J. (1990). Vygotsky, the zone of proximal development, and peer collaboration: Implications for classroom practice. In L. C. Moll (Ed.), *Vygotsky and education: Instructional implications and applications of sociohistorical psychology*. Cambridge, MA: Cambridge University Press.

Tudge, J., & Rogoff, B. (1989). Peer influences on cognitive development: Piagetian and Vygotskian perspectives. In M. H. Bronstein & J. S. Bruner (Eds.), *Interactions in human development*. Hillsdale, NJ: Erlbaum.

Uzgiris, I. C. (1992). Fostering development in early childhood: An interactive approach. *Proceedings of the Conference on New Directions in Child and Family Research: Shaping Head Start for the Nineties* (pp. 390–392). Washington, DC: The Administration on Children, Youth, and Families.

Vygotsky, L. S. (1978). *Mind in society: The development of higher psychological processes.* Cambridge, MA: Harvard University Press.

Wertsch, J. V. (Ed.). (1985a). *Culture, communication, and cognition: Vygotskian perspectives*. New York: Cambridge University Press.

Wertsch, J. V. (1985b). *Vygotsky and the social formation of mind*. Cambridge, MA: Harvard University Press.

Wertsch, J. V., McNamee, G., McLane, J. B., & Budwig, N. A. (1980). The adult–child day as a problem solving system. *Child Development, 51*, 1215–1221.

Wertsch, J. V., Minick, N., & Arns, F. J. (1984). The creation of context in joint problem solving action: A cross-cultural study. In B. Rogoff & J. Lave (Eds.), *Everyday cognition: Its development in social context* (pp. 151–171). Cambridge, MA: Harvard University Press.

Wood, D. (1989). Social interaction as tutoring. In M. H. Bronstein & J. S. Bruner (Eds.), *Interactions in human development*. Hillsdale, NJ: Erlbaum.

Wood, D. J. (1988). *How children think and learn*. Oxford: Basil Blackwell.

Wood, D. J., Bruner, J. S., & Ross, G. (1976). The role of tutoring in problem solving. *Journal of Child Psychology and Psychiatry, 17*, 89–100.

CHAPTER 7

A Pedagogy of Caring and Thoughtfulness

Living and Sharing Our Lives with Our and Other People's Children

VICTORIA R. FU AND ANDREW J. STREMMEL

> Parenting and teaching derive from the same fundamental experience of pedagogy: The human charge of protecting and teaching the young to live in this world and to take responsibility for themselves, for others, and for the continuance and welfare of the world. (van Manen, 1991, pp. 6-7)

> It is the responsibility of every adult . . . to make sure that children hear what we have learned from the lessons of life and to hear over and over that we love them and that they are not alone. (Edelman, 1992, p. 15)

Human development is embedded in the social and cultural activities that we participate in daily (Vygotsky, 1978). As children are growing up in a variety of changing family, social, and cultural settings, we, as parents and educators, must ask ourselves, "How can educating and bringing up children remain a rich human and cultural activity?" (van Manen, 1991, p. 4). Although parents have the primary responsibility for a child's development, teachers living daily with children from diverse backgrounds are also influential in their development. Teachers must try to support parents in fulfilling their primary pedagogical responsibility in bringing up children.

93

The links between parenting and teaching have always been recognized in some societies more than others. As children spend more time outside the home—in schools and child-care programs—the importance of these linkages in childhood socialization is becoming more crucial in this society. In this chapter, we wish to explore a pedagogy of living with our and other people's children. This pedagogy calls on us to be caring and thoughtful in our relationships with children.

Van Manen (1991) clarified that although pedagogy has most often referred to teaching, the term *pedagogue* derives from the Greek, and refers not to the teacher but to the watchful guardian whose responsibility it is to lead the young child to school. Literally this meant showing the child how to get to and from school. In a richer sense this meant accompanying or being with the child and caring for the child. This is a responsibility that we have transferred increasingly to teachers and other professional caregivers, but pedagogy is at the very core of the adult–child relationship. For, according to Van Manen (1991), it is in the adult–child relationship that "the adult provides a sense of protection, direction, and orientation for the child's life" (p. 38). This is a fundamental feature of adult life; in every human society, children have lived in some pedagogical relation to their elders.

PEDAGOGICAL RELATIONSHIPS

Regardless of the culture, bringing up children is a complex process. The burden of the responsibility to care for children who are entrusted to us should be taken seriously. Ask any parent, "What would you like your children to become when they grow up?" and you will get a range of responses. In general, parents hope their children will grow up to be adults who are educated, responsible, productive, healthy, happy, caring, loved, and able to love others. We also would like them to be prepared for change, to develop their own values that will serve them and others well in a democracy, and to be "concerned with" (care for) the well-being of oneself and others. Ideally, all these qualities are ingrained in children's lived-experiences with parents, teachers, and other people who care for them. This notion of living and learning is reflected in the writings of Dewey (1944). He said, "The good life is not a vision to be held before the pupil as a distant reward for enduring and suffering the hardship of education. The qualities of the good life should be inherent qualities of the educative process" (p. 3).

A pedagogical relationship between an adult and a child is built on a commitment to act in the best interest of the child. Van Manen (1991) described this relation as follows:

> The pedagogical relation is an intentional relationship between an adult and a child, in which the adult's dedication and intentions are the child's mature adulthood. It is a relation oriented toward the personal development of the child—this means that the pedagogue needs to be able to see the present situation and experiences of the child and value them for what they contain; and the pedagogue needs to be able to anticipate the moment when the child can participate in the culture with fuller self-responsibility. (p. 75)

A pedagogical relation is two-dimensional in nature, in that both players (parent and child, teacher and student) contribute to the construction and maintenance of a relationship in a spirit of collaboration, intersubjectivity, and mutuality. The realization of such a relationship depends on the adult to be thoughtful and caring in guiding the child's development. It calls for an adult to be a "carer, who in attempting to apprehend and feel for the other person's reality, (is) committed to act in behalf of the other" (Noddings, 1984, p. 16).

These pedagogical experiences, unfortunately, are not available to many children, for not all adult–child relationships are pedagogical in nature. Countless children do not have opportunities to form significant relationships with adults who are both concerned with and are able to guide their development.

Children first experience the world through their parents. Parent–child interactions reflect parents' beliefs, attitudes, and expectations, the origins of which can often be found in the lived stories of their childhood. This relationship is also contingent on the adult's commitment to the child. Even in the best situations, parents and children can be in conflict with each other. Conflicts usually occur around issues of inclusion, trust, acceptance, love, power, and control. In negotiating these issues at home (and other places), children begin to construct their notion of who they are, living among people in different sociocultural contexts. In these contexts, children may experience opportunities that either promote growth or put them at developmental risk. The following stories illustrate these concerns.

This is a familiar story in which we have all been players. The script is an episode of action–dialogue between a baby and her mother (or father, caregiver, etc.):

> The baby thrashes her arms, kicking her legs, opening her mouth, cooing and babbling, trying to catch her mother's attention. The mother approaches and responds to her by calling her name, nickname, or other names of endearment, smiling with delight, cooing and babbling, modeling the baby's vocalizations and gestures. The baby coos, she coos; the baby sticks out her tongue, she sticks out her tongue; the baby opens her mouth, she opens her mouth wide . . . pausing for the baby to take her turn, who in turn pauses to let the mother take her turn . . . and the interaction goes on with each player trying to engage the other in a shared–interest relationship.

In these episodes, mother and baby are in tune with each other, staring deeply into each other's eyes, engaging each other by signaling and responding to each other's vocalizations and gestures. Through mutual give-and-take, together they are creating and maintaining a synchronic relationship. Does this not reflect the beginnings of a relationship of loving, caring, sharing, having a voice, respect, and equal participation? Is this not an example of a pedagogical relation? Is this not reflective of the dynamics of democratic conversation? How does living in this relationship contribute to the baby's construction of her social world?

On the other hand, we have also observed adults who rebuke their baby's attempts to make connections. The following script begins like the earlier one, with the baby greeting and trying to get her mother's attention. But, in this case, the mother ignores the baby's gestures and attempts to connect:

Sternly the mother tells the baby, "Be quiet! It's not play time!" The baby looks perplexed and begins to cry. The mother goes to the baby, spanking her hand and saying, "Quit!" The baby cries more.

This mother may only want to play with the baby when it is convenient for her. She may take a rigid stance with respect to all routine caregiving and playing, or perhaps she is too concerned with whose turn it is to be with the baby. These interactions reflect a lack of reciprocity, spontaneity, respect, care, voice, sharing of power, and participation. Garbarino (1992) suggests that such interactions tend to reflect a parent's taking control of the relationship, frequently as a result of struggle for power and control in the family. This predominantly one-directional relationship is not pedagogical in nature. How would this relationship jeopardize the baby's development? How would it influence the baby's construction of her social world? Of her place in the world?

These two divergent scripts are also enacted in early childhood programs and schools, the next social contexts in which children live their lives. Noddings (1993) believes that "teachers not only have to create caring relations in which they are the carers, but that they also have a responsibility to help their students develop the capacity to care" (p. 18). In Noddings' view, the aim of life and education is not happiness or achievement, but the maintenance and enhancement of caring.

Teachers and parents can provide opportunities for children to learn to care for themselves and others. On one level, children experience caring in adult–child interactions, for example, in taking the responsibility to care for pets and plants, and in sharing classroom or family chores for the benefit of the self and the group. On another level, children can construct the ethic of care through listening, telling, talking, and sharing their ideas and feelings in a variety of stories. These are stories that have meaning to children: (1) lived-experiences of their own lives, (2) lived-stories of their parents, teachers, and significant others, (2) stories from books, including fantasies, and (4) stories they have created and written by themselves.

Paley (1981, 1993) illustrated in her books how children construct, through "storying," notions of caring, justice, fairness, and other complex concepts that affect their developing sense of self and others. She also shows us that caring teachers listen to their students' stories. Noddings (1993) said, "Caring teachers listen and respond differentially to their students" (p. 19). If we reflect on what we hear and see in the children we care for, we can begin to create teaching–learning relationships that accommodate the student's multiple interests, capabilities, and realities.

DEMOCRACY AND DISCIPLINE

In parenting and teaching, we live and share our lives with children; therefore, telling and sharing our stories with them is a crucial part of the pedagogical relation. Edelman (1992) stressed that it is our responsibility to tell children our stories. These stories may serve as connections to the past, present, and future of our and their lives in a rapidly changing world. Thus, storying is a wonderful way to create and demonstrate democratic conditions for living and learning.

However, just like those parents who want to control their children, some teachers believe their role is to control their students. These teachers often get into power struggles with students, who react by being disruptive, rebellious, and belligerent. This conflict often results in what is known as, "The teacher's having a discipline problem." These teachers often relegate their disciplinary problems to blaming the children for their sense of not being in control. In this process, many children experience rejection, ridicule, punishment, isolation, invisibility, and labeling in their lived-world of school, and their development is at risk. These same scenarios are also played out in many families. In essence, an adult who constructs discipline in terms of power fails to empower children to develop self-discipline. On the other hand, a teacher or a parent who sees discipline as an opportunity for democratic learning and growth, may use pedagogically significant discipline.

Pedagogically significant discipline requires the adult to consider how situations and events appear from the child's vantage point, how the child's response to a situation influences the adult to act, and how the adult's choice of action affects the child. Van Manen (1991) reminded us that reflecting on the pedagogical moments we share with children as teachers and parents may help us to heighten our thoughtfulness in pedagogical situations and increase the likelihood of demonstrating appropriate understanding in our every day living with children. It is the caring and compassionate adult who is able to see the situation from the child's perspective, while reflecting on the possible effects her actions may have on the child's welfare and developing self-image.

Let us now share with you a couple of stories for reflection:

> A mother called a radio call-in show and asked the hosts, "What kind of paddle should I get to discipline my children?" She believed her children need to be paddled so that "they will learn to behave properly." She believed that the only way to make them behave is to paddle them. She based her conviction on three observations: (1) She considered her preacher's children "perfect" and "very well behaved" because they were disciplined with a stick; (2) she said that the Bible says "spare the rod spoils the child," therefore, using the paddle is the way to discipline; (3) she was disciplined with a switch by her parents. Thus, she was convinced that paddling is the way to discipline children, and she only wanted to know what kind of paddle was more appropriate.

This story shows the powerful effect one's lived-story has on one's perception of a parent's role in disciplining children. Her perception of discipline is one-dimensional and limited in its effect on the child's future development. Our lived-stories often provide scripts for living and sharing our lives with children. Revisions in our scripts may depend on our commitment to children and our willingness to reflect on our past and current experiences. This is a pedagogical experience when we share and reflect on our stories with other teachers and parents in reconstructing our knowledge about child guidance. This notion of sharing stories with one another as a means of education has traditionally been a part of the parent education movement in the form of parent discussion groups. We believe it is effective because it promotes social construction of knowledge. In telling and retelling stories, parents and teachers begin to see possibilities for change.

> Tim's mother called me one day saying that she was "devastated." Tim's kindergarten teacher said that "He's a problem!" According to the teacher, Tim would not sit still through circle time, could not and would not try to color within lines, and would not follow classroom rules. Above all, her "assertive discipline" strategies had no effect on him. "Tim," she said, "is a problem! He will fail kindergarten! What can I do? He doesn't care about anything I do to make him behave. He doesn't care that his name is written repeatedly on the blackboard! He doesn't care whether he gets a sticker for good behavior. I've tried everything!" She suggested that Tim be withdrawn from kindergarten, stay at home for a year, and re-enroll the following year. She believed that Tim needed "an extra year to get ready for kindergarten."

This teacher and the mother in the previous story both lack a sense of thoughtfulness and caring in using discipline with children. The adults are rigid, controlling, and manipulative in approaching children. Instead of orienting differentially to each child, they expect all children to experience and learn in the same manner. Children who do not meet their expectations are rejected and labeled. What possible effects would these interactions have on Tim's development? What are the causes of the teacher's perception of the situation? How can we help teachers develop a pedagogy of living with other people's children? How can we help teachers and parents develop a pedagogy of living with their own children? Adults who are sensitive and responsive to children like Tim need to be sensitive to their backgrounds, life histories, and particular characteristics. They need to develop a reflective capacity to understand the meaning and significance of children's experiences.

> Dennis was enrolled in the "three-year-old" group in a nursery school. His teacher thought he was too young and too immature to be in her class of threes. She tried various behavioral strategies to get Dennis to fit into her classroom, without success. The parents were told that Dennis was not ready for school. Other children began to treat Dennis in ways that modeled the teacher's attitudes, behaviors, and expectations. He was often excluded from their play groups. They made comments such as, "Dennis can't do it. He doesn't know how." A substitute teacher, who taught in the room one day a week, was concerned with the way Dennis was being perceived and treated. When she was there she would respond to Dennis in ways that focused on his interests and level of development. For example, one day Dennis finished eating his spaghetti lunch and was sitting at the table with his chair tilted back. He had spaghetti sauce on his nose. The substitute teacher looked at him and began to say, "Dennis . . . " He immediately sat straight up in his chair, looked away and said, "No!" She said, "Dennis, do you know what I see on your face?" Still avoiding her eyes, he said, "I look stupid, don't I?" She reassured him, saying, "No, Dennis . . . " He again said, "I look stupid, don't I?" She said, "Come. Let me show you what I

see." She took his hand and he reluctantly followed her to the bathroom. They stopped in front of a mirror, and she said, "Dennis, look in the mirror." He had his head bowed, and again said, "I look stupid, don't I?" The substitute teacher said, "That's not what I see. Please look in the mirror." Finally, he looked, and stared at his image with sauce on his nose. She said, "What do you see?" Dennis pointed his finger to his nose. She said emphatically, "Yes. That's what I see. Spaghetti sauce." He grinned. She then asked, "What can you do about it?" He began to pull a paper towel from the rack, wet it, and wiped his nose.

This story shows the powerful influence teachers have on children's perception of themselves and others. The effect of being rejected, "not ready" for school, affected both Dennis and the other children's perception of him. It also shows that schools can be hostile and uncaring communities that can put children at risk. Dennis, at age 3, began to live the script or story the teacher had written for him. He developed a negative self-image and responded to others readily in a self-defeating manner, "I look stupid, don't I?" This story also shows us that caring and thoughtful guidance, like that given by the substitute teacher, can contribute to changing a child's sense of self. She patiently and thoughtfully provided opportunities for Dennis to disprove and reaffirm his assumptions about himself. In this way she empowered him to reconstruct his sense of self by seeing it with his own eyes. She further empowered him by letting him take care of cleaning the sauce off his nose. Is this not a pedagogical relation?

Blevins-Church (1993), who teaches writing at Hollins College and Virginia Western Community College, describes her vivid memories of teaching in the public school:

> It's maddeningly unattractive to think that we could so carelessly send our children into a place where they will be shunned and shouted at, where they will be encouraged to memorize and spit out bits of information they are not often taught to use for the purpose of living more kindly and peacefully and more knowingly, and where they will be judged by their willingness to keep quiet and not make a fuss" (p. A7)

Of course, this is not a description of all schools. Yet, for schools to be the caring and supporting environments necessary for instilling dispositions of caring and thoughtfulness, we need caring teachers who possess a caring orientation towards children. Moreover, Greene (1986) pointed out that a caring attitude is essential to providing a curriculum aimed at building a more just society.

Kessler (1991), in describing curriculum as "technology," stressed that schools place a heavy emphasis on preparing children for the future by fostering the skills that will enable them to function successfully at the next level of schooling and in the larger society. Though few would disagree with this assertion, perhaps it also is true that schools overemphasize the fostering of autonomous thinking and problem-solving skills to the exclusion of such dispositions as caring and thoughtfulness. In particular, the knowledge and perspective of women and other disenfranchised groups have been excluded from the school curriculum—for example, responsiveness, and the knowledge of caring, compassion, and concern for others (Belenky, Clinchy, Goldberger, & Tarule, 1986; Noddings, 1984). According to Noddings (1984), a curriculum of caring will require these traditionally female themes to be viewed as legitimate and essential ways of thinking about teaching children.

CONSTRUCTING A PEDAGOGY OF LIVING AND SHARING OUR LIVES WITH CHILDREN

Where do we begin to examine our own pedagogy of living and sharing our lives with children? We believe that one way to start is to reflect on our childhood to better understand our stance and intentions as parents and teachers. Just as telling and sharing stories with children can build pedagogical relations, sharing stories with friends, colleagues, spouses, and others can also be pedagogical in nature. We can learn through these reflections on our lives as teachers and parents.

Recently we, the authors, were telling each other stories of our childhood, as we often do. We told stories of things we remembered doing with our parents and grandparents. Trading stories, as always, led to more stories, reflections, and trying to find meaning in them. How are these stories pedagogically significant? How are telling these stories acts of creating meaning of who we are?

Vickie's Story

I remember, as a young child, moving to Hong Kong to escape the ravages of war. My parents were trying to rebuild a life for us from scratch. My father was holding down three teaching jobs to make ends meet. Many of his former university students had also escaped to Hong Kong; jobless and hungry, their futures were dim. There was always room for one more at the dinner table, and we shared our meager meals with them. They were like part of the family. Father was always trying to find positions for them and tried to help them financially, if possible. Through the years, they have become successful. For more than 40 years they kept in touch with their former professor, sharing their lives and families with him and his family. Even after my father's death they still kept in touch with my mother. What made these professor–student relationships meaningful?

When I was a child, my father would take me to the university with him. We'd catch the bus, take the ferry, and ride another bus that took us up the hills to the University of Hong Kong. As we made these trips, he would listen and respond to my continuous chatters and questions. In between my chatters, he told me stories of his childhood and his work. I remember sitting in his office reading storybooks and drawing pictures while he prepared his lectures and talked with his colleagues and students. I felt included when he introduced me to them. On the trips back home we would have afternoon tea at the Glouchester Hotel. I guess those were my "special" times with him, and I always had his undivided attention. What do these interactions inform me of parenting, teaching, and pedagogical relations?

Somewhere, somehow, in my special times with my father, watching him teach and interact with his students, a seed was planted in me that many years later influenced me to go into teaching as a profession. I am sure that it was more than his knowledge as a sociologist that made his practice as a teacher meaningful to his students and to me. Maybe it was because he was also caring and thoughtful in the classroom and in other situations? Are these pedagogically significant moments?

I also remember when I misbehaved in school, or didn't do my work, or tried to get out of doing things. I used to dread the times when my mother said, "Let's talk about it." The "talking through" sessions were painful experiences that my mother patiently guided me through so as to understand the situation and the consequences of my actions for me and for others. Those talk sessions had made lasting impressions on me. How were intersubjectivity, reciprocity, and mutuality achieved between my mother and me in these sessions? Is it because there is a history to the relationship? Does having a voice make a difference? Were these disciplinary incidents pedagogical moments? How do they reflect my parents' views on discipline?

Andy's Story

In thinking about the many experiences I have had growing up in a small Pennsylvania town, it has become painfully clear to me that, in my living and dealings with parents, grandparents, and other adults and children, I have not always understood the significance of these pedagogical moments. Only when I have reconsidered these experiences with Vickie and others, have I begun to reach some understanding of their meaning.

In my current position as a university professor, I often receive comments from students about the caring ways I have advised, taught, and interacted with them. But I never really thought about what made these interactions "caring," or how in my own development I may have "come to be" a caring teacher. Van Manen (1991) described pedagogy as the caring and thoughtful orientations we have toward others that assist those persons in the process of becoming. I have lately reflected on how I have been assisted "in my becoming" a caring adult.

I certainly look back with great fondness on my childhood and my relationships with family and friends, relationships that even today seem strong and vital. I am fortunate to have had parents who were nurturing and encouraging of most everything I did and to have friends who were genuine and who allowed me to be a listener. But it is only in more recent years as a caregiver, first working at Head Start, then as a preschool teacher in a university lab school, and now as a teacher–researcher and parent, that I believe my dispositions of caring and concern have emerged and blossomed. Without question, my associations and apprenticeships with several remarkable women have helped me to construct my current values and beliefs related to caregiving and teaching. I could relate many stories of experiences shared with these individuals but choose instead to describe here an interaction with my son, Joel, who at the time of this writing, was 7 months of age. I have learned a lot about myself, reflecting on the pedagogical moments I have shared with Joel. I share with you one such moment:

> Joel is sitting on the floor, with many toys scattered around him, waving his arms and smiling, so delighted with himself that he is recently able to sit up. He enjoys the attention he receives from me as I express my joy at his accomplishment. Soon he begins to cry. What does he want? Could he want me to pick him up? No, surely he is pleased with his ability to demonstrate competence in sitting. Should I give him a toy which is just beyond his reach? Talk to him? Make him laugh, as I often do? Play with him in some way with one of the toys? What do I do here? I choose to offer him a toy, but this does not console him. In this seemingly common and taken for granted encounter, I struggle with finding the "right thing" to do. Finally, I pick him up and walk with him, and after a time his crying ceases. Is this what I should have done?

Reflecting on this experience later, and in my writing here, helps me to consider more carefully what I might have done; consequently, this and similar interactions with him help me to decide how I want to be. How I am now as a caregiver, both as father to my child and as a teacher to my students, is never clear to me until I have further opportunities to act in more appropriate (caring and thoughtful) ways. Joel has helped me with this, as do my students, every day.

CONCLUSION

What Are the Next Steps?

Parenting and teaching are ever-changing, dynamic activities. If we are committed to a pedagogy of living with children, we are committed to change—to an ongoing reconstruction of pedagogy of caring and thoughtfulness. The next two steps are (1) reflecting on and reconstructing our daily interactions with children and (2) sharing and reflecting on our stories of pedagogy with parents and colleagues. These two steps are related. Insights gained in one setting will help us with our reflections in the other.

Many situations common to parenting and teaching require reflection. For example, we are often confronted with the dilemma of deciding when to actively intervene or leave children to their own devices. The dual role of actively guiding children and of letting them find their own direction is a constant challenge to reflection (Van Manen, 1991). Pedagogical reflection and action consist in continually distinguishing between what is good or appropriate and what is not good or less appropriate for a particular child or group of children. However, we usually act on the spur of the moment and have little time to sit back and consider what we did in a given situation. Reflectively talking or writing about our experiences can be extremely useful.

Keeping a personal journal can help us record significant incidents and our reflections regarding their effects on us and on the children with whom we interact. It will chronicle our change and the factors that effect change. Are our practices oriented toward the child? Are children active participants in this relationship? Have we been thoughtful and caring in our intentions? Have we relegated to blaming the children for our failure to approach them differentially?

The pedagogical relation is intentional; thus, reconstruction of our pedagogy of living with children is also intentional. Lived-stories provide the context for us to reflect and reconstruct this pedagogy to meet the needs of children from diverse backgrounds in constantly changing social contexts. We are all participants in this living story of cultural transmission of caring for the young, as Dewey (1944) wrote so poignantly:

> Society exists through a process of transmission quite as much as biological life. The transmission occurs by means of communication of habits of doing, thinking, and feeling from the older to the younger. Without this communication of ideals, hopes, expectation, standards, opinions, from those members of society who are passing out of the group life to those who are coming into it, social life could not survive. (p. 3)

We wish to leave with you the following questions:

1. How can we as individuals and as members of society be thoughtful and caring in living with our and other people's children?

2. How do we foster caring dispositions in a broken, shattered, untidy world full of violent crime, cruelty, and disregard for human life?

3. How do we help children become adults who will approach difficult and complex issues in thoughtful and caring ways?

Perhaps there are too many answers to questions that are not important and not enough questions that require important answers.

REFERENCES

Belenky, M. F., Clinchy, B., Goldberger, N., & Tarule, J. (1986). *Women's ways of knowing: The development of self, voice and mind*. New York: Basic Books.

Blevins–Church, A. (1993, September). Not all memories of school years are fond. *Roanoke Times & World News*, p. A7.

Dewey, J. (1944). *Democracy and education*. New York: The Free Press. (Originally published in 1916)

Edelman, M. W. (1992). *The measure of our success*. Washington, DC: Children's Defense Fund.

Garbarino, J. (1992). *Children and families in the social environment* (2nd ed.). New York: Aldine de Gruyter.

Greene, M. (1986). In search of a critical pedagogy. *Harvard Educational Review, 56,* 427–441.

Kessler, S. A. (1991). Early childhood education as development: Critique of the metaphor. *Early Education and Development, 2,* 137–152.

Noddings, N. (1984). *Caring: A feminine approach to ethics and moral education*. Berkeley, CA: University of California Press.

Noddings, N. (1993). *The challenge to care in schools: An alternative approach to education*. New York: Teachers College Press.

Paley, V. G. (1981). *Wally's stories: Conversations in the kindergarten*. Cambridge, MA: Harvard University Press.

Paley, V. G. (1993). *You can't say you can't play*. Cambridge, MA: Harvard University Press.

Van Manen, M. (1991). *The tact of teaching: The meaning of pedagogical thoughtfulness*. Albany, NY: State University of New York Press.

Vygotsky, L. S. (1978). *Mind in society: The development of higher psychological processes*. Cambridge, MA: Harvard University Press.

CHAPTER 8

Children, Schools, and Social Class

DORIS MARTIN AND MARY CHERIAN

Freddy was different. His hair wasn't combed. His shirts were wrinkled and dirty. Even Freddy's hands were dirty. And it was not because they got dirty on the way to school. He hadn't washed them before he came to school. Freddy usually didn't have his homework done either. When the teachers asked him, "Why?" he would just shrug his shoulders. We thought Freddy was lazy.

When Freddy talked he sounded kind of funny, as if he were mumbling or something. He had to go to speech to learn how to speak correctly. Sometimes he made disgusting noises to get attention, like clamping his hand in his armpit, just to make kids laugh and to annoy the teachers. I think the teachers did not like Freddy very much. We didn't like Freddy very much either. But we did pick Freddy to be on our kickball team. He was a good runner. We did not mind playing kickball with Freddy, but not Red Rover. Red Rover was where you had to hold hands!

While both authors contributed to this chapter, for the sake of readability, any first-person personal pronouns will refer to the first author, Doris Martin, unless otherwise indicated.

Tim was another boy in my class. He went to speech lessons like Freddy, but it was only because he stuttered. Tim was different from most of us too, but he was clean and he wore really pretty plaid flannel shirts. His eyes got very small when he smiled. He smiled a lot. Tim always said "please" and "thank you" and he always had his homework done. The teachers did not seem to mind that Tim never got good grades. They said that Tim tried and was doing the best he could. We all liked Tim even though he was "slow." The teachers liked Tim too because he never caused any trouble. He always did whatever they told him. I figured Tim was a nice boy, because he lived in a nice white house, and his mother was always outside to meet him at 3:30 when the school bus dropped him off.

I grew up in a rural/suburban community in southeastern Pennsylvania that was racially and, in many ways, culturally homogeneous. But as with any community, there were differences of social class. As a young child I was rapidly gaining experiences of how the people around me behaved differently toward one another based primarily on economics, education level, and occupational status. My early childhood perceptions of Freddy and Tim as having different statuses were not unique to me. Most children observe in others or experience for themselves differentiated treatment based on socioeconomic status. In addition, children's constructions of social class are mediated by the images and models of behavior and beliefs of the significant adults around them, particularly parents and teachers (Rogoff, 1990).

Mary recalls, "Even in kindergarten I knew which of my friends were Chinese, Indian, Malay, or Eurasian (all whites). I was also conscious of the class differences although we didn't talk openly about them. I recognize the 'Freddy' whom Doris remembers. In my world Freddy might have been Indian, Chinese, or Malay, but he was definitely 'low class' or 'labor class.' There seemed to be implicit agreement about who was 'low class' and who was not. School uniforms were to be the great equalizer but there were the other signs: the schoolbag, handkerchiefs, fingernails, and the smells."

ISSUES OF SOCIAL CLASS

In this chapter, we seek to illustrate how children of various ages are in one way or another affected by the social class of their families, especially as class is experienced in the context of schooling. We will begin by briefly addressing issues related to the study of social class and its relationship to race and gender, followed by how children develop perceptions of social class in ways consistent with their growing social cognitive skills. Drawing from the literature and our own and others' personal stories, we will examine examples of social class and the effect of social class through families' involvement in the schools. The chapter will conclude with a discussion of the hindrances to democratic conversations around the issues of social class and pose questions that may stimulate solutions.

For our purposes here, the distinctions of class are significant to the extent that an individual is perceived to be stationed above or below others; that is to say, whether one thinks one is more or less privileged or powerful than others because of identification with a particular group of like status. The many kinds of labels that have evolved to reference income, education, and status of family heads (e.g., upper class/underclass, rich/poor, white collar/blue collar) illustrate the inadequacy of these terms to represent people in terms they wish to call themselves. Though admittedly inadequate, but for lack of a better alternative, we will refer to families and children who are denied middle-class privileges, for reasons of status, income, and education, as either *working-class* or *poor*. *Lower classes,* despite the term's negative connotations, will be used to designate the range of groups who have in some way been marginalized by the dominant groups. For our purpose here, the social class designators are not intended as specific qualifiers. They are at best broad generalizations which fail to recognize a range of individual differences.

Children are assigned to a social class according to the status of their adult family members, a classification that is subject to change when they themselves become adults. Yet, despite the myth of education as an opportunity to rise above ones' beginnings, children whose families are labeled under the rubric of lower class are more than likely to remain as lower class when they become adults (Nieto, 1992). The overwhelming evidence is that children in the lower classes do not have the resources and opportunities to succeed in society in the way that middle-class children do. Health care, child care, and housing represent only three of the severe inequities faced by children and their families in the lower classes.

Wilson (1987) argued that the term *lower class* fails to acknowledge the realities of the group whose "behavior contrasts sharply with that of mainstream America," the so-called underclass (p. 8). Children born into this growing segment of society face discrimination on an individual basis as well as at the policy-making level, an area this paper does not attempt to address. Extreme poverty laced with drug abuse, physical and emotional violence, homelessness, long term unemployment, welfare dependency, and teen-age pregnancy are common experiences of the urban underclass. For further reading on the experiences of homeless children, see the work of Boxill (1990). Current educational terminology has dubbed children of the underclass as being among those who are "at risk," meaning their chances for failure are elevated by virtue of their particular circumstances, one of which is often poverty (Stevens & Price, 1992). With nearly one fifth (21%) of this nation's children living in poverty (Children's Defense Fund, 1997), social class, as it affects the lives of children, must be brought into the foreground of our democratic conversations.

Though we have chosen to focus on social class, we recognize that gender and race have equally significant consequences for children's lives and that the three are inextricably related. The high percentage of people of color living in poverty must be recognized as an indication of the connection between racism and classism. Though gender and race cut across the stratifications of social class, little is understood of how these phenomena interact. Both structural and cultural theories fail to explain the grossly disproportionate number of African, Latino, Native American families, and families headed by women that constitute the so-called underclass (Giroux, 1983; Solomon, 1992; Weis, 1988). Equally perplexing is the lower school performances of minority students regardless of social class (Ogbu, 1993). New interpretations regarding the interactions of race, gender, and class are needed to address the question of the role of public education in "equalizing" opportunities during and after the formal school process (McLaren, 1989).

According to Weis (1988) and Ogbu (1993), more research attention has focused on the phenomenon of social class in education than on race or gender. However, on the personal level there is little consciousness of class discrimination by people who work with or set policies that affect children. Race and gender discrimination have been highlighted by media coverage of events such as the videotaped beating of Rodney King by Los Angeles police and the Anita Hill testimony during the Senate hearings of now Supreme Court Justice Clarence Thomas. Over the years of teaching education classes, I have found that pre-service teachers have a vocabulary and a relative willingness, if not eagerness, to address how race and gender affect them personally. Discussions of social class on the personal level, however, are highly taboo. The current attention to multiculturalism and diversity within education circles fails to address social class as a personal issue except in minimal and rather perfunctory ways (Derman–Sparks, 1989). Race, gender, ethnicity, religion, family structure, and national origin are more specifically noted in teacher education materials than is the possibility of discrimination and hidden prejudices with regard to social class. Government policies and legal precedents have made strides to address racism and gender, but classism has been virtually left to run rampant (Davies, 1992).

CHILDREN'S DEVELOPING PERCEPTIONS OF SOCIAL CLASS

The developing recognition of the relative status of others is paralleled with the development of a sense of one's own family or group status. In the intimacy of the parent–child relationship, children begin to hear words and sense affectations that reflect adult family members' perceptions and acceptance of their own status and identity as a member of a group. Young children are the unwitting recipients of their parents' projections of themselves, which can reflect a range of feelings from pride to shame. These perceptions of self are further developed when others respond in accordance with one's own expectations. Children develop a sense of their own and others' relative status or class through their observations and first-hand experiences with others who have different behavioral styles (Fishbein, 1992). The development of prejudice and discrimination in children is arguably inevitable, but that does not mean that they are not modifiable (Fishbein, 1992).

A 2-year-old boy stuck out his chest and proudly lifted his pant leg to display a current designer clothes symbol on his socks. From his tone of voice and posture it was clear that he was not simply indicating a fascination with the particular animal that was stitched on them. His manner and the knowledge that his socks represented something to show others were learned from the people around him who purchased the socks and who expressed pleasure at seeing the symbol. This toddler would not have been able to explain why these particular socks were "better" than any other pair of socks, but he could and did understand that his mother reacted in a way that made the possession of these socks very important. And by association, he, the wearer of the socks, was important too. The symbol on the sock took on a particular significance as the child constructed his own meaning in the social context prescribed, in this case, by his mother (Rogoff, 1990).

In the classic children's story *The Bridge to Tarabithia* (Paterson, 1977), Jesse, a farm boy from a struggling working-class family, confronts the very different values and practices of Leslie and her middle-class parents, who are professional writers. Leslie and her parents are renovating an old farmhouse having just left the big city to establish a simpler life style in Jesse's rural community. Jesse demonstrates an awareness of his family's lower status when he struggles to do the right thing during a visit with Leslie's family and again when he apologizes for his family's behavior when Leslie joins them. In contrast, Leslie is curious about Jesse's family, but remains confident with her own and her parents' ways, despite their having just moved into new surroundings and into a less-than-familiar culture. Paterson's portrayal of these two fifth-grade children demonstrates the social acceptance and status each child had acquired for themselves through the class perspectives and broad social context of their own families. Leslie's middle-class family represents self-determination and a deliberately chosen lifestyle, whereas Jesse's working-class family lives a simple lifestyle in the country, because it is all that they can afford.

As children grow older, the expectations and behaviors modeled by the important adults in their lives continue to be influential. Consideration of their peers' perceptions also increases with age. As children construct new cognitive schemas, their abilities to make judgments about the self more nearly mirrors the complexity of reality. As a child growing up on a small farm, my family was not considered poor, but we shared many of the habits of the poor such as going barefooted in summer. I remember clearly that my father would not let my siblings and me ride "to town" with him without first putting on our shoes. Going barefooted was appropriate when we were at home or with other farm families, but it was not okay when we were around families who did not share our simple lifestyle. When I started school I realized that my "town" classmates wore shoes all the time, regardless of the weather. When they rode their bikes to our farm to play, I was too embarrassed to join them until I had first put on my shoes. My construction of socially accepted behavior was influenced by my father's rules and then reinforced by my peers' behavior and my desire to be like them.

Children gradually shift their explanations of poor and rich from possessions and appearances in early childhood to the use of traits, thoughts, and motivations during early adolescence (Leahy, 1983). In simplistic ways, children begin making connections between how people talk and act with one another and how they dress. Although young children may be tacitly aware of other differences such as speech and behavior patterns, these differences are less tangible and therefore less likely to be consciously and directly attributed to how others are different.

Mary remembers that most minority children learned Malay as a second language. "In those classes there were always a large number of Indians and Malays. For three years in a row, I had a Malay teacher who constantly shouted at some of the Indian children and yanked the girls' long plaited hair to the ground. Their faces would contort in silent pain. Although I too am Indian and had long hair, I never feared that she would treat me that way. The children she picked on were 'labor-class' Tamils or Sikhs whose fathers were wealthy but were non-English speaking businessmen. They were a different class."

Leahy (1983) interviewed more than 700 children from a range of age groups. His research revealed that 6-year-olds readily make distinctions with regard to the relative status of individuals based on concrete associations of clothing and other material goods. Joe, a 6-year-old, described the rich and poor using material items or the lack thereof as delineators. "'They [the rich] got yachts, got big yachts, got crazy outfits. They got horses, dogs, and cats.'" Of the poor he said, "'No food. They won't have no Thanksgiving. They don't have nothing. They don't have no shirts'" (p. 80). As is typical of the child at this age, Joe saw rich and poor in absolutes, as either having or not having.

Leahy (1983) suggested that children who are confronted daily with the disparity between rich and poor people are more likely to take the perspective of others who are in similar situations. On the other hand, upper middle-class children are more likely to mention the concrete traits of the poor, suggesting that they are more likely to see poor children as the "other." The experience of "not having" in a world portrayed as a land of plenty creates a disequilibrium of which the poor child must cognitively make sense.

In earlier times, the isolation of rural families in small communities of similar means allowed many adults to recall, "We didn't know we were poor." However, with the prominence of television and the ease of travel, one's wealth relative to the rest of society is readily apparent. The public's concern and pressure to have the media reflect the diversity of our society, as we know and observe it, has brought about some changes, but by no means do the images that most children see in the media reflect the contexts of their own lives. However, not long ago I saw a commercial that featured a man and young boy, implying a father and son, trying out a familiar small product. The first frames of the advertisement clearly portrayed them sitting on the front steps of a mobile home before focusing in on the people. This housing context was not the usual middle-class bungalow or wide porch with wicker chairs and potted plants we are accustomed to seeing, and for many lower-class children the mobile home in this commercial came closer to their reality than media portrayals of suburban houses.

> In the seventh grade we attended school in a new building, and as a result of that, the school bus route changed. Now Freddy rode on my bus. That's when I first saw Freddy's house. It made me sad. Freddy's family didn't bother to mow their yard, and there was an old junk car sitting there beside the house. I felt sorry for Freddy. Freddy's family was lazy. All this time I had thought that Freddy was lazy. It wasn't his fault! It was his mother and father's. They hadn't taught him how to work.

As a young child, I was judgmental of Freddy in a way similar to how I heard the adults around me address Freddy and families like his. Seeing Freddy's house reminded me of the role of parents in teaching their children "good behavior and good habits." My parents had taught me how to mow the lawn and made sure that I did it. Obviously that was not a priority for Freddy's family. As a young adolescent I had a new sympathy for the boy whose hair always needed combing and whose clothes were shabby. I transferred my blame from Freddy to his family. The messages and modeling of my family and larger community were providing a basic context by which I made sense of what I saw. At this point in my experience, the guides in my learning (Rogoff, 1990) had not yet helped me to make associations between Freddy's family circumstances and the larger political, social, and economic systems of which his family and mine were a part.

In *The House on Mango Street,* Sandra Cisneros (1984) relates the young Esperanza's desire to have a different house than the one she lived in. She dreamed of living in one of the fine large houses in the wealthy part of town. As a young adolescent she no longer enjoyed the weekend family outings that included a drive through the rich neighborhood where her father worked. Instead of pride in her father's work, she felt shame and even disgust, and eventually refused to accompany her family on these rides. The young girl in Cisneros's story had difficulty reconciling her family's circumstances relative to a community of fine houses that survived, in part, because poorly educated and poorly paid minority adults like her father were forced to work very hard, long hours for low wages to support their families.

The older adolescent who is now able to think abstractly and hypothetically is able to identify attributes of the rich and the poor which include attention to the systems of which they are a part. In Leahy's (1983) study, Bill, a 17-year-old from a working-class family, describes the rich: "They only know the good side of life. They miss the bad side. They feel that they are over poor people and they shouldn't be in their society. That's why rich businessmen in New York who run this city don't live here. They don't know about the apartments, what's bad about them. They live in the suburbs." Bill adds, "Some are very nice, they care about people, help people. But then there is the bad, too" (pp. 79–81).

Bill describes the poor, "Poor people have to struggle. Every day is a bad day it seems like to them. Some don't really care if they are poor or not, as long as they are living. Then the kids, they forget they need education to get out of poorness. Without it they won't make it. Since their parents are poor, they should realize that" (pp. 79–81). Bill discusses the differences between the rich and poor: "One is money. They [the rich] can go where they want when they want. I feel they have certain more rights than poor people. They can get better lawyers than poor people. Poor people get lawyers who don't really care because they are not getting the money the city is paying. They have better advantages. Rich people's life is easy for them."

Leahy asks Bill whether there are any similarities between the rich and poor. Bill responds: "They pay taxes. They work. Everyday life. They care for their family, they love them, try to look out for them. They want their kids to be better than they are in life" (pp. 79–81).

This 17-year-old recognizes the way in which individual families are part of a larger system—businessmen live outside the communities that they have power over. The opportunities for rich and poor are different and are not simply afforded because of individual effort or intent. The poor get lawyers whose pay comes from the city and therefore they aren't motivated to win the case. Bill attributes education as the way out, but acknowledges that the poor may forget even that, although they, like the rich, also want a better life for their children. This older adolescent describes the rich as having more opportunities, again a recognition that class is not simply a result of individual effort, although effort has its part. Bill also acknowledges that despite differences, both the rich and the poor have common goals and some common experiences. Bill acknowledges that not all people within a class are the same. Some rich are bad and some are "helpful" and "care about people." The older adolescent view is that classifications are based on relative wealth and status, but that within any economic classification individual traits are still operant.

Children construct their own realities based on the practices, postures, beliefs, and attitudes of their families and the other influential people in their immediate environment (Bruner, 1986). All children develop an awareness of class, but it is primarily for children of working and underclass families that this awareness is also experienced as a disregard for who one is and how one has come to think and behave. Growing up in a working-class or underclass family and then joining the world of school that is dominated by a different set of values and social expectations is like entering into a game in which the rules have changed, but no one has bothered to explain them. As teachers, the responsibility to guide children's thinking by posing questions is as critical in the social arena as in any other. Vygotsky (1978) recognized the importance of social interaction with more skilled partners (adults or peers) as the means by which children become encultured in the use of intellectual tools of their society. And, a critical intellectual tool to enhance development is an openness to learn from the ideas of others regardless of their social class. The teacher's valuing of each student's contribution to the learning community, regardless of status, serves as a viable and important model for the students. Not only is the teacher in effect saying that higher status students can learn from all other students, she or he is also giving the message to all students that their voice has a valued place in this group and that democratic conversations are important here.

SOCIAL CLASS AND THE EXPERIENCE OF SCHOOL

Entrance into school often marks the initial experience in which children must function as individuals in society apart from the familiarity of their families or close community units. School brings children into face-to-face interactions with a teacher who, like the primary caregiver, is the all-important line of defense against the rest of the world. For children whose teachers use familiar language and whose expectations are similar to the parent or caregiver they left behind, this transfer of trust to the new adult is relatively smooth. The child who comes to school with social skills practiced and taught in middle-class families has an immediate advantage over the child whose family functions differently from that of the general expectations of the school. Children who do not grow up in the "culture of power" lack access to their codes or rules regarding "linguistic forms, communicative strategies, and presentation of self; that is, ways of talking, ways of writing, ways of dressing, and ways of interacting" (Delpit, 1993, p. 122).

A young woman (T. Williams, personal communication, Fall 1994) recalled: "In first grade there was this little black girl, and she always seemed to be very quick-witted—she was always back-talking to the teacher. The teacher was white, middle-aged and very prim and proper. I feel that that's where they were at odds. I remember one day this little girl said something back to the teacher and the teacher literally washed her mouth out with soap. I remember the suds coming out of her mouth and the little girl was like you know, this little girl was so spunky, and after that—she was taken off guard. That day she was stunned. It was scary. I'll just never forget that incident."

The student continued to reminisce, "She talked with an attitude. I know it sounds stereotypical, but that's what a lot of black children—my best friends were black girls—and I would come home and say, 'No! I'm not going to do that!' and my mom would say, 'Where did you learn to talk and act like that?'" Given the setting of southern Virginia during the mid-1970s and the very beginning of court-ordered desegregation, one can be certain that race played a significant part in this school incident, but clearly class and cultural expectations also came into conflict. The African-American child's behavior was outside the limits tolerated by the "prim and proper" white, middle-class teacher who could not and would not see that the child's behavior was a part of who she was as a member of a group—a group whose communication patterns were different from her own. The young middle-class white girl was reprimanded by her mother when she imitated the language of her black peers. From both her mother and her teacher she was given clear messages of what behavior was acceptable. As a middle-class child with a white, middle-class teacher, the expectations from home and school were consistent. Though even as a child she thought that the teacher was being unfair to her classmate, the message that only compliant, "polite" behavior would be tolerated was dramatically reinforced. To a degree, all of these first-grade children were silenced, but for the one who spoke with an "attitude," the silencing was devastating. Her talk, her attitudes, her ways, were wrong and they would be punished. And for those observing, the lesson was clear.

Bowman (1991) wrote, "When children and adults do not share common experiences and common beliefs about the meaning of experiences, adults are less able to help children encode their thoughts into language" (p. 20). The following anecdote illustrates how children make meaning of the language and its usage according to the culture in which their learning is embedded. A 5-year-old asked his teacher, "Is butt-hole a bad word?" "Well, its not really something nice to call someone," the teacher replied. Overhearing the conversation a second child of a working-class background chimed in, "I know a bad word, fuck, but only Mommy and Daddy can say that." The second child's serious breach of social convention, despite his apparent intention of "helping" to clarify "a bad word" caught the teacher off guard. She had responded instantly to the first child, but to the second child, an awkward silence was followed by a partial agreement, "Yes, that is a bad word" and for further clarification, "We don't say that at school." The final phrase solidified the distinction between the language used at home and at school, by parents and by teachers.

The way that teachers and children responded to Freddy and Tim were at least in part a response to the social class lifestyle and values that each child's family practiced. Despite his difficulty with learning, Tim was supported and encouraged by his teachers and peers because he had learned the middle-class rules for polite social negotiations. Tim's middle-class family had prepared him well by teaching him the "magic words" of *please, thank you* and *excuse me.* He had further learned that compliance to adults brought its own rewards. In contrast, Freddy faced ongoing reprimands for not having his homework done, for speaking out of turn, and for using "bad" words.

The tendency to blame those who are considered "lower class" as frequent trouble makers is a familiar experience to many. Not only do teachers attribute misbehavior more to some children than to others, even more insidious is the child's growing image of self as being one who causes trouble. When I was in ninth grade my friend failed to catch the eraser I had tossed to him, and it fell out of the open second-floor window behind him. Just then the bell rang, and we took our seats. Minutes later the principal who happened to be walking under the window at the time, came into the class and demanded to know who had thrown the eraser. I raised my hand to confess, but ignoring my hand, he repeated, "I want to hear from the person who did this." Still with my hand raised, I blurted out, "I did." Later in the office after hearing my story I was dismissed with a kindly smile and told to be more careful next time. Had I been Freddy who by now was firmly in place in the lowest track, it is unlikely that my explanation would have been requested or believed.

Children from working-class families have the extra burden of learning the rules and social conventions of middle-class society if they are to be viewed positively by middle-class teachers. Middle-class children, on the other hand, learn these conventions in the context of family. For example, a 6-year-old was observed pulling out a chair for the teacher to be seated and on another occasion reminded another child that it was "bad manners" to interrupt the teacher. When used judiciously, compliments, such as "Teacher, I like your hair," are also powerful tools that children can use in winning an adult to their side. In a city school in a very poor neighborhood, a large sign on the front door read, "REMOVE YOUR HAT BEFORE ENTERING." A third grader was heard explaining to his teacher, "But my daddy wears his hat in the house." His teacher had just reprimanded him and several other boys for failing to remove their hats when they entered the building. She offered by explanation, "because it is the polite thing to do." By inference children could deduce that what is done at home was not "the polite thing."

Though my family did not emphasize good grades or higher education and lacked the refinements of "educated middle-class society," I was taught the social skills that were interpreted as respect for adults. As a child I "knew my place." That, I am certain, put me in good stead with my teachers. Unlike Freddy, my behavior did not conflict with the power of those in authority. Like Tim, I knew the payoff for compliance and politeness. Unlike Freddy, Tim and I were rewarded with teacher behavior that was generally supportive of our relative successes in school. The values and beliefs of our teachers and the school at large were readily adopted by us because, for the most part, they matched what we had already experienced within our families.

TEACHER BIASES TOWARD CHILDREN OF THE WORKING CLASSES

When one examines the gross inequities of funding bases for public schools, one wonders how we as a society can in good conscience claim our schools as contributors to the great American dream. For many of the working-class children in our society, the disparity is akin more to a nightmare than a dream. Tales about the horrors of schools and the despicable treatment of individual children on the basis of race and class abound in the literature and in the cinema. Research too contributes to our image of teachers who blatantly throw prejudicial statements and beliefs on the already humongous heap of discrimination. Fifth-grade teachers in Anyon's (1981) classic study said this about their working-class students, "They're lazy. I hate to categorize them, but they're lazy." Another teacher explained why she taught history by having the children copy notes from the board: "Because children in this school don't know anything about the U.S., so you can't teach them much" (p. 7). Prejudice toward working-class children cannot be blamed on teachers alone. Their behavior reflects our society. However if working-class children are to receive a more equitable experience of schooling, it must come primarily from those in the front line—the teachers.

To cope with the relatively large number of children in their classrooms, teachers categorize or develop typifications of the children to make the numbers cognitively manageable. Using their individual "self themes" or "filters" (see Chapter 5) teachers make connections to students on the basis of their own experiences as they appear alike or different from those of the students. For example, the "ideal pupil" model is a construction drawn primarily from the teacher's own lifestyle and culture (Wright, 1992), which in most cases is white and middle class (Ryan & Cooper, 1992). Other students assume positions that are relative to the position of the ideal. The common practice of testing children before they enter school is one way teachers assess children's level of skills and basic knowledge. Described as a necessity in planning, early screening can fairly accurately determine who has and who has not learned their colors, shapes, alphabet, and so on. Unfortunately, for children whose language and dress indicate working-class or underclass status, the screening results are too often interpreted not as what a child has been taught, but what he or she is capable of learning. With low expectations, low performance is almost sure to follow.

Teachers speak despairingly of children from "broken homes" and as having "bad home lives." For a middle-class family, the description is more likely to be that "the parents are divorced or separated." An education student reported her interactions with a kindergarten child, "When I asked what he was making he said, 'a building in New York City.'" She continued, "You could infer that he has been to New York, although I would doubt that from what I have seen of him. He seems to be from a family that is lower middle class." Several weeks later she concluded her report, "He is doing about as well as one could expect considering his background."

An adult student shared that as a child she never had friends come to her house or told her teachers or friends where she lived "because Ninth Street was known as the poor area where no one who was any good ever came from. I was a good student, but I thought that they wouldn't think so if they knew where I was from." During career week in a rural second grade, a teacher told her student intern not to bother listing "things like doctor, lawyer, or actress" on the board these "these children will never have those anyway. They'll probably be just like their parents and work on the farms." Even had the children not aspired to one of those "impossible dreams," one has to wonder what else this teacher has "predestined" that "her" children would never become.

A kindergarten teacher asked me to review a long list of information that she planned to share during home visits. Among the items was the statement that "classical music is played in the classroom." I smiled to myself as I recalled my first introduction to classical music in seventh grade. I applauded the teacher's intention to introduce classical music to her children, but at the same time I feared for the child who might offer to sing all the verses of the popular country-and-western song "Achy Breaky Heart" as a little girl in another classroom did. Would this teacher honor the music of another culture and thus the child who so proudly sang it? Would she also play music of the children's own cultures, or was she intent on playing only classical music as her statement implied?

In my own family, I had learned the valuable lesson of obedience and respect for adults. I came to school in clothes that were sometimes hand-me-downs, but they were always clean and neat. Although I forgot the rules and was distracted, there was no possibility of my intentionally speaking assertively, much less aggressively, to an adult. That was unthinkable. Not so with Freddy. For Freddy, his family interactions included children questioning and challenging adults—a practice or habit which destined him to be labeled a troublemaker. His clothes, his speech, his lack of cleanliness, his posture, all made him a target of class discrimination. As teachers, like all of us, we will always discriminate, but when, in the interactions of the teacher and student, does class move to the background and the person move to the fore? What training/experiences do educators and others who work with children and families need for them to be truly egalitarian and democratic in their interactions with others?

CLASS DIFFERENCES IN THE INTERACTIONS OF SCHOOLS AND PARENTS

Through parental contact or involvement with the school, the two worlds or systems of which the child is a direct participant come together. The interaction of these two systems indirectly affects the child's experience of school. Lareau (1989) detailed the expectations schools have of parents and contrasted the expectations and involvement of parents at a working-class school with parents of a predominantly middle- and upper middle-class school. Lareau (1989) contended that the differing patterns of parent involvement of the two groups demonstrated "the enduring power of social class in American society" (p. 170). "Researchers presume (incorrectly) that once parents are taught the importance of being involved in their children's education, all parents would have an equal chance to participate in ways the teachers would approve. [However,] social class—specifically, education, occupational status, income, and the characteristics of work, provides parents with unequal resources and dispositions" (p. 171).

Of the two groups, the working-class parents were not as active in their children's education as were the middle-class parents. Principals and teachers assumed the reason to be that working-class parents simply did not value education as did the others. Contrary to this assumption, interviews with the working-class parents reflected a strong interest and valuing of education. Parents expressed intentions for their children's graduation and to "get a good education" and to "be smarter than me." While both groups valued education, the middle-class parents had higher educational aspirations. Lareau (1989) concluded however that the value that parents placed on education was not sufficient as an explanation of the practice of separation that working-class parents adopted toward schools.

Another common explanation of class differences in parental involvement in schools is institutional discrimination. For example, children who are placed in lower-ability groupings are disproportionately from working-class and minority families. Similarly, children who are the participants in special programs for the gifted and talented are overwhelmingly from middle-class families. Lareau argues that after children's ability is removed as a factor, support for such discrimination is not sustained. However, the issue then becomes how ability is determined, i.e., the validity of tests and measurements used in determining ability. In addition Oakes (1985) argued that research supported the integration of different abilities to optimize learning, especially for those in the lower groups. "Problematizing social inequities and making them the subject of academic exploration and involving the community in such discussion means talking about merit, intelligence, testing, gifted programs, differential skills, and social justice" (Sapon–Shevin, 1993). Conceivably, cultural capital, (Bordieu, 1977) the very element that keeps working-class children from full participation in the best of schooling, is also the issue responsible for the lack of full participation by their parents.

As mentioned earlier, teachers are predominantly from white, middle-class backgrounds, and their white, middle-class values and beliefs dominate in the classrooms (Ryan & Cooper, 1992). It is their middle-class language and ways of presenting themselves that make parents and children of the same class relatively comfortable in their communication and interactions with them. Apart from any distinctions related to material possessions, the language effectively separates persons of different social classes. One program intending to foster working-class parents' involvement in their children's schooling included instructions for the children to make a collage at home and then bring it school. Misinterpreting the word *collage* as *college,* one parent and child pair proudly presented their three-dimensional representation of the nearby community college building (Hearson, 1992). Parents with less education and less status are not only not as welcomed, but are also less likely to experience a classroom as a comfortable place to be because what they see does not mirror who they are.

Frequently I have heard education students and experienced teachers alike use the phrase "They just don't care" to describe some of the parents of the children in their classes. More often than not, the families they speak of are working-class families who did not conform to the teachers' expectations of what caring parents do. For most teachers, parents who care provide for their child's basic needs; respond to school invitations, especially parent conferences; and return notes and letters requiring parental signatures. By categorizing a parent or family into the group of those who "don't care" the teacher and school conveniently absolve themselves of further responsibility to attempt to connect with the families. By sheer habit, but not out of expectation, the newsletters, invitations, and requests continue to be sent home. No other alternate efforts seem warranted, because "they don't care anyway."

The privileged have power that is not dependent on the teacher's approval or acceptance. For middle- and upper middle-class children the family very often can provide other options. A student recalled, "I had a friend who came from a good background and, as it turns out, his parents were very well educated. I started high school with him, but in seventh or eighth grade he didn't feel challenged. He didn't make good grades because he was unmotivated and disinterested. So his parents pulled him out and sent him to a private school where he ended up doing very well."

Coming from another family context, Ira Shor fared differently. In *A Pedagogy for Liberation*, Shor (1986) described how at age eleven he started an unofficial school newsletter, which fueled student resistance to the status quo. The principal promptly banned the newsletter, and his mother was called in to discuss his behavior and to pressure him to be quiet. "My mother took the day off from work and complained that the school was boring me, but the teacher embarrassed her by saying she would have to find the money to put me in a private school if I needed special classrooms. Ashamed of being working-class, my mother backed down and told me to obey the teachers. I caved in and kept quiet for a long time" (p. 19). Overcome by pressures to comply, the young Shor discovered the benefits of "going with the flow." Initially seen as a troublemaker, he became the teachers' favorite. In this case, intervention from his mother failed to instigate a more appropriately challenging program, because she lacked the social status to influence the school, and she did not have the financial resources to "buy" an alternative.

On the larger educational and political scene, the issue of school choice, which has a ring of democratic decision making, is actually an assurance for those who have the cultural resources to be able to get and keep what they want. The middle and upper classes have always had choices. Instituting choice will not grant equal access to choice for those who have limited resources with which to claim their choice. We must not delude ourselves with appearances.

The working-class representation on school boards or committees that have decision-making responsibilities for the school is rare. A publicly supported child day-care board had several parent representatives on the board, and in all cases those parents were college-educated "professional" individuals, even though children from the working-class families constituted more than half the day-care enrollment. Whereas at least token efforts to be inclusive with regard to race and national origin are frequently evident, inclusiveness with regard to socioeconomic status is seldom, if ever, considered. If the interests of the lower class are served in any way, it is from the perspective of those who are "trying to help," not from the direct personal experiences of individuals representing others who are in similar circumstances. Those in decision-making positions fail to see working-class people as having worthy ideas, opinions, or the desire to contribute to schools and programs serving children. The one notable exception has been Head Start, which has involved parents in decision making since its inception. Otherwise, working-class parents are almost systematically shut out of the decision-making processes of institutions that serve their children.

A final example of a generalized disregard for families of lower status is the lack of confidentiality. While not only an issue of the lower classes, they, more then the middle classes, seem to be the object of "othering." During day-care board meeting discussions, for example, children who posed particular behavioral difficulties for the staff, or children whose families were behind in their tuition payments, were spoken of by name or with enough detail to eliminate any anonymity. The confidentiality usually afforded the middle class was not offered those of lower status, a status that also did not warrant their being given representation on the board. Similar incidents can be observed across schools and school systems throughout our country as teachers share incidences of family circumstances that stand out as different and therefore "worthy" as a conversation topic. The "aberrant" behaviors of lower-class children's families are not likely to be among them.

Too many children are too often the victims of the prejudices of their peers, their teachers, and their society by virtue of their families' social class. Individual teachers are both the instigators and defenders of democratic conversations and interactions in the classroom. It is we who must examine our personal themes and, through reflection, reject the limiting projections we place on our students.

CONCLUSION

The *words class, race, gender, national origin, religion, sexual preference, disability,* and so on are combined any number of ways in our now-frequent discussions of multi-culturalism and diversity. In truth, it is difficult to isolate social class from issues of race, gender, and so on. How one identifies oneself is usually a blend of many of these variables. Of the many classifications, the one that seemingly has the most inherent properties of personal choice and change is social class. While many categories are or have been the basis for negative discrimination, social class, more than any other variable, seems to resist open discussion between individuals of different social classes.

Perhaps part of this reluctance is due to the commonly held notion that one's social classification is indicative of one's individual worth. The association of social classes as representing the rungs of a ladder which one must climb in order to be placed above, and by connotation better than another, may help explain our reluctance to converse openly and freely about our class differences. The notion that one person is inherently better than another flies in the face of "all men [and women] are created equal." According to the great American myth, one can move upward by sheer determination and the will to do so. Obstacles are acknowledged but are seen as surmountable by those who truly want more for themselves. The consequence of this myth is that those who do not arrive at the top, or who do not at least progress up the ladder, are seen as fundamentally flawed. They have seemingly given up or have resisted the American motto to "be all that you can be." They have sold themselves short. To those who have arrived at or have at least maintained their middle-class status, the "seemingly" minimal achievements of the lower- or working-class are the result of personal failures and lack of aspiration. The adult individual is to blame. And in the case of children—they are to be pitied.

By contrast, one's race, nationality, or disability are seen as attributes outside the individual's control and therefore "excusable," or "no fault of one's own." There is the assumption that "You cannot help that you were born in Mexico or that you have brown skin, but you can work hard or study hard and make something of yourself."

Despite overwhelming evidence to the contrary, we still hold to the ideals of Horace Mann as the schools being "the great equalizer." And the great equalizer myth fits well with our ideals of what constitutes a democracy. Our discomfort and our uneasiness comes when we compare the myth with the inequities we see around us (Kozol, 1991). We are immediately uncomfortable when confronted with the sharply contrasting resources of a suburban middle-class school and a school in Appalachia or in a poor urban area. If we are among the privileged, and most of us reading this are, we do not want to face the hard choices of how to remedy these obvious inequities. We cannot tolerate the apparent contradictions between the idea that those who worked hard deserve what they have and the recognition that the opportunities to "work for it" are themselves unequal. It makes us uneasy to realize that a democracy works better for some than for others. We fear that we will be expected to give up something of our own. We reconcile our relative privilege (money, status, or education) by convincing ourselves that we worked for it and therefore deserve it. We fail to recognize that an equitable distribution of resources would elevate all of us, not take us down.

What is the lesson that our schools provide for the poor and working-class children? Is it that democracy exists for the benefit of the middle and upper classes and not for them? Wood (1992) reminded us, "If we want children to learn how to function democratically they must experience, in school, a democratic setting." What can we do to support democracy in schools, a democracy in which students, regardless of differences, have decision-making rights and responsibilities and are free of the discrimination which belies egalitarian participation? We have models and ideals that address the difficulties and possibilities of creating situations in which students have access to the rewards and benefits of full participation in quality schooling (Goodman, 1992; Kreisburg, 1992). Why has democracy in schools not become common practice?

The problem of discrimination by social class affects all of society; these problems are not the property of schools alone. Yet, it is perhaps the school more than any other institution that has the most immediate potential to influence children and families in ways that can make a difference. One place to start is in teacher education, by employing such approaches as "hermeneutic listening" (see Chapter 2), which promotes change within the individual. For several semesters, in a similar effort, I have invited students to a class that I call "telling our stories." Students are asked to recall and share an incident in which they believed they had been the object of prejudice or discrimination. In one such class, which was all female, mostly white, and middle class, numerous students began relating the "discrimination" they experienced by virtue of privilege: being members of a Greek organization, living in a certain upscale neighborhood, having gone to a prestigious high school, and so on. One story prompted another, and the range of experiences usually related in this class quickly narrowed. Sensing that these stories were discouraging to students who were not among the privileged, I interjected that these were indeed examples of prejudice in which individuals had been judged by association with a group and not on their individual merit. I asked the students to then consider examples that were the result of circumstances beyond their own families' control or circumstances in which they were not seen as "better than." For these students, the leap from understanding the prejudice they experienced because of privilege, to understanding marginalization because of race, gender, and class, was a difficult one, but their own experiences provided a place (the only place) to start our exploration of discrimination. Two very different stories followed, which illustrated racial minority discrimination. As the students continued to listen to each other's stories, the recognition of discrimination by virtue of privilege, versus discrimination by lack of privilege, began to become clear. Prejudice regardless of its reason produced common feelings among the young women. These common feelings allowed students regardless of their status to identify with each other's experiences and to begin to know in a new way the individuals who were their classmates. In the telling of our stories, democratic conversations had begun.

Clearly the effect of our social class continues throughout our lives. As shareholders in a democracy, we relish stories in which the hero or heroine has climbed out of a lowly station to "make it big." Those who make it big, however, are the exceptions. As a democratic society we owe it to all children, and to the ideals of democracy, that within our own professional influence and within the limits of personal opportunities, we will do all that we can to make education the opportunity that it can be. We must not be lulled by classist and racist arguments such as those of Herrnstein & Murray (1994) who would have us believe that the poor are poor because they are genetically inferior. " 'Democracy,' said Jefferson in 1782, 'could not serve without those talents which nature has sown so liberally among the poor as well as the rich. . . . ' " (Wood, 1992, p. 19). As a society we cannot afford to systematically restrict the opportunities of a large segment of the population without adversely affecting the whole. When the poor are discriminated against, we all are losers; when society seeks to rectify its inequities, we all stand to gain. For us, the having of democratic conversations is about listening and responding to "the least of these" as described by Cleave (1994)—that is to all those whose voices have traditionally been drowned by the din of the more privileged.

REFERENCES

Anyon, J. (1981). Social class and school knowledge. *Curriculum Inquiry*, *11,* 3–41.

Bordieu, P. (1977). Cultural reproduction and social reproduction. In J. Karabel & A. H. Halsey (Eds.), *Power and ideology in education* (pp. 487–511). New York: Oxford University Press.

Bowman, B. (1991). Educating language minority children: Challenges and opportunities. In S. L. Kagan, *The care and education of America's young children: Obstacles and opportunities* (pp. 17–29). Chicago: University of Chicago Press.

Boxill, N. A. (1990). *Homeless children: The watchers and the waiters.* New York: Hawthorne Press.

Bruner, J. (1986). *Actual minds, possible worlds.* Cambridge, MA: Harvard University Press.

Children's Defense Fund. (1997). *Annual report, the state of America's children.* Washington, DC: Author.

Cisneros, S. (1984). *The house on Mango Street.* New York: Vintage Books.

Cleave, M. V. (1994). *The least of these: Stories of school children*. Thousand Oaks, CA: Corwin Press.

Davies, B. (1992). Social class: School effectiveness and cultural diversity. In J. Lynch, C. Mogdil, & S. Mogdil (Eds.), *Equity or excellence: Education and cultural reproduction* (pp. 131–147). Washington, DC: Falmer.

Delpit, L. (1993). The silenced dialogue: Power and pedagogy in educating other people's children. In L. Weis & M. Fine, (Eds.), *Beyond silenced voices: Class, race, and gender in the United States Schools* (pp. 119–139). Albany: SUNY Publications.

Derman-Sparks, L. (1989). *Anti-bias curriculum: Tools for empowering children*. Washington, DC: National Association for the Education of Young Children.

Fishbein, H. D. (1992). The development of peer prejudice and discrimination in children. In J. Lynch, C. Mogdil, & S. Mogdil (Eds.), *Prejudice, polemic or progress* (pp. 43–74). Washington, DC: Falmer.

Giroux, H. A. (1983). *Theory & resistance in education: A pedagogy for the opposition*. New York: Bergin & Garvey.

Goodman, J. (1992). *Elementary schooling for critical democracy*. Albany: State University of New York Press.

Hearson, P. (1992, January). *They said to make a collage*. Paper presented at the Qualitative Interest Group Annual Conference, Athens, GA.

Herrnstein, R. J., & Murray, C. (1994*). The bell curve: Intelligence and class structure in American life*. New York: Free Press.

Kozol, J. (1991). *Savage inequalities*. New York: Crown Publishers.

Kreisberg, S. (1992). *Transforming power: Domination, empowerment, and education*. Albany: State University of New York Press.

Lareau, A. (1989). *Home advantage: Social class and parental intervention in elementary education*. New York: Falmer.

Leahy, R. L. (1983) The development of the conception of social class. In R. L. Leahy, (Ed.), *The child's construction of social knowledge* (pp. 79–107). New York: Academic Press.

McLaren, P. (1989). *Life in schools*. New York: Longman Press.

Nieto, S. (1992). *Affirming diversity: The sociopolitical context of multicultural education*. New York: Longman Press.

Oakes, J. (1985). *Keeping track: How schools structure inequality*. New Haven, CT: Yale University Press.

Ogbu, J. (1993). Class stratification, racial stratification, and schooling. In L. Weis (Ed.), *Class, race and gender in American education* (pp. 163–182). Albany: State University of New York Press.

Paterson, K. (1977). *Bridge to Tarabithia*. New York: Harper Trophy.

Rogoff, B. (1990). *Apprenticeship in thinking: Cognitive development in social context*. New York: Oxford University Press.

Ryan, K., & Cooper, J. M. (1992). *Those who can, teach* (6th ed.). Princeton, NJ: Houghton Mifflin Company.

Sapon-Shevin, M. (1993). Gifted education and the protection of privilege: Breaking the silence, opening the discourse. In L. Weis & M. Fine (Eds.), *Beyond silenced voices: Class, race, and gender in the United States schools* (pp. 25–44). Albany: SUNY Publications.

Shor, T., & Freire, P. (1986). *A pedagogy for liberation: Dialogues on transforming education*. New York: Bergin & Garvey.

Solomon, R. P. (1992). *Black resistance in high school: Forging a separatist culture*. Albany: State University of New York Press.

Stevens, L. J., & Price, M. (1992). Meeting the challenge of children at risk. *Phi Delta Kappan, 74*(1), 18–23.

Vygotsky, L. S. (1978). *Mind in society: The development of higher psychological processes.* Cambridge, MA: Harvard University Press.

Weis, L. (Ed.). (1988). *Class, race and gender in American education*. Albany: State University of New York Press.

Wilson, W. J. (1987). *The truly disadvantaged: The inner city, the underclass, and public policy*. Chicago: University of Chicago Press.

Wood, G. (1992). Democratic schools at risk. *Educators for Social Responsibility Journal, 1*(1), 12–21.

Wright, C. (1992). Early education: Multiracial primary classroom. In G. Dawn, B. Mayer, & M. Blair (Eds.), *Racism and education: Structures and strategies* (pp. 5–41). Newbury Park, CA: Sage.

PART Three

Journeys in Diversity

CHAPTER 9

Photo Elicitation of the Heuristic Meaning of Multiculturalism

C. B. CLAIBORNE

The meaning of multiculturalism is a lived experience for each of us. A lifetime of events and relationships inform what we understand as transcultural or multicultural experiences. In this chapter, I explore the meaning of *multiculturalism* as lived experience using a heuristic research approach. Photographs are used to elicit vignettes of past events and relationships. Current understandings of multiculturalism are interpreted using the vignettes as text. Finally, a creative synthesis captures the discoveries evoked by this process. This heuristic research process complements democratic conversations. The process may include interviews, reflexive thinking, and discussion with others. A search for understanding is the essence of both heuristic research and democratic conversations.

HEURISTIC RESEARCH AS A CONVERSATION WITH THE SELF

Heuristic research is an investigation of human experience. It is a process of internal search through which one discovers the nature and meaning of experience (Moustakas, 1990). The process usually involves self-search, self-dialogue, and self-discovery. Moustakas eloquently described this process:

> I began the heuristic journey with something that has called to me from within my life experience, something to which I have associations and fleeting awareness, but whose nature is largely unknown. . . . In the heuristic process, I am creating a story that portrays the qualities, meanings, and essences of universally unique experience. . . . In the process I am not only lifting out the essential meanings of an experience, but I am actively awakening and transforming my own self. Self-understanding and self-growth occur simultaneously in heuristic discovery.

The heuristic process begins by identifying the focus of inquiry. A "dialogue" ensues with this focus through an inverting of perspective, that is, taking the position of the situation, object, or other person (for example, by asking what it is like to be a cancer virus). After a period of "indwelling" or living with the phenomenon, insights are explicated via a creative synthesis that represents a comprehensive expression of ideas that underlie the tacit dimensions of the focus.

As mentioned earlier, multiculturalism is the focus of this chapter. A set of photographs representing different multicultural experiences will be presented. The photos act as windows to lived experience, an existing text waiting to be interpreted (Ellis & Flaherty, 1992). In this study the dialogue involves the creation of short stories or vignettes stimulated by the images. The short stories serve to "bracket out" memories associated with the images. I then synthesize the vignettes to explain the meaning of multiculturalism by stepping back and identifying themes that emerged during the process.

The five images used are of (1) my grandmother's funeral, (2) a boyhood friend, (3) a Venezuelan priest, (4) a Japanese bow, and (5) a Turkish barber. I employed no systematic search for the images; they simply emerged out of the hundreds that were considered. An image "waved," and I had to stop. Sometimes the vignettes emerged with the images, needing only to be developed. At other times, the vignettes were the results of an effort to understand the significance of the image.

REFLECTIONS ON FIVE IMAGES OF MULTICULTURAL EXPERIENCE

Introduction

I grew up in a town that prided itself on being the last capital of the Confederacy. Danville, Virginia, always struck me as a quaint but backward place. Backward because it longed for the past and quaint because it retains part of that past. Growing up black in such a place was a constant reminder of the antebellum South and slavery. I felt a part of the mainstream culture but also different and less important. A pervasive aspect of everyday life was the constant flow in and out of the two cultures: white society on one hand and black society on the other.

When I was young, black society was more real. White society was "out there." I read about it in school books and I saw it on television. But black society was more palpable. It had sounds and smells like hair grease, pork chops frying, and Miss Verna's perfume. Some people that I knew never or seldom ventured outside black society. Until about 1950 this was still possible, because the black community in Danville was separate to the extent that it had its own mayor, post office, and community services, such as a fire department. This community, called Almigro, was physically separated from the rest of town by a railroad track and Industrial Avenue, one of the largest roads in the city. This was the road that all the open-bed tractor-trailers used to bring in tobacco to be processed. Danville also prided itself on being the "world's best tobacco market." In the autumn, when the tobacco season was at its peak, parked trucks lined both sides of Industrial Avenue and the aroma of freshly cured tobacco filled the air. Crossing Industrial Avenue and the railroad tracks was venturing into another culture, one that shared many historical events but in custom and manner were very different.

My grandmother lived in Almigro. By the 1950s the community had been annexed and was part of the city. However, going to visit her was still crossing that cultural border. Everything was different when you crossed the railroad tracks. There was "community." My grandmother represented an old black culture that would not or could not be assimilated simply by annexing Almigro. She, in a way, embodied that community. The following two vignettes are about the two cultures I experienced growing up in Danville. The first was written in response to a photograph made at my grandmother's funeral.

My Grandmother's Funeral

"Precious Lord, take my hand . . . ." The choir sang a resounding chorus. It was her favorite song. The choir should have sounded good, for this was a special choir made up of the Liberty Hill Gospel Chorus, the Shiloh Choir, and the White Rock Youth Choir. She had wanted it that way. All the best choirs had to be represented. No one was to be slighted, especially not the preachers. Three preachers that she had worked with most over the years would offer eulogies at the funeral.

My grandmother always sat in the first seat of the first pew, right by the aisle, closest to the pulpit. Except on communion Sundays, when as a deaconess she sat in the front on the side opposite the deacons. She was the matriarch of the church. She took personal responsibility for the minister. He came to our house for chicken dinners on Sundays after the service. The Rev. R. J. Wilson, who offered the final eulogy, was the last to come. There was also the Rev. Watkins before him, the Rev. Venable before him, and the Rev. E. M. Wilson before him. The Rev. E. M. Wilson would pat me on the head and encourage me to grow so that I could play basketball. Now, the tallest one in the church, listening to the Rev. R. J. Wilson, I remembered that succession of preachers and others too. This group represented a "who's who" across the podium.

This funeral had been planned for years. She would sit by her bed and review and adjust the program and the order. As the sun went down and the

Figure 9.1

room turned dark, she would doze off with a smile on her face. I think she knew it would be a magnificent funeral.

Two people were entrusted with this information—the director of Brooks Brothers Funeral Home and me. "See that it happens just this way. James will help you," she would say. Today, the funeral occurred. The procession was the longest I had ever seen. At one point, as we started up Liberty Hill, I looked back. It seemed as if the procession stretched all the way to the railroad tracks, to the edge of "the community," perhaps beyond.

In the church, I sat in the first pew by the aisle, and although she did not specify it in her funeral instructions, I took the photograph in Figure 9.1.

My Friend Red

In 1954 baseball had desegregated most of its teams. Willie Mays, Roberto Clemente, and Larry Dobie were all household names. Boys played baseball and saw themselves one day becoming their favorite major league hero.

Somewhat oblivious to its effect on youth, the world of sports had begun to drop its racial and cultural barriers. Among the sports, baseball was leading the way. When I say baseball had begun to drop its cultural barriers, what I meant was that there were two games. The black game was unorthodox and exciting. The white game was fundamental and consistent. Willie Mays epitomized the black game—underhand catches, taking chances on the base paths, "say hey."

Figure 9.2

Mickey Mantle epitomized the white game—bat right-handed against left-handed pitching and bat left against right-handed pitching. He was consistent and let the odds take care of the outcome. These two ways of playing were struggling to merge as the major leagues integrated. It was in this atmosphere of blending sports cultures that I met my friend Red.

Red Bastine was a freckle-face kid that lived two blocks behind me. We had several things in common. We both came from working-class backgrounds. Our friends granted us a certain amount of leadership because we played ball better than average. We also had one major difference—he was white and I was black. We loved to play baseball. We both organized games among our respective peers. After school, I prided myself on being the first onto the field so that I could locate home plate and position the bases and foul lines. This would have to be done each day because whatever rocks or markers we had used were moved during the day by kids using the field for gym classes. I also collected and made sure the necessary balls, bats, and gloves were available. Usually we made sure the first baseman and catcher had gloves, then others, like the third base-man and center fielder. At one point I had enough equipment to furnish an entire team, including first baseman's and catcher's mitts, shin guards, a chest protector, and a mask.

Red did the same thing for his group. They played beside the school, and we played behind it. Often the games would run simultaneously. Occasionally, we would foul a ball onto their field or they would hook one onto ours. During one of these chance occurrences, I met Red. The ball had run down the hill in the third base area. I was standing on third. Calling time, I retrieved the ball and threw it to the kid who appeared at the top of the hill. We exchanged glances. Some days later, after setting up our fields and while waiting for our compatriots, we wandered around the school and bumped into each other. I'm not sure who initiated the contact or what we initially said to each other. It was on this day, because we didn't have enough guys for two games, that we decided to play together. Some guys on both sides saw this as a symbolic challenge, black against white, Willie Mays against Mickey Mantle. We played games of epic proportions. Every day was the seventh game of the World Series. Not since Joe Louis fought Max Smelling had so much racial pride hung on the balance of a sporting event. We kept tally of who won each day and that inspired the losing team to play harder the next day. It was a great series. My friend Red and I were happy just because the games happened.

A few years ago I took the photograph in Figure 9.2 of a boy enthused with baseball. He reminds me of Red Bastine.

Domingo Dias Porta

Domingo Dias Porta (see Figure 9.3) is a model of compassion, intelligence, and courage. In his life he has been a professor, psychologist, priest, and humanitarian. He is originally from Venezuela, I believe, but he transcends cultural limitations. When I met him, his "humanness" overwhelmed me. It's hard to say exactly what this was, yet many other people talk of experiencing this quality.

In 1978 I had a job driving Domingo Dias Porta to several speaking engagements in the Midwest. One of these was on the south side of Chicago. It turned out to be on the second floor of a building in a commercial district. After circling the block, we found a parking space not too far away. When we got out of the car I felt the weight of many eyes on us. This was a black part of town. All around were afros, colorful clothing, and Cadillacs double-parked by the curb. Not being from Chicago, I felt as if I had walked into a Lou Rawls song. The "maestro's" appearance accentuated this. Dressed in his priest's habit, a white tunic top, white leggings and sandals, he stood out. Coupled with his shoulder-length hair and full beard, it is no wonder we drew so much attention. Oblivious to all the stares, he started walking the two blocks to our destination.

As we walked, my attention was drawn ahead to the next block where there was much commotion. A gang of youths had spread out over the sidewalk, heckling and harassing passersby. The sidewalk must be twenty feet wide on these commercial streets, so the gang was formidable. I say youths, but some were older. They were in no way small. They were intimidating in their jackets, although I don't remember what was on them.

People from the community crossed the street or walked out into the street to avoid the gang. Domingo Dias Porta did not waver. He continued to walk

Figure 9.3

down the street toward them. I wondered if he knew that this was a gang and that gangs ruled and protected the space that they occupied. Right now the sidewalk belonged to them. Ten years earlier, in Brooklyn, I saw a gang similar to this one congregated around the exit from a subway stop. An elderly woman came out of the subway and tried to walk through the gang, asserting her right to the sidewalk. The gang pushed the woman around, took her purse, and ran away. I noticed some shopkeepers had stepped into their doorways, sensing such an impending confrontation.

When we reached the gang, Domingo Dias Porta seemed to engage each member personally. Some stepped back. The way opened. No words were spoken. As we walked away, I heard someone articulate, "Whoa, who is that?" Looking back then, I saw the ranks close as things reverted to their previous state. A couple of gang members walked down the street to read the sign beside the door we entered. It read: UNIVERSAL GREAT BROTHERHOOD.

Learning to Bow

Aikido is a Japanese martial art originated by Morehei Ueshiba in the 1930s. Aikido synthesizes hand fighting techniques like jujitsu, with sword fighting techniques like kenjitsu, and philosophical perspectives like those of Zen Buddhism.

My aikido instructor once said, "If I could only teach you one thing, it would be how to bow properly." Statements such as this are not rare in a martial art that promotes nonconflict and nonaggression. Yet, to have an essential aikido skill identified as bowing was surprising.

Bowing reflects a certain attitude, shows respect for the other person, displays an openness, and shows discipline, all while symbolizing one's rank. Bowing incorporates complex cultural aesthetics into one gesture. Much of learning aikido is acquiring gestures such as bowing. For example, distance (*ma-ai*) is important in a practical and a symbolic sense. To defend yourself, a proper distance must be maintained. An attacker outside this distance is not yet a threat. An attacker inside this distance must be dealt with. Distance in a more symbolic sense represents relationship—how formal or informal interactions are. The ideas of aikido are ideas of Japanese culture as well.

The first time I visited Japan the subtlety of the culture stood out. Every nuance was informed by a more subtle nuance. Bows differ by situation, social status, age, and so on. The possible interactions between these factors and their symbolic implications are complex. Aesthetics are also subtle. I once saw fresh-cut flowers in the men's room in the Narita (Tokyo) airport. This was surprising because Japanese toilets are generally given less attention than the rest of the house. Different shoes are worn in the toilet than in the house. The toilet would never share the same room as the afro (bath), as they do in our homes. So to find fresh cut flowers in a public toilet was a wonderful but surprising subtlety.

One day while walking in Kyoto, I saw two women interacting. They appeared to be old friends who had met while shopping. They had a wonderful

Figure 9.4

visit, laughing and joking. They reacted physically to the tenor of the conversation, gyrating back and forth, touching each other in what was a very informal distance. Yet when they were about to part, they stepped back to bow to each other. One woman, who was dressed in more modern attire, appeared to have less status and bowed very deeply. The other woman, dressed in traditional attire, only seemed to nod (see Figure 9.4). Having bowed properly, they turned and walked off down the street in opposite directions.

Ali Uludag the Barber, Being Welcomed

Merhaba! Greetings! Each time I walked in, the barber's greeting was so warm and infectious. Ali had a shop on a side street that led to our hotel. He frequently sat in front of the shop talking to the baker who ran the business opposite his. This was plausible, because the baker worked primarily in the early morning and early afternoon (fresh bread is made twice a day in Turkey). Ali, on the other hand, worked sporadically, whenever a customer came for a haircut or shave.

We shared these casual greetings for two days, whenever I left and returned to the hotel. It was at one of these passings that he held up his teacup and motioned for me to come and have tea with him. People share the tea drinking ritual many times a day in Turkish business. Tea is catered through an elaborate distribution system. Hot tea can be delivered within minutes of the request. Furthermore, this call is not by telephone, but by direct line to the tea vendors. I attempted an apology offering that I was late for a meeting with my family. I suggested, as well as I could with 50 words of Turkish available, that we would share tea when I returned. And so later that day, I went past the barbershop with the idea of stopping for tea. This time Ali was busy shaving a customer. We finally did get to share tea. With our limited vocabularies we tried to make the kind of talk that men make in barbershops all over the world. Are you Saudi, he asked? No, American, I replied. He looked surprised, but his attitude did not waver. I noticed this reaction, because there was considerable anti-American sentiment in Turkey around the time of our visit. Some people had decided not to attend the international conference that took me there because of the killing of several tourists the previous week. Ali exhibited none of the coolness often directed to foreigners. Rather, he saw me as a Moslem brother. Even if I had been Saudi, we shared a common religious heritage. I don't mean to imply that the link was that we were of the same religion. Rather, that a strong layer of Moslem values permeates and underscores Turkish society, guiding individual behavior regardless of the individual's adherence to Moslem traditions. With Ali and others in Turkey, I experienced an acceptance, openness, and equality that I had only experienced in the black community. In the United States, even in the town where I live, I often feel invisible when a clerk, or shopper, or colleague, looks through me to address someone else. I understand Ellison's (1952) lament about being an invisible black man when a mechanic ignores me and goes to a white customer who has just walked in and asks, "Who's next?" Though I was a foreigner in Turkey, I was neither invisible nor insignificant. Ali, while exceptional in his warmth, epitomizes the welcoming attitude I experienced in Turkey.

Figure 9.5

After tea, he invited me to sit in his barber's chair. Gently he rocked the chair back. His demeanor changed. While he still had a kind and generous look, he was all business now. He lathered my face, took out a straight razor and began to sharpen it on the strop that hung from the chair. It had been many years since I had had a shave with a straight razor. I remembered, mostly, the burning sensation of the blade scraping over my skin. In contrast, Ali's touch was velvet. He made many short strokes, very quickly. It was hard to feel when the razor touched my skin. All finished, he turned me around to look at my newly coiffured beard in the mirror. It was the best shave I'd ever had. I offered to pay him. He refused. He held up my camera and motioned to take a picture as a complimentary service. I suggested we go outside his shop where the light was better. He called to his friend the baker. We made the photograph in Figure 9.5 of Ali with his plentiful moustache and his friend the baker.

CONCLUSION

How can the five photographs and vignettes aid in understanding multiculturalism? These images, chosen out of thousands, "wave to me." They have some fascination.

The vignettes epitomize special moments within the context of experiences that sometimes lasted years. These moments, though vague, are what I bring from the past. They also inform the future.

My grandmother taught me to care for others. Although her life was spent in a highly segregated and sexist world, her compassion knew no bounds. My friend Red showed me that we can share goals more important than racial pride. We wanted the game to go on, above all. Domingo Dias Porta represents, more than anyone I have met, what it means to be compassionate and loving. Learning how to bow continues to emphasize the subtlety of cultural differences. Such *subtle* differences cannot be stereotyped. Finally, Ali Uludag taught me the meaning of being welcomed.

Two themes connect the experiences here. One theme captured in giving, openness, care, affection, and empathy represents a meaning of multiculturalism. The multicultural ideal is the complement to ethnocentrism, both conceptually and experientially. If other people are different, they are special because of their differences. The second theme is the more personal meaning contained in the lived experience. This meaning is ever changing. Garrison and Kimball (1993) suggest that we are conditioned by historical circumstances *and* by future events. Events that follow an episode in time determine its meaning just as those that precede it do. Unless all events stop, no meanings will ever be final. The five stories presented have meaning for me because my life story has included, and continues to include, different cultures. I am the keeper of my grandmother's funeral ceremony, but I am also learning to bow properly when I practice aikido. Sharing these stories opens a discussion with others and a dialogue with myself. Any sense of whom I am includes the past and extends into the future. My two selves dialogue, the future self with the past self, as I struggle to see the significance in my story and to transform the mundane into the meaningful. The meaning that I describe here is a type of personal myth. My personal myth is multicultural. It always has been. When Red Bastine and I touched, I wondered what it felt like to have freckles. I remember, as a kid, being fascinated by judo advertisements in the back of comic books. When I look into the future, I see myself like Ali Uludag, warm and loving, accepting, without cultural biases. Or even like Domingo Dias Porta, transcultural, loved, and admired by all.

The meaning of multiculturalism is to have a personal myth that carries you beyond your historical values, beliefs, and circumstances. I once heard that only 4% of the world's people ever spend significant time outside their culture. If this is true, this group must be composed of those people with multicultural personal myths.

Myths have a strange way of becoming reality. I remember thinking as a kid that the way to solve the problems of race relations was to blend people so that they were all the same. I later read a science fiction novel called *The Blue Barbarians* (Coblentz, 1958), which had accomplished this by turning all the survivors of a nuclear war blue. The change in skin color accompanied a genetic adaptation that allowed them to survive exposure to nuclear fallout. This change took many generations. Some people who had access to fallout shelters were not exposed to the radiation; therefore, they did not develop the blue pigmentation. However, generations of life underground had rendered these people sterile. They referred to those who

Figure 9.6

could still reproduce as "barbarians" and sought to sterilize or exterminate them, although the future of the race depended on this group's capability to reproduce.[1]

The Blue Barbarians was written in the 1950s. A recent special issue of *Time* magazine (Fall, 1993) featured a computerized image of a woman who was a mix of several races (see Figure 9.6). She represents, in the words of the magazine, "the face of the world's first multicultural society." Current digital technology has done what science fiction could not do. Racial and cultural differences are integrated, not by turning everyone blue, but by perfectly blending characteristics. The ultimate multicultural myth now has an image to solidify it. Can reality be far behind?

REFERENCES

Coblentz, S. A. (1958). *The Blue Barbarians*. New York: Avalon Books.
Ellis, C., & Flaherty, M. (1992). *Investigating subjectivity: Research on lived experience*. Newbury Park, CA: Sage Publications.

---

[1]This is perhaps a reference to the Eugenics movement in this country that sought to sterilize people seen as inferior so that they could not reproduce "inferior" offspring.

Ellison, R. (1952). *Invisible man*. New York: Random House.

Garrison, J., & Kimball, S. (1993). Dialoguing across differences: Three hidden barriers. *Philosophy of Education 1993: Proceedings of the Forty-Ninth Annual Meeting of the Philosophy of Education Society.* Urbana, IL: Philosophy of Education Society.

Moustakas, C. (1990). *Heuristic research: Design, methodology, and applications*. Newbury Park, CA: Sage Publications.

CHAPTER 10

Toward Multicultural
Understanding
A Reflective Journey

ANDREW J. STREMMEL AND LYNN HILL

V ivian Paley (see Ayers, 1989) stated that if teachers are to continue to grow, they must begin to examine themselves. This chapter is, on one level, the story of Lynn's journey toward a more multicultural perspective. But it is also the story of the collaborative process used to study the journey and how this process provided a space for two people to learn about themselves in the attempt to comprehend the reality of the other. In this chapter we show how the self-reflexive storying of life experiences can be a powerful—and empowering—tool in the continuous and lifelong growth toward multicultural understanding. We emphasize the term *growth* in an attempt to focus not on an end state, but on the process of developing a higher mental and emotional consciousness that frees one to negotiate new meanings, appreciate variations in human perspective, and develop dispositions of tolerance and inquiry (Wurzel, 1988).

Reflection can be viewed as a dialectical mental process that allows one to challenge, reinterpret, reframe, and reconstruct assumptions, attitudes, beliefs, and values. Through reflection, individuals subject their action and belief systems to critical assessment, by asking themselves: "What do I believe?" "Why?" "How have I come to believe this?" and "With what result?" Because reflection invites self-examination, it may lead to greater self-awareness, open-mindedness, introspection, and an enlightened attitude toward diversity. More importantly, reflection frees and empowers one to think and feel without constraint.

We believe that the telling of stories prompts reflection and encourages the authentic expression of lived experiences. Gomez (1992) suggested that story making is a means for monocultural teachers to break silences and become multicultural in belief, thinking, and actions. She suggests that, by listening to each other's stories, "teachers and students can construct responsive relationships that can open the insights of each to the other" (p. 165). This also applies to the sharing of stories among teachers. But, for the most part, teachers' stories have been told *to* researchers in the service of *their* interests and research purposes, not to other teachers who are more likely to be hermeneutic listeners (Carter, 1993; Kimball & Garrison, 1999). Consequently, many of these stories have presented teachers in less-than-desirable ways, as characters who are "deficient in some basic knowledge or human capability that would enable them to be effective at what they do or able to make the necessary change toward enlightened practice" (Carter, 1993, p. 9).

Thus considerable care is taken in this chapter to let Lynn tell *her* story, without amending or unduly imposing structure and meaning to her words. As a male academician, it was difficult for me to avoid assuming a privileged, more-knowing attitude toward Lynn and her story. Like others who have undertaken collaborative ventures (e.g., Miller, 1990), we both struggled with internalized "images" of our roles as university professor/teacher (the "expert" and transmitter of knowledge) and director/student (the caregiver–nurturer and learner) in our work. This is evident in the words chosen by Lynn in the telling of her story. Such socially constructed roles often reflect, as Miller (1992) suggested, assumed hierarchies within our relationships to one another, and within the university community, the conventions of educational research, and the constructions of teaching–learning that guide our practices.

It should be noted, therefore, that the original purpose of this chapter was to present Andy's perceptions of the changes in Lynn's practices and beliefs as she moved toward multicultural ways of thinking and being. However, our dialogues increasingly allowed for Lynn's voice to surface and ultimately take the form of the resultant narrative. It also provided space for Andy's story to emerge in response to Lynn's social construction of personally meaningful events. Through our continued meetings and conversations, and the revelations of this story, we have come to accept and understand the possibilities that can exist within true collaboration, that we are and can be co-participants and co-constructors in the creation of knowledge and meaning.

> A lost coin is found by means of a penny candle; the deepest truth is found by means of a simple story. (de Mello, 1986, p. 23)

LYNN'S STORY

Lynn: I first met Andy (the professor) when he placed students into internships in the child-care center that I (the director) owned and administrated in Blacksburg, Virginia. Andy teaches a curriculum course which provides students with practical experience working with young children. My initial contact with Andy was minimal. I observed him in the center as he observed his student interns. I remember feeling slightly ill at ease with his presence in the center. I wondered if in the course of his observations he might also be assessing the center. I often tried to imagine what he might be thinking. For me, Andy represented an authority figure and someone of great knowledge and insight. I desperately wanted his approval. About a year later my center, Rainbow Riders Childcare, underwent the self-study process for accreditation by the National Association for the Education of Young Children (NAEYC), the leading professional organization of early childhood practitioners. During the course of this challenging experience, I decided that I needed to further my education, so I enrolled in the master's program in Andy's department of Family and Child Development. Almost immediately I was assigned to work with Andy on a reflective teaching research project. And in my second semester, I took a class titled "Contextual and Interactionist Perspectives on Multiculturalism," which was team-taught by Andy and his colleague, Victoria Fu. As a result, Andy and I began meeting regularly to discuss the issues and challenges associated with promoting a multicultural climate in an early childhood setting. The conversations took place in Andy's office; they were often taped, and in the beginning, they took the form of an interview, with Andy as interviewer. These informal interviews encouraged reflection on my experiences as a center director and the understandings that I had gained from participation in the multicultural class. Our conversations were the beginning of an ongoing collaborative relationship.

Conversation as Teaching

Andy: Before continuing with Lynn's story, I feel it necessary to mention that I had hoped that, through conversation, I could further support Lynn in her evolving understandings about multiculturalism. This was an opportunity for teaching and learning, only I saw myself primarily as the teacher. What will become evident in the following pages is that I also was learning about the power of conversation as a means of identifying our common stories, establishing shared meaning and knowledge construction, and synthesizing our perspectives. But I will let the story reveal this.

Finding a Perspective

Lynn: When I try to understand the changes that have taken place in my center, I find that I must also try to understand myself. This is not an easy assignment for me. I was challenged by Katherine Allen (see chapters 3 and 12) to "find your perspective." This challenge allowed me to confront my childhood and to see more clearly how I became the adult of today. When I think back to my childhood, the thing that stands out for me is the constant moving that we did. My father worked for a large company and was transferred frequently. I was always the "new kid on the block." This led to a very solitary and quiet life. It became increasingly difficult to form new attachments and friendships as we moved. I remember being desperately lonely and trying to figure out a way to gain the approval of yet another group of children. I became very "watchful." I would observe and analyze from afar these would-be playmates. And I became a chameleon. I never wanted to stand out in the crowd or to be different. I never wanted to draw attention to myself, I was much too insecure for that, and so I patterned myself after the favorite child and tried to win approval by association.

I have resented my childhood at times and have regretted not having had roots with consistency and security. But now I think I know how I can best use my perspective. I can understand the plight of the child who "doesn't fit in." I can recognize the signs and symptoms of the child who is in pain. I can empathize with the insecurity that comes with being different. And now that I am an adult who works with children, I can try to make a difference. This is the perspective that I took with me as I tried to redevelop the multicultural position at Rainbow Riders.

In 1986, after having worked for almost 10 years at the local Department of Social Services with the Foster Care and Protective Services Programs, and after my marriage and the birth of my two daughters, I decided to open a child care center. While my work as a social worker had been challenging and meaningful, I was at the point in the system where I no longer could follow the rules and regulations set out by the bureaucracy. Ironically, on opening my own center, my first order of business was to set out the rules and regulations. I developed a staff handbook and a parent handbook, and I expected that everyone would be willing to follow them. I also quickly put together a curriculum plan that I thought would be most marketable. My impression was that owning my own business would mean that I would earn a lot of money, and I wanted to make sure that my center met consumer expectation. I admit that at this point, after having worked with economically impoverished families for so long, I was ready to work with families who could afford to take good care of their children. Because I wasn't a student of "quality care" as yet, my expectations for enrollment came directly from the licensing regulations set out by my old nemesis, the Department of Social Services. I followed the guidelines for ratios that I found there and planned a 2-year-old classroom with 20 children, one teacher, and one assistant teacher. When purchasing my supplies and equipment, I did what most new center directors do, I went to yard sales and auctions. Money was tight, and I needed to take advantage of every deal I could get my hands on. I bought all the major equipment first, including tables, chairs, bookcases, teacher desks, cots and toy shelves. We stored them all in a storage unit until we had a building. My husband, Scott, is a building contractor, so we worked together on the building design and construction. We were really excited about the project and worked long ridiculous hours to complete the building in time to equip, staff, license, and open it by September. My daughters, Kate and Megan, who were 5 and 2 at the time, spent hours sorting toys and making executive decisions about which age group would be most likely to play with which toys. They were our first consultants.

I did all the interviews for new staff in a room at the local library. We showed the prospective teachers a blueprint of the new center and asked them to use their imaginations. My interview questions for potential teachers were basic and unimaginative: "What is your education?" "What experience have you had?" When we finally had a staff, we began our training program. The components for the training, again, came directly from the licensing manual.

I put an ad in the paper for enrollment. In looking back, I'm surprised that so many families were willing to commit to us when we didn't even have a classroom or a playground to show them. But on opening day we had 60 beautiful children in our care. That day was a whirlwind. One wonderful teacher, Gail Olinger, who was there on that first day and continues to be an inspiration today, loves to tease me about all the details that we had failed to think about ahead of time. Gail and I found that there were a thousand and one things that the licensing manual didn't mention. Every time we ran into one of those questionable issues, I had to think up an answer. The answers didn't come easy for me. Once again I was "new on the block" and desperately wanted to please all my new friends. I found out quickly that there would be no way to please everyone. With all the decisions to make and all the people to please, I spent a lot of sleepless nights. The blanket solution to many of my problems at that time was to keep it simple. In my mind I had a vision of the perfect child care center where everyone followed the rules and everyone wanted the same things and everyone was happy. Of course this vision left no room for any diversity. It wasn't long until things got boring. I found that the day-to-day effort to promote a quality environment for children was strenuous and demanding, but after the first couple of years, it became a more manageable proposition. I soon noticed that I was less satisfied with my daily work and felt a need to shake things up a bit. I think, now, that extrinsically my needs for a job had been met but that intrinsically I felt needy.

Introducing a Multicultural Component

I was fairly pleased with the environment we had created for children at Rainbow Riders. By now I had figured out that the 20:2 ratio for 2-year-olds would never work. And after several discussions with teachers and parents and a major decision to forget about my previous vision of "getting rich," we changed the group size in the classroom to 15 and employed three full-time early childhood educators to work with them. I'd also realized that team-teaching was more equitable and promoted a more collaborative spirit among the staff. I was feeling confident enough to have open meetings with the parent body—we called them "State of the Center Meetings." It was at this point that we began the self-study process for NAEYC accreditation.

One component of the accreditation is that a multicultural curriculum should be in place. We didn't have any such thing, but we began to investigate it. From what we could tell, children should be exposed to all cultures to diminish prejudice in our environment. This was something we believed we could offer. We called the International Studies Department at Virginia Tech and asked them to send us a selection of international students for an afternoon of multicultural experience. We specifically requested that the students wear their "native costumes" and bring music and food associated with their countries. We declared the afternoon a big hit and vowed that we would do this at least once a year. During our validation visit for the accreditation, we were surprised to hear the validators comment that we did not have a "true" multicultural experience for the children. They did not seem impressed by our attempt at International Day. Criticism and lack of approval seem to be the impetus for me to make changes. Because of my childhood need to win approval and because conflict seems to be the reason for my actions, I began to research the issue further. At the time, good books and articles on the topic were not readily available and so I talked with several authorities. I could not find a consistent attitude anywhere. But the research and discussion encouraged me to continue my search for knowledge, and I applied to graduate school.

Almost immediately on entering graduate school I found myself becoming more intentional about my work at the center. I began to work with Andy (the researcher) on the reflective thinking and teaching project and I (the student), in my turn, became more reflective. My own reflections, generally, are practical in nature. When I stumble on a new and exciting concept, I immediately want to figure out how to apply it to my real world.

CONFRONTING CONFLICT

Lynn: In my second semester, I enrolled in the multiculturalism course of which I spoke earlier. This class challenged me enormously, and I found myself becoming more and more aware of the prejudice in the world around me. As a part of the course, I began to keep a reflective journal. Because I am generally one of the quieter students in a classroom setting, I found journal writing to be an avenue of expression for me. Issues that I had trouble presenting verbally in class could more easily be shared through the journaling experience. I remember that we were required to submit our journal on several occasions, thus enabling a space for dialogue between the student and the instructors.

In one journal entry I had described an encounter with the licensing specialist from the Department of Social Services. She had ridiculed and mocked a lesbian family that was enrolled at Rainbow Riders. I described this encounter in my journal and had expressed my own inability to deal effectively with the situation. I noted that although I felt extreme distress with the situation, my hands were tied as she held the strings to my license. In the margins of my journal, Andy wrote back, "Why not tell her how you feel? What have you got to lose?" I remember feeling furious after reading his comments. Wasn't he just another professor who never dealt with real-world situations? What did I have to lose? I had everything that I had worked so hard for up to this point to lose! I was irritated with his question, and I could not get it out of my head. I played it over and over and answered it in a million different ways, until one day I realized that he was right. If I were ever going to make a difference, I was going to need to stand up for the things I believed in.

I ended up calling the licensing specialist and requesting a meeting with her, and at the meeting I made my perspective known. The specialist denied making the mocking statements that had caused me such discomfort. We were at an impasse of sorts, although I believed we had made some progress because the issues were now out on the table. Future encounters with her continued to be uncomfortable, and she seemed to adhere to the licensing standards to a greater degree after our meeting. But I still felt a new sense of power in having brought my concerns out into the open. After doing it once, I think it comes easier the second and third times. I think it will be easier to confront prejudice head on next time.

A Reflective Turn

Andy: Lynn has described a confrontation of differing views that challenged her to take a risk and to move toward a heightened awareness of self. It is here that Lynn's story takes a "reflective turn" as she attempts to analyze her prior actions and beliefs and examine her practices against the experiences, values, and beliefs of others (Schon, 1991). When interpretation and understanding of the patterns of activity that make up one's experience are not shared by others, conflict emerges, a tension that arises from the confrontation of differing knowledge systems, perspectives, or beliefs. Movement toward multicultural understanding begins with acceptance of the inevitability and universality of conflict resulting from exposure to different cultural realities and the attempt to reflect on and question one's own ways of understanding (Wurzel, 1988).

This experience was significant on at least two other levels. First, it afforded an opportunity to talk with Lynn about the questions I had asked in her journal. When Lynn expressed her initial feelings about my challenge, I was unaware that I had struck a nerve. My own reflection on this incident made me mindful of the insensitivity with which I posed my question, "What have you got to lose?" She did have much to lose in her view. And yet the disequilibrium resulting from my questioning seemed essential to reflective action that can lead to change—in this case a new courage to confront. And, for me, it led to a new understanding of Lynn's vantage point within the context of *her* personal and professional experience. Second, it was at this point that I also began to sense how I, too, was on a parallel journey. I was constructing new understandings about the way I viewed my position as a teacher and researcher. Perhaps, for the first time, I was beginning to truly understand the importance of conversation as a pedagogical tool for establishing relationships of the kind that can allow students to have an active voice and presence and help me to move forward as a more sensitive teacher. Lynn's emerging multicultural perspective was now directing her daily life, as she continues with her story.

Awareness and Understandings

Lynn: I started to recognize prejudice everywhere—in the stores on packaging, on commercials, in children's books, in the movies, and so on. And then one day, I was giving a prospective family a tour of Rainbow Riders when I heard a comment that I had heard several times before, but this was the first time that I had really listened to it. The parent said, "My goodness these children all look like they could be siblings. Do you only take blonde and blue-eyed children?" I laughed a little and said, "It sure looks like it, doesn't it?" But inside I was appalled. Could it be true? Could I have excluded children based on their color or nationality? I ended up scrutinizing my waiting list after that episode and discovered that I had tended to skip over several names when I was working on enrollment. Those names often tended to be foreign ones. I made an immediate pact with myself that I would make up for this slight by actively seeking to include all children in our program.

Another episode that had enormous impact at this time came from my relationship with T. J. Stone and Katherine Allen. We had been friends and colleagues since their move to Blacksburg (see Chapter 12). In what I considered my open-minded and forward-thinking way, I supported their lifestyle and enjoyed our friendship. One night when Scott and I were out to dinner with T. J. and Katherine, we began discussing their upcoming commitment ceremony. We were excitedly planning the details and imagining the day, when they casually asked, "You'll bring your children to our ceremony, won't you?" I remember feeling confused and uncertain as to the "politically correct" response. T. J. was my daughter's first-grade teacher at the time and I felt somehow that their bond might be damaged by too much intimate knowledge. I hadn't ever talked with my children about gay and lesbian issues. I felt "put on the spot" and I could see that T. J. and Katherine were very upset by my hesitation. I needed time to figure out where my insecurities were coming from. I know now that I was dealing with homophobia, something that I thought "other people" had, not me. Scott and I finally realized that we had a golden opportunity to make a step toward ensuring that our children wouldn't be confronted with these same ambiguous feelings. They loved T. J. and Katherine, and that love wasn't going to change because I thought I had to explain to them something that they already knew, that T. J. and Katherine loved each other. I thank them for helping me to take another step in my journey.

During this time, Andy would call me periodically and set up appointments to discuss my progress. He would usually have prepared typed questions that he wanted to ask me and I would respond off the cuff. He would constantly say that he wanted to make this project "more collaborative." I wasn't sure what he meant by that. I felt insecure about my place in the research.

A FEW WORDS ON COLLABORATION

Andy: As noted earlier, I had another purpose in mind for our conversations when they began. I viewed our collaboration as an opportunity for us to engage in teacher research, only I was the one calling the shots. I had even planned to present Lynn's journey at a national meeting, as a way of discussing how movement towards multiculturalism involves the inevitable recognition, acceptance, and resolution of cultural conflict. But what was missing was Lynn's voice, her own telling of her experiences in a way that was devoid of academic jargon and untidy interpretations. We soon stopped meeting with a planned agenda and began conversing more naturally and openly about Lynn's experiences, as well as my own. At about this time, I noticed our relationship begin to change. As Lynn relates:

> Our meetings together were now opening up somewhat. We still met at Andy's suggestion and always in his office, but now I began to have a short agenda of my own. The conversation still centered on the multicultural issues at Rainbow Riders and for me, but Andy was now sharing more personal issues as well. He

and his wife were about to become new parents, and the changes and challenges that come with this new role were often discussed. This was a topic where I felt knowledgeable and felt that I could contribute more equally. I felt good about being able to give something more to the relationship.

I was still the professor and she the student, but I was becoming increasingly aware through our conversations that in trying to comprehend the realities of Lynn's experience, I was learning so much about myself. Lynn's evolving story prompted me to think of my own encounters with diversity and how I had attempted, and often failed, to work through some of the conflicts I had been dealing with, particularly related to becoming a new parent. For example, it was my sincere desire and intention to share responsibility for the care of my newborn son, and yet the multitude of responsibilities and continuous demands of my position at the university prevented me from meeting this expectation, much to my dissatisfaction. This frustration was forcing me to confront and accept other contradictions and ambiguities in my daily experience. I was changing too, and Lynn was assisting me in this sojourn. We increasingly were becoming partners in addressing shared concerns.

As the relationship between Lynn and me was requiring a shift in power from traditional roles as teacher and student to those of co-constructors of knowledge and understanding, so were the relationships between Lynn and her staff changing. Lynn was striving to create a center climate conducive to democratic conversation, in which everyone is free to have a voice, to raise and explore issues, and to listen "carefully" with the hope of achieving shared understanding. Her story resumes.

EXPANDING A VISION OF COLLABORATION

Lynn: In the fall of 1992, Rainbow Riders was awarded a grant to mentor other child care centers in the southwest portion of the state. We would design, develop, and implement an individual training plan for each center. The plan would be offered in the spirit of friendship and camaraderie. Because we believe that learning takes place within a social context, this training plan offered an opportunity for child care professionals to connect on both a personal and professional level. Teachers from other centers would be traveling to Blacksburg to observe in our center. This was cause for greater introspection. We were challenged by the necessity to articulate our philosophies for these teachers in training. We knew what we did and why we did it, but we had never been asked to share the information with lots of different people who all tended to learn in different ways. Trying to relate to each person as an individual was not as easy as I had expected. Collaborative ventures are truly multicultural experiences. Learning to cooperate, share, be flexible, nonjudgmental, and tolerant of other philosophies were outcomes of this training experience. But they were not easily learned. For instance, there was a teacher in our training program who had been in the profession for 13 years. "Sally" had always "taught" the 3-year-olds in her classroom in a rigid, structured, academic style. She was demanding and inflexible in her daily schedule and in her curriculum goals. I tried on numerous occasions to get her to see the benefits of a more child-centered approach to the environment, but I couldn't sell her. I couldn't make her see that her interactions with the children needed to consist of more than flash-card exchanges. I found myself thinking about her all the time. What was it that made her need to control the environment so completely? Why couldn't she loosen up? And then one day during a training session on childhood sexuality, it all came out. Sally had been sexually abused as a child. As an adult and a teacher of young children, she was fearful of close contact with the children in her care. She went to great lengths to ensure that she never touched them or supervised them alone. Such normal situations had turned into compromising situations for her as a child. Through the support system of our mentoring project, we were able to discuss Sally's fears and, over the course of several months, we were able to help her make some changes in her classroom. This was a lesson in collaboration as a multicultural experience. Because we were tolerant and caring, Sally felt supported and more able to effect change in her own life. Because we were willing to reserve judgment, Sally got the strength she needed.

About this time, Andy started to ask me about democracy within my center. I told him that of course we were democratic in our approach. All children, families, and staff were treated in a fair and equal manner. But was that the truth? I found myself examining staff policies and hierarchies. Our staff meetings could definitely use a shot of democratic spirit. Too often, they were no more than information dissemination from the director down to the staff. At our next meeting I tried to talk with the staff about what they wanted from their staff meetings. They wanted more open communication and a chance to connect with each other.

We decided to initiate a new component at each staff meeting: "Our Best Work." At each meeting, teachers would have the opportunity to tell the rest of the group about a noteworthy occurrence in their classroom. The story could be about a developmental breakthrough, a hilarious episode, a new technique that worked for them, or an endearing incident. These stories fueled our staff meetings with a new sense of solidarity. We could all relate to each narrative and we experienced great joy in this new oral history that we had developed. This was a good start, but I could tell that we were all hungry for more.

As summer drew near, I began thinking about the possibility of taking the staff on a retreat. We had "retreated" once before when we were preparing for our accreditation, but it had been a while since we had all been together for an extended period of time. With the new idea of a democratic staffing system filling my head, I talked with the teachers about the possibility. They were in favor. So, one Saturday in late July, we all met on the top of a mountain in a neighboring county for a day of thought and food and sharing. This experience sparked our new democratic flame! The day consisted of opportunities to get to know each other. We discovered things about each other that awakened a new understanding and empathy. We felt comfortable enough on that day to share our real stories—not just the ones that come out in everyday work environments. We laughed and cried together and felt a bond and team spirit that was almost spiritual. Then we set professional goals for ourselves. We realized that it was ludicrous to expect that each teacher would be interested in the same training opportunities at the same time. If we were to truly embrace a multicultural form of staff development, that meant making the training plan individualistic. Just like the individual attention that is shown to the children in our classrooms, we had to have a similar system in place for our teachers.

Next we tackled our center-wide problems. Using a nominal group process of decision making, each staff member offered suggestions for improvements. After lengthy discussion and debate, we were able to democratically narrow these ideas down to 10 goals. These goals became the basis for our staff committee for the year. Teachers were encouraged to sign up to serve on at least three committees. Each committee elected a chairperson to lead its discussions. The committee discussed, analyzed, and researched the problems presented to it. Once they were prepared, they presented their findings to the entire staff. The staff then had a chance to deliberate and vote on an outcome.

This process has been inspirational to all of us. For teachers who feel some discomfort in large groups, it allows for small-group interaction where they feel safe and confident enough to voice their opinions. For teachers who are ready for some additional professional challenge, it has provided an outlet. And for the administration it has been a respite. Where administrators once planned meetings, ran meetings, provided follow-up information, and set policy, now we are able to provide consultation to the committees and trust that the details will be handled by the appropriate people. Now, I believe I can truly answer Andy's question about democracy within the center with a resounding "Yes!"

ON FREEDOM AND EMPOWERMENT

Andy: Democratic conversation and reflection can promote change. And, as is demonstrated here, mentoring relationships and staff meetings may provide safe contexts for collaborative conversation and reflection, particularly on issues that puzzle and perplex and which lie at the core of teachers' common experiences. Like Lynn, I had been noticing in my own classroom of student teachers that when given time and space to talk about their daily experiences with children, without restrictions imposed by content, assessment, or rules for behavior, students would more freely discuss the problems that really mattered to them as teachers; these conversations were more likely to promote the process of meaningful change.

Smyth (1992) outlined four forms of reflective action that are necessary in developing a more socially, culturally, and politically sensitive attitude toward teaching. He suggests that if teachers are to free themselves from the constraints that prevent them from seeing multiple possibilities and diverse ways of thinking, they must engage in a process of examining the assumptions and beliefs that are informing their practices. This involves (1) describing what they do, (2) analyzing what they do to make sense of their actions, (3) confronting and challenging "operational theories" of practice, and (4) reconstructing teaching practice to be able to act in a more open-minded, responsible way. In the following section, Lynn alludes to empowering and liberating aspects of this reflective process as she relates the experiences of encouraging and using reflection with her staff and in her mentoring program.

Implementing a Reflective Approach

Lynn: As a part of the Model Center Grant, all the Mentor Teachers began keeping journals of their experiences. We decided we would use them during this first year to help to sort out the myriad puzzling circumstances that were bound to come up and also to be used as historical reference. Because I had enjoyed the journaling experience that I had in Andy and Vickie's multicultural class, I decided to pattern this new experience after it. The Mentor Teachers would submit their journals to me at several points during the grant year. I would read and make comments in the margins. Because I was becoming more reflective, I wanted to encourage this trait in the people that I worked with every day. I read everything I could get my hands on about "Encouraging the Reflective Practitioner" (e.g., see Schon, 1983, 1887) and set out to emulate Andy. What happened was very interesting to me, and it seems to point out the power of the collaborative relationship.

Remembering how empowering it was for Andy to take note of my reflections, I did the same for the Mentor Teachers. Sometimes, I would even use the same powerful phrases that Andy had used with me to comment on their writings. I watched as they became more and more empowered. Their reflections moved from mere descriptions of events to insightful analyses of the events. And then the leap occurred when they began to ponder the future based on their reflective experiences. These were the same stages of thought that I am sure that I traveled under Andy's guidance.

And now these Mentor Teachers were sharing this skill with the proteges in their own care. I heard them using the same powerful phrases, and we watched together as these proteges blossomed and unfolded. I knew we were making some headway when one participating director in our project commented that she had heard her staff (our proteges) modeling our phrases with other teachers in their center. For me, this was the ultimate evaluation of our project. Shared learning and shared experiences made it worthwhile.

Toward Multicultural Ways of Being

Another aspect of this grant included developing new training workshops. Katherine Bucca, one of the Mentor Teachers, and I worked together on the workshop designed to focus on the multicultural aspects of teaching. Our main thrust was to teach teachers to recognize that many examples of bias, stereotypes, and prejudice exist in the children's environments. The second part of the workshop was designed to teach resistance to these environmental effects. A noteworthy change that occurred as a part of my journey is that Katherine and I changed our approach to the Multicultural Training Workshop. We moved beyond both the "tourist approach" (see Derman-Sparks, 1989) and the "preachy" approach to recognizing and resisting bias toward a more democratic approach. Our main goal in our discussion began to center on the individual child's self-esteem and in promoting a democratic community within the classroom. We then offered 50 "Teacher Ideas" that might meet this goal.

I believe Katherine and I have collaborated in a way similar to the partnership that I have with Andy. As Andy has led me through the paces, so I have led Katherine.

As Andy has loosened the reins and offered me additional challenges, I have tended to do likewise with Katherine. From planning and organizing to implementing and evaluating, we perceive each other as equals who challenge each other!

Because I had made a pact with myself to be more democratic about the enrollment process, we now had a diverse group of families at Rainbow Riders. Many of these families were bilingual and were placing their children in settings where the dominant language would not be their own first language. This was a problem for the teachers as they were having difficulty communicating with the children. As a solution to this problem, I spoke with each of these families upon enrollment and suggested that they might want to reinforce the English language as much as possible in the home. My thought was that if the child was completely immersed in the new language, the learning process would be faster. I thought I was making my suggestion based on what was best for everyone involved. But, now I realize that I was one-sided in my perspective.

After taking a cognitive development course and choosing bilingualism as a topic for a research paper, I began to see the error of my ways. By denying children and their families their language, I deny them their self-esteem and set up the possibility that they may also lose their cultural heritage. Some families, on coming to the United States, find that after placing their children in U.S. schools they can no longer communicate within the family. The children grow stronger in their English skills due to the immersion technique, but the parents do not have the same opportunity, so they continue to use their own dominant language. Often, the children "disown" their parents' language in an attempt to fit in. The pressure is so great to conform, that they will do so at the expense of losing their family. This scenario is particularly poignant for me, because at Rainbow Riders we had a 3-year-old child who went from speaking fluent Spanish to speaking English and Spanish, to refusing to speak at all. Silence was where she waged her private war on our system. This heartbreaking dilemma was cause for much debate within our center. Somehow we had denied this child her individuality, and we set out to plead for a second chance. After several months of failed attempts, we were awarded with the breakthrough that we had sought. This child became a happy and content 4-year-old who chattered nonstop in the language of her choice.

Holidays and how to handle them in a nonbiased, culturally relevant way has always been a dilemma for our center. We have been through many stages of thinking and reaction. At one time we decorated the entire center for Christmas including lights on the building and stockings for every child. We sang carols and put up trees in every room. After realizing that this technique may not have been appropriate for some families, we went to a "round robin winter holiday festival." During this phase of our thinking, each winter holiday that we knew of was celebrated in a different room of our center. There was a Christmas room, a Chanukah room, a Kwanzaa room, and a Solstice room. The children rotated through the building visiting each holiday. Surely, we thought, this should satisfy everyone. Then, because of the class on multiculturalism, I started to read more of Derman-Sparks' (1989) work and to study the concepts used at the Reggio Emilia schools. It became obvious to me that I had been promoting a stereotypical view of the holidays. By having the children "visit" the holiday rooms, we were treating them like tourists and giving them little "tastes" of what we determined to be the most important aspect of each event. After much debate within our staff committees, we developed a new strategy for handling the holiday dilemma. We decided not to use the idea of holidays as a curriculum topic. We decided instead to listen carefully to the children and to their conversations and questions. If a child brought up the topic of decorating the Christmas tree or lighting the menorah, we would follow their lead and provide ways to expand on this emergent interest, but the topic would not be initiated by the teachers. Then we asked each family to decorate a panel during their winter holiday. We asked that the panel be a representation of their time together—to "document" the time. After the holidays the panels started coming into the center by the droves! The entire main hallway was decorated with the illustrations of each family's special memories. There were photographs, recipes, lists of family members visited, maps of travel, ticket stubs, bits of cookies, and anecdotes. They were absolutely beautiful, and they came from the heart and soul of every family. We did not have to develop a curriculum for the holidays; the families did it themselves. Each family was celebrated for its unique qualities. Before my immersion into the idea of a multicultural community through my work with Andy, I'm sure that this type of project would never have been a reality.

There is no end to the journey toward a more multicultural existence. I believe it is a lifelong road. I've come a long way on my journey. I've taken some shortcuts that didn't pay off. I've gotten lost and forgotten my way at times. I've stalled out and made no progress for long periods of time, and I may find out tomorrow that I'm on the wrong road and headed in the wrong direction. But because I've learned to be more reflective, I know that I'll find my way eventually. I feel as if Andy (the friend) has been holding the road map for me, showing me that there are lots and lots of options out there. Pick a road and enjoy the scenery; learn from your experiences and keep trying.

CONCLUSION

Andy: Who is the multicultural individual? What does he or she look like? Perhaps these are questions to which there is no known answer. Within these pages we have tried to present multiculturalism not as an end state but as a journey, a movement toward a way of perceiving, thinking, feeling, and being. Lynn's story has provided us with one such journey. The attainment of a multicultural perspective, as Lynn implies, is a long and sinuous road with many obstacles an offshoots. Wurzel (1988) suggested that achieving multiculturalism involves movement to a higher mental and emotional plane of being that enables one to recognize and accept variations in perspective, the ambiguities of knowledge, and the contradictions embedded in the human condition. The reflections shared here by Lynn, and by me, are consistent with such movement.

And while I may have been holding the map, as Lynn states, each turn taken and each hill climbed has enabled both of us to view new countryside and encounter similar terrain. The navigation has been an assisted performance. Being a part of Lynn's journey has allowed me to examine my own development as a multicultural being, and our collaborative conversations have revealed that moving toward multi-culturalism is a dynamic and developmental process that can be mutually assisted by participants in reflective, communicative interaction.

Today, Lynn and I continue our journeys as colleagues in the Virginia Tech Child Development Laboratories. I am the director and she is the curriculum specialist. We continue to learn from each other and reflect on our experiences and those of the children, parents, staff, and students with whom we work.

REFERENCES

Ayers, W. (1989). *The good preschool teacher: Six teachers reflect on their lives.* New York: Teachers College Press.

Carter, K. (1993). The place of story in the study of teaching and teacher education. *Educational Researcher, 22*(1), 5–12, 18.

de Mello, A. (1986). *One minute wisdom.* New York: Doubleday.

Derman-Sparks, L. (1989). *Anti-bias curriculum: Tools for empowering young children.* Washington, DC: NAEYC.

Gomez, M. L. (1992). Breaking silences: Building new stories of classroom life through teacher transformation. In S. Kessler & B. Swadener (Eds.), *Reconceptualizing the early childhood curriculum: Beginning the dialogue* (pp. 165–188). New York: Teachers College Press.

Kimball, S., & Garrison, J. (1999). Hermeneutic listening in multicultural conversations. In V. R. Fu & A. J. Stremmel (Eds.), *Affirming diversity through democratic conversations* (pp. 15–27). Upper Saddle River, NJ: Merrill/Prentice Hall.

Miller, J. (1990). *Creating spaces and finding voices: Teachers collaborating for empowerment.* Albany, NY: SUNY Press.

Miller, J. (1992). Teachers, autobiography, and curriculum: Critical and feminist perspectives. In S. Kessler & B. Swadener (Eds.), *Reconceptualizing the early childhood curriculum: Beginning the dialogue* (pp. 103–122). New York: Teachers College Press.

Schon, D. (1983). *The reflective practitioner: How professionals think in action.* New York: Basic Books.

Schon, D. (1987). *Educating the reflective practitioner.* San Francisco: Jossey-Bass.

Schon, D. (1991). (Ed.). *The reflective turn: Case studies in and on educational practice.* New York: Teachers College Press.

Smyth, J. (1992). Teachers' work and the politics of reflection. *American Educational Research Journal, 29*(2), 267–300.

Wurzel, J. S. (1988). Multiculturalism and multicultural education. In J. S. Wurzel (Ed.), *Toward multiculturalism.* Yarmouth, ME: Intercultural Press.

CHAPTER 11

A Journey in Understanding Teaching

ELIZABETH STREHLE

> Stories invite us to come to know the world and our place in it. Whether narratives of history or the imagination, stories call us to consider what we know, how we know, and what and whom we are about. (Witherell & Noddings, 1991, p. 13)

Teachers communicate through telling stories. This chapter is the journey of a teacher as she comes to understand her students through reflecting on classroom stories. Reflection in this context is viewed as a dialectical mental process that allows one to challenge, reinterpret, reframe, and reconstruct assumptions, attitudes, beliefs, and values (Stremmel & Hill, 1999). The ongoing reflection about one's own teaching makes possible the rethinking of what it is to be the classroom teacher. Stories very early become a way of establishing questions about one's classroom practices. These stories become valuable cornerstones of inquiry and provide evidence of change in one's practice of teaching. The stories in this chapter unravel the complexity of inquiry, the joys of connecting with students, and the ongoing process of change. This teacher explores teaching through relationships with students in the role of university supervisor, researcher, and then as a college instructor. This story comes full circle in understanding the connection of the teacher with her students.

As a beginning teacher, I felt confident I could offer the students all they needed to know. This changed as I began to see that all students did not learn the same way. I was pushed to discover ways of teaching I had not explored before. The challenge of the classroom became making learning equitable to all students. At the time, this seemed an impossible task, but the joy came as I explored teaching through reflecting on my stories. I discovered as I got to know the students in the classroom that my beliefs and practices about teaching were changing. I was growing through listening to the stories of the students. I allowed myself to be drawn into their world in hopes of making my teaching more meaningful to them. My teaching began to focus on listening to the students and making connections with the lessons I taught.

Now, as a teacher of college students, I find my learning in the classroom rests on my students. The questions they ask and their different ways of understanding allow me to connect with what they know; their diversity opens windows for me to understand their world. They now are my teachers and I am the learner.

I have been around good teaching all my life. Growing up with a teacher as a mother I learned early about the dedication of a good classroom teacher. I remember the long evenings we spent in her room putting up the Christmas bulletin board or putting work together for the next day. My mother's teaching always seemed to be a family project—whether we were getting ready for the next day's lesson or accompanying her to evening graduate classes. It seemed like a job that encompassed her life, spilling over into the evenings and weekends when we were dragged into teachers' stores to look for additional classroom materials. This did not discourage me from entering the teaching profession but helped frame the question, "What is a good teacher?" I began to think of other questions too: "Were good teachers born that way and just knew what to do?" "Were they so dedicated to their work that it was impossible to separate their lives from their jobs?" "Did they do things intuitively, or did they have a plan of action?"

I have wondered about these questions since I embarked on the journey of becoming a teacher. These early images of teaching played a significant role in how I have come to understand teaching. The more I understand this profession, the more complex and multidimensional a shape it has taken. It appears to me that it is something that takes time and reflection to understand.

EXPERIENCES IN TEACHING

Knowing the Students

I was teaching in Dallas, Texas, armed with these images of teaching. I had been teaching for 5 years and was at a point where I could think about what I was doing and if it made sense with what I wanted to achieve as a teacher. I remember one day, as I stood in the cafeteria eating lunch with my second-graders.

How proud I was of them as they sat there so well-behaved, talking with each other, eating their lunch quietly. I had worked hard to organize my teaching to become familiar with the basal reading text, the spelling book, the math book, and most of all to develop manipulatives that enhanced the phonics program. As I watched the children, however, the question occurred to me, "What had I done in my teaching to get to know my students?"

As a beginning teacher, I focused on establishing management techniques for the classroom. Good management techniques created time for me to think about the students as individuals. I began considering a classroom design that would make connections between the student and the curriculum, an environment that would provide students opportunities to build relationships with other students as well as the teacher. In this design, all students would be members of the classroom and share in conversation. This seemed easy enough. What appeared to be a simple task, however, turned into a complex agenda in listening.

Learning to Listen

As we stood in the hall outside of our first-grade classroom, I held Tina's tiny hand as tightly as she held mine. We were both frightened and unable to move. I could feel her tiny body shaking, but I was so overwhelmed I could only hang on to her hand. I stared in disbelief at the angry young mother who stood before me shouting at her daughter. She was a single mother, and it was all that she could do to keep food on the table. She was attending class at night and working full time. There was no excuse for this type of behavior from her daughter, and if she continued to act like this in school, Tina's mother threatened to call social services and have her taken away.

Her mother was responding to a note I had written about Tina's change in classroom behavior. Tina had always been quiet and withdrawn, but lately she had been doing things like sitting under her table and walking around the room aimlessly. In this school, I was expected to notify parents when my students did not comply with rules of the classroom. The school felt the parents had responsibility for their child's behavior.

This mother cared for her child, but she was at the end of her rope with Tina at home and with the stress of everyday life. She was doing the only thing that she could. She believed she was being responsible for Tina. Now I wondered if I should have notified the mother. We both cared so much for Tina, why was this happening?

I had carefully designed my classroom, I examined what I taught, and I consistently implemented school rules. At this point, however, I had failed to understand Tina. The message Tina's mother heard was not the message I wanted to send. The message I sent was that Tina's behavior belonged to her mother. When this incident occurred, I realized that as teachers we frequently have to reassess decisions we make in the classroom. Classroom decisions, I realized, will affect the relationship the teacher has with the student. Through these decisions, the student will discover if the teacher can be trusted.

I learned that to understand my students I had to listen. Listening goes beyond arranging the classroom and observing student behavior. Listening is intertwined with understanding the student and making decisions that will allow the student to feel a part of the class. As I began to listen to my students and hear their voices, I discovered constraints that restricted my decision making. School rules place an added responsibility on me. In this case it was the note I sent home reporting Tina's behavior in school. How could I support a rule that could possibly break down a relationship between me and my student?

Teaching was beginning to appear problematic. More than ever, decisions seemed to be contingent on knowing the child. I discovered that through knowing children, trusting relationships could be built and a curriculum designed to meet their needs. It became apparent that decisions must contribute positively to the learning of each child. I wondered if this was possible. Consider, for example, a former and very special student of mine:

> Kim was the smallest child in the room, and yet her presence seemed to fill the room. She had a spark in her eye that always tipped me off that something might be about to happen. Kim was a constant concern of mine. As I struggled with the groupings in the classroom and special students being pulled out, I felt I was losing the class's need to become a community. The pull-out programs left some children uncertain about their relationship to the classroom. I believed there was not enough time for our class to develop our interests as a community or get to know each other. Concerned with how to make up for the class time that these students lost, I chatted briefly with the speech pathologist. We landed on the idea of spending a concentrated amount of time offering some language experiences for the class. Twice a week the class would be broken into groups and would concentrate on activities that offered opportunities to work collaboratively by using language as a tool for communicating. The speech pathologist would take one group in the front of the room, and I would take another group in the back of the room. The dynamics of the group changed as the membership of each group shifted from week to week, along with the arrangement of chairs and contributions that the students made. The lessons included all members of the group and their contribution to the lesson. However, what seemed to be such a good idea that centered on the concern for reaching several children ended in a tense angry session where hands were raised, chairs were pushed, and Kim ended up falling over my leg and spitting in my face.

Knowing the child and making connections with learning are valuable components of understanding the classroom environment. Yet unpredictable situations arise in the classroom that must be handled as they occur. I was upset and confused by the circumstances, because I knew all the good intentions that had started this project were not meeting the needs of this child. Language was a part of the picture, but feeling comfortable as a member of this community was somehow out of reach for her. She needed time to become accepted as a member and valued for her contributions, and she needed more than two opportunities a week to be a contributing member of a community. Kim was important to me because I knew it was my responsibility to help provide her with a successful learning environment.

The ominous responsibility of teaching every child and understanding the rules of the local school is difficult without talking with others. I began wondering why students with special needs are pulled out of the classroom. The pieces of teaching were coming together but understanding them was not. As I learned to listen to my students, I knew the value of conversation and making sense with the student. It was important to find the next piece in my understanding the classroom. I turned to other teachers who were thinking about these concerns, also.

GRADUATE EXPERIENCES

Conversation with Other Teachers

It was not until I entered graduate school, and I met a professor who valued experience acquired from practice, that I recognized the piece that had been missing from my understanding of teaching. The professor valued individuals and what they brought to the classroom. He talked about the fact that learning in the classroom needed to be authentic and important to each individual and then modeled this for us, his students. Through this professor I was able to see what I had been working so hard to obtain within my own classroom.

According to him, teachers are individuals who believe in their students. They value, trust, and remember students' concerns. Teachers are people who trust, without question, the decisions made by the students. Teachers like each student's work—not because of how it compares with the work of all the others but because it is the student's own work. The students do not have to be loud to be heard. They do not have to be embarrassed if they make a mistake, but they always want to do their best. They don't want to let their teacher down.

As a graduate student, I was invited to be a part of a reading class his students were taking. In this class, I observed the professor extend to his students an invitation to a yearlong journey, one in which he entrusted to them to make good decisions and then to learn from the experience. He never prescribed the journey but allowed it to develop according to individual experiences and the dynamics that occurred naturally within their own boundaries. The students had powerful opportunities to reflect and engage in conversations that drove the curriculum and molded their experiences. He many times opted for a longer "time" for us to figure things out rather than offering advice or direction. I learned that this process gave all students the confidence to make the question, as well as the answer, their own.

We all define a good teacher differently. Our construction of this concept comes from being a student most of our lives. On entering graduate school, I had strong images of a good teacher. They were those of a kind and caring person. These images also included concepts I could not articulate, but through my own teaching experiences, I knew they were valuable characteristics. Seeing people model these teaching practices helped me to understand my own teaching. Good teachers, I now understood, believed in their students and valued the experiences that their students brought into the classroom. Watching others teach and reflecting on their practices became valuable tools for me to understand my teaching. As a teacher myself, I could recognize good teaching. But being taught by a good teacher, I found, is a remarkable experience. To have someone listen to my words and take time with me leaves an unforgettable impression. To be given the opportunity to sit and listen, as well as to talk and think, emphasizes that the process of "coming to know" is as valuable as "knowing the right answer." I knew that it took a special individual to be a teacher.

As a child I understood teaching being connected to one's life; as a classroom teacher I saw the value of knowing and listening to the students. As I moved out of the classroom, teaching took on a broader perspective. Teaching was being able to talk about the connections between your personal and professional experiences. Through opportunities of observing other teachers, I began to construct an understanding of teaching. This reflective approach began adding a new dimension to my understanding of myself as a classroom teacher.

Observing Beginning Teachers

As I observed a student teacher interacting with the children in her class, I realized that behind every decision is a value judgment. The student teacher was talking to a group of boys, negotiating whether they would be able to work in the same group. I felt the tension between making a good working situation and the self-esteem issue of the "special needs" child within this group of boys. I noted the care and thoughtfulness this student teacher portrayed as she waited for answers from the group. When no one answered, she allowed the students who were clustered into groups to discuss the question.

As a supervisor of student teachers, I began looking, listening, and observing beginning teachers. I knew I would be able to look with them and listen as they developed their ideas about teaching. I would try to use the qualities of teaching that I valued. I would try to listen and let them talk and make sense of their experience.

From the perspective of a university supervisor, the classroom took on a different appearance than it did for me as a classroom teacher. I was able to observe classroom teachers as well as observe student teachers as they embarked in the process of learning to teach. I noticed that teaching was a process of solving problems.

My responsibility as a supervisor was to be a liaison between the university and the local schools where the student teachers taught. The reflective teaching model allowed the student teachers the opportunity to reflect on their teaching as they began to make decisions concerning the classroom. My goal was to listen to the student teachers by giving them an opportunity to verbalize the thinking that went into planning their lessons, as well as the reasons for the adjustments they made during their lessons. I asked questions during our conference time such as, "How did your lesson go?" "What would you change if you could do it again?" and, "If this were your class, what would be different?"

I saw student teachers take ideas from reading literacy textbooks or talking with their colleagues and develop them in their classrooms. Ideas were plentiful, but many times the concerns were more pragmatic, like how to carry out the new idea in their classroom. Classroom management, as well as the content of the lessons, were items that these student teachers developed by observing their cooperating teachers' classroom design. Many times our conversations began with discussions of management concerns or the curriculum. The conversations often began with the activities that were planned and ended up focusing on an individual student's need (Wildman & Niles, 1987). The concerns voiced by the student teachers were the same concerns I had in my own teaching.

Observing and reflecting on others' teaching gave me an opportunity to think about my own teaching. I was understanding my own teaching through being connected with these student teachers and their teaching. I was learning as much as they were.

As a facilitator for the student teachers, I found my job included asking good questions after observing and listening to the student teachers in the classroom. Most student teachers took this process seriously, wanting to talk about their lessons as well as to receive feedback. Some merely tolerated the process, believing it had no direct effect on them and that it was just something that was required. Some resisted the dialogue approach, preferring a more prescriptive method. They wanted to be told what to do and how to do it.

The student teachers who did take the conference seriously appeared to be eager to spend the time to think out loud, because they had spent so much time on their own thinking about their lesson. The individuals who took time to listen and consider alternatives to their lessons were eager to make adjustments in their classrooms. These student teachers who valued the "listening" themselves tried to foster this trait in their students. Listening appeared to be the beginning in understanding teaching. "Teaching" was not about finding the right answer. Teaching was making good decisions based one's value system and one's willingness to make changes if it did not work. How could this be done without the conversation and questions of other educators, I wondered.

Observing the Experienced Classroom Teacher

Experienced classroom teachers are autonomous within the confines of their classrooms. They determine how the classroom is structured and how learning will take place. They determine if a positive student teaching experience will take place. The cooperating teacher interprets school policy for her classroom and decides the amount of structure that is needed for success in the classroom. The cooperating teacher also allows space for teaching to take place. How much space she allows the student teacher to use is entirely left up to her. Many cooperating teachers happily share their space by introducing the student teacher the first day and saying to the children, "We are your teachers." Also many cooperating teachers allow time for the student teacher to try out ideas. The student teachers are given a voice and are allowed to make decisions in the classroom. The student teachers in these contexts tend to have a positive experience in which they are free to think about teaching. A close relationship develops with the cooperating teacher, and questions and concerns of the classroom are a matter of daily conversation between the experienced mentor and the novice.

Cooperating teachers who do not share their space readily fail to integrate the student teacher into the classroom as an important part of the teaching day. The student teacher's responsibilities in these classrooms many times include clerical duties, which pushes the student teacher into a position of assistant. When the cooperating teachers decide on the classroom experiences without the input of the student teachers, the opportunities for the student teachers to learn in a collaborative manner are restricted. Student teachers placed in situations like these are not allowed to make their own decisions, which limits their opportunities for risk taking. Student teachers are then forced to think and articulate their understanding of teaching outside the realm of their own classroom experiences. These situations limit learning and are uncomfortable for the student teacher.

Observing the School Culture

One of the cooperating teachers offered to have a morning breakfast for the student teachers at her school. At this breakfast, she was going to share with them tips on being a teacher. This seemed like a good idea to me. When I was asked for my thoughts in making this decision, I encouraged the breakfast. My encouragement "mandated" that student teachers attend the breakfast and suggested that I, as the university supervisor, supported the cooperating teacher. This endorsement on my part made a statement to the faculty that I endorsed the suggestions of the cooperating teacher. This situation placed the student teachers in an awkward relationship with their own cooperating teachers.

I quickly discovered that each school had its individual culture. As the student teachers entered into their schools, they created their place within the school network. As a supervisor of the student teachers, I found that the relationship the student teachers had with their cooperating teachers was carefully constructed by the two. I was an outsider to the culture, and I did not realize all the ramifications of the decision I was being asked to endorse. To understand the members of a community and how they interact with one another, I learned that I must listen to them talk and observe them. Regardless of the length one goes to create a dialogue, it does not make one a member of the culture. The student teacher creates bonds at school, and the relationship between the supervisor and the student teacher is only a small part of the school network.

The school environment produces the foundation for student teachers to examine their individual belief systems as well as to consider that of their cooperating teachers and peers. The school environment also encourages student teachers to make their beliefs explicit, as well as affords the opportunity to acquire a language to discuss teaching issues. Student teachers are given time to fine tune their teaching.

Observing and Building Relationships with the Learners

After an introduction to measurement, Kathy broke her students into groups to experiment with this concept. I decided to join a group of students who had settled beside my chair. The group consisted of two boys and two girls. I didn't know any of them, although I had seen them work at their desks during my weekly visits. Bart and James began immediately making decisions about how they would measure a book. Because it was large, it should be measured with crayons, they said. One of the girls assigned herself the task of recorder. "Who has the crayons?" Miss Taylor asked. Bart had his school box open displaying a set of new crayons. James immediately grabbed a handful to measure the book. Students immediately began the activity. Several times Miss Taylor stopped by to see how the task was going. Bart had measured John with fourteen crayons; now it was time for James to measure Bart. James put the fourteen crayons beside Bart. The crayons stopped just about at James' ear lobe. "Bart is fourteen crayons long," yelled James.

Kathy has the beginning of understanding how to structure a classroom that allows opportunities for individuals to find out what they know and to explore what they don't know. This environment allows students to begin to know each other and their teacher by listening to each other. As the teacher constructs a classroom that allows time and space for conversation, the dialogue that begins is the foundation for a relationship. The relationship that emerges from working collaboratively builds bonds that develop over time. During the conversations that take place, students begin to understand the genuine concern of their teachers. Are their concerns remembered? Are their voices heard? These are the questions that students ask as they begin to cross the line to participate in learning.

Relationships are under girded with a common dialogue that the learners enter into, freely exchanging ideas and questions about teaching and learning. Whether the relationship is between the student teacher and the cooperating teacher or the student teacher and the university supervisor, a dialogue is established that will reflect the growth that occurs between the learners. This dialogue is used as a tool for understanding teaching.

Many times as the teacher, we forget that there are other ways to look at a situation. Being autonomous in the classroom makes the teacher the decision maker. Rarely does anyone question decisions made during the day by the teacher. The teacher's conscience lies in listening to the responses of the students. Are we making an effort to listen to the learners and see their perspective?

After many years of experience we perceive ourselves as the expert and forget that the learner is inexperienced and has not developed a complex understanding of teaching. The language a teacher uses is laden with meaning understood by the teacher. The preconceived understanding of what a teacher should look like clouds the picture of what is happening. As expert teachers come back and observe student teacher behavior, these complex understandings become a wall, preventing connections between learners. As illustrated in the following vignette, we often see teaching through our own lens:

His face was fire-engine red, which made his blonde hair seem almost white. I was shocked to see this new supervisor of student teachers seated comfortably telling stories of his day being in the local elementary school observing student teachers. He told the story of visiting one classroom and the sequence of events that occurred throughout the lesson. It seemed as if it had started out to be a good lesson. The student teacher in front of the classroom talking to the children, making connections with what they knew and their work, and writing on the board. But as the story unfolded the supervisor described not the lesson as he saw it but the lesson as he would have taught it.

The supervisor had his story and his questions, but where were the questions and concerns of the student teacher? This story reminded me of my own experience with Tina. I had been unable to see what Tina needed from me or how I could help her. I couldn't understand Tina's behavior as she twisted and turned and crawled away from me in the classroom.

The university supervisor, telling his story to an audience, was an expert teacher observer looking for specific behaviors. When he made this observation, it was obvious that the expectations he had for the student's lesson had not been fulfilled. So when he evaluated the lesson, he deemed it a failure because his expectations of the lesson were not met. When the supervisor's expectations of student teacher behavior is uppermost in the supervisor's mind, then often the observation is spent looking for those behaviors and overlooking what actually occurs during the lesson. This happens in the classroom when a lesson is considered a failure because what was taught was not what was learned. But what *was* learned?

When we know someone, what that person knows becomes valuable information. It is important for teachers to know and think about the things we do and how they affect the ones we care about. Can the ones we teach trust us to make decisions that are for their good? The key to understanding another perspective is to listen to what one says. Many times a simple question or silence reveals our concern for understanding what one is saying.

Observing Myself as a Teacher

I stood by the copy machine with another graduate student discussing the teachers we so admired in graduate school. We also reflected on the classes we ourselves were teaching. Our professors had made learning a journey in which we all eagerly participated. As we talked and critiqued our own teaching, being a "good teacher" seemed an unobtainable goal even though we were experienced teachers! "It seems as if I take over the conversation too often," "It is not easy to wait for them to get the courage to contribute an idea." We mused over the texts we were selecting and the articles we were assigning the students to read, wondering what success we were having. We knew it would take a long time to become the kind of teacher who values the individuals and their contributions to the class.

As a teacher of undergraduate students I tried to change the structure of the class to help students begin to make decisions about their own learning. Going through the process themselves would make it easier for the students to understand how important it was to allow their own students an opportunity to make decisions.

The students in my class had difficulty moving from a structured university classroom to one where they participated in designing the class. I knew they must begin to participate in their own education and feel comfortable with making decisions about their own learning.

There were only a few students in this education course first semester. The students expressed concerns about the intimacy of the class and being on the spot more often. The students were unsure what to expect and anxious about their own part. One student dropped the class.

As I read their reflective journals, I became familiar with their fears and their concerns about understanding how to teach. The biggest breakthrough in this class occurred when the students wrote on a topic of their own choice. Through this writing, I felt for the first time that a window had opened into who they were. As their writing progressed and more questions were asked, the students began to trust the process. They were still unsure about the assigning of grades and how process of learning could be assessed, but they had started to think about their teaching. The class made several turns that I had not anticipated. As I spent more time talking and responding to their concerns it seemed they trusted me more. This allowed them the freedom to reflect on the learning taking place instead of the final product they were to turn in.

GOOD TEACHING REVISITED

I suggest we venture into defining *teaching* within a paradigm where one is allowed to grow and think about teaching. As good teachers ask questions, they begin to hear their voices. As they hear their voices, they begin to recognize the importance of hearing the voices of those they teach. As they listen and care for those within their classrooms, they find that teaching is a struggle.

The good teachers discover that only by tearing down the boundaries in the classroom that prohibit learning will a community of learners begin to form. Boundaries are all the things that teachers perceive to be restrictions to learning. Many times these restrictions are as simple as understanding how school rules fit into the design of one's own classroom. The good teachers move from being classroom managers to being active constructors of learning. Once teachers feel comfortable making decisions, they will grow confident in allowing individual voices to be heard and to contribute to the construction of their own community.

Good teachers are not born that way. They have constructed a history of caring and concern for others, and they make decisions daily that reflect that concern within the classroom community. A thread woven throughout the teaching day is necessary to creating opportunities for learning. Good teachers are always concerned about the dialogue of their students and are willing to give time for this dialogue to develop into a culture that offers understanding and support to its members. They develop a skillful ability to listen and ask questions that allow their students to feel good about their own abilities. Enthralled with the process of learning and empowering others to be learners, good teachers value their learners and worry about their concerns. Their lives as teachers begin to spill over into their lives outside school. The two merge as they bring their interests into the classroom. Teaching becomes a process of understanding our classroom design and the students we teach. With this comes an ability to make changes.

If we listen to the concerns of our students, they will open a new world to us—one we cannot see except through their eyes. If we begin to hear them, they may begin to trust us and allow us to be a part of their world. It will only mean growth for us as teachers.

What are you looking for as you look in a classroom? Do you see the richness, the joy, the sadness? Do you hear the voice of the teacher? Can you win her confidence so that she can trust you and invite you in and share her stories with you? Only if you are quiet and listen can you see the picture. Be willing to be surprised, be willing to worry and be concerned. Don't judge her too hastily, but listen to her stories. What you look for you will find.

CONCLUSION

My journey of teaching has allowed me to understand my role as a classroom teacher and the importance of making connections with the students. Learning comes through listening to your students and finding that the diversity they offer adds richness to the classroom. This diversity provides an opportunity for the teacher to acquire a more complex understanding of teaching. Listening does not come easy. To listen and understand means to step outside of your own understanding.

> I also believe that greater self-knowledge can help us to separate our thoughts and feelings from those of our research participants, to be less judgmental, and to appreciate experiences that deviate greatly from our own. Confronting oneself and one's biases was one of the most difficult and thought-provoking aspects of being a qualitative researcher for many students. (Ely et al., 1991, p. 122)

The journey of understanding teaching from another perspective began as I observed student teachers in the classroom. Being a teacher, I understood the dynamics of the classroom. But as a researcher I had to move beyond understanding teaching as I taught. While looking at teaching through the eyes of four student teachers, I found I had to become them to tell their story. I did this through understanding my own journey of a teacher and the growth that I went through. I believed my journey of teaching allowed me to acquire a language of my practice and acknowledge the importance of change that occurs over time. As an observer of teachers, I was able to recognize and accept diversity as well as the propensity to change in others. To move beyond one's own realm of understanding is freeing because it allows us to gain another perspective. These multiple perspectives create a need to rethink how we teach students in the classroom. Change is a powerful agent that does not let one go back. Once we begin to understand through the eyes of others, our beliefs and practices are changed.

This discovery opened up new windows of looking at ordinary events in truly an extraordinary way. Because of my own journey, I could look at the classroom and not be bound by my understanding as a teacher, supervisor, researcher, or college teacher. I was pressed to remove my own perspective so I could listen to the voice of others. I began to celebrate the richness of diversity that each contributes to the classroom.

REFERENCES

Ely, M., Anzul, M., Friedman, T., Garner, D., & Steinmetz-McCormack, A. (1991). *Doing qualitative research: Circles within circles.* London: Falmer Press.

Stremmel, A. J., & Hill, L. (1999). Toward multicultural understanding: A reflective journey. In V. R. Fu & A. J. Stremmel (Eds.), *Affirming diversity through democratic conversations* (pp. 141–155). Upper Saddle River, NJ: Merrill/Prentice Hall.

Wildman, T. M., & Niles, J. A. (1987). Reflective teachers: Tensions between abstractions and realities. *Journal of Teacher Education, 38*(4), 25–31.

Witherell, C., & Noddings, N. (1991) *Stories lives tell: Narrative and dialogue in education.* New York: Teachers College Press.

CHAPTER 12

Parenthood and Pregnancy

The Journey of a Lesbian Couple and Their Children

TAMARA J. STONE AND KATHERINE R. ALLEN

L esbians and gay men typically are not invited to join in conversations about diversity. Consequently, prejudice and stereotype often stand in for the real families in which gay people live. As two women raising our children together in a committed partnership, we are cognizant of the constraints and possibilities confronting the families of lesbians and gay men. We witness lesbian and gay identities discussed openly on television, in the press, classrooms, and other social settings. Issues related to sexual orientation and families are no longer completely silenced or invisible, yet lesbian and gay families remain controversial fodder for public commentary.

In a review of more than 8,000 articles in nine social science journals that publish research on families, Allen and Demo (1995) documented that little is known about the family lives of lesbians and gay men. Laird (1993) has called for rich, detailed, ethnographic descriptions of the day-to-day lives of same-sex couples and their children to correct this deficit in empirical knowledge. Our story is a response to Laird's observation that new information about the families of lesbians and gay men is needed to expand the conversation about family diversity.

The purpose of this chapter is to describe our family's journey in diversity around the particular transition of preparing for and incorporating the birth of a second child. To join the conversation of diversity, we use the methodology of personal narrative to tell this story. This method allows us to address the tension between public and private experience (Laird, 1989; Sollie & Leslie, 1994; Witherell & Noddings, 1991). As social scientists and members of an oppressed group (lesbian mothers), we use a case study approach to provide a microscopic description of how we have struggled to incorporate the normative transition of adding a new member, while at the same time dealing with the nonnormative issue of *heterosexism,* which is the biased belief that everyone is and should be heterosexual (Herek, Kimmel, Amaro, & Melton, 1991). In this story, we become participant observers of our own lives, seeking to connect our particular experience to the theme addressed by all the authors in this book—journeys in diversity.

Our story begins with an analysis of living biculturally—as members of both oppressed and privileged groups—an experience common to lesbian and gay people (Brown, 1989) and to many members of different racial–ethnic groups (see Carrasquillo, 1994; Peters, 1988). Next, we describe the process of planning for a second child within the context of a lesbian relationship. This portion of the chapter is in the form of a journal kept by Tamara (T. J.) and includes pre-pregnancy planning and her experience of pregnancy. We explore this process mostly through conversations we had with ourselves, with each other, with our friends and families, and with our first child, Matthew, who was six years old at the time of T. J.'s pregnancy. Finally, we reflect on ways our family's journey in preparing for the birth of our second child enriches the conversation about diversity.

PREPARING TO TELL OUR STORY

As lesbian mothers, we experience a tension between safety and danger that requires us to second guess our decisions about our family. For example, T. J. wants to emphasize our boldness—detailing the promise and accomplishment of our ability to create a new kind of family. Katherine wants to emphasize our vulnerability—what are the risks of telling a story most others will find different, at best? To what kind of jeopardy do we subject our family by telling our story? Like other families headed by lesbians, ours is bound by a fierce and liberating love that is still unprotected and often denigrated by the society in which we live (Burke, 1993).

We could take many paths in telling a story about our family. We could play it safe and not tell it at all. But then we would be guilty of not acting on our privilege as educated professionals, and we are feminists who have learned the necessity of taking calculated risks. Without telling the truth of our lives, we would be less than authentic—denying ourselves the inner strength that comes from claiming a life, partnership, and family of our own choice.

We could tell the truth with a positive cast and leave out the inner tales of homophobia. We could tell the socially acceptable truth by minimizing the vulnerability that accompanies living on the margins. We could tell the fretful and worrisome truth, so aptly revealed in Margaret Atwood's (1986) best-selling novel, *The Handmaid's Tale,* a harrowing account of patriarchy gone awry. Atwood describes independent women being carted off by men in white uniforms affiliated with religious extremists intent on destroying women who loved other women.

The story we will tell about our experience as two women who are in a committed relationship and raising children together will have all of these features to it: truth packaged with a smiling face, truth peeking from under a blanket of fear and reservation, and truth hoping for change in the structural and legal conditions of our society. The changes we work for include the right to marry, the right to a legal relationship with each other's biological child, and the right to be free from the threat of harassment based on gender and sexual orientation.

In telling our story, we risk being reduced to the label "lesbian" because ours is a story yet to be heard by many members of society. Although Parents, Families, and Friends of Lesbians and Gays (PFLAG) estimates that one in four people in the United States has a gay or lesbian family member (Goodman, 1991), most of us have little preparation for understanding the experience of being lesbian or gay until we realize that we, ourselves, or someone we know, may be lesbian or gay.

Planning to have another child has made the disclosure process more deliberate and subjected us to more intense scrutiny. And we are able to tell this story because we have spent many years as "out lesbians," meaning that we have acknowledged our sexual orientation to our families, friends, and co-workers, and we have spoken with many groups about our experiences. We have written, deliberated, and sought professional counsel about integrating a lesbian identity into our lives. We have confronted legal, familial, economic, and societal institutions and prejudices.

There are benefits to being open about our family. As mothers and lesbians, we do not take our class and race privilege as educated white professionals for granted. Our examination of the paradox of privilege in the context of persecution has deepened our commitment to social change on behalf of all families. This commitment is one of the empowering benefits of our journey as a diverse family.

Our story contains a paradoxical mix of peril and privilege. Knowing what to tell has not been easy because of our fear of potential consequences if this story falls into the wrong hands—hands that have not held ours. We fear for our physical safety, our children's security, and our careers. Yet, as contributors to a democratic conversation on diversity, we have learned that when people share true emotions, thoughts, and experiences, they open a window to understanding that, although maybe tentative or incomplete, is empowering.

GETTING TOGETHER

In the beginning of 1989, we stood on the library steps at the university where we met and simultaneously realized: "We are in love with each other!?" This explained so many feelings neither of us had completely explored before. There was a calm sense of knowing ourselves. Yet, quickly, there was a sense of danger and fear. Would we be hurt? Would we be ridiculed? Would our careers be over? Would our families reject us? These questions provoked anxiety, yet the strength and power of our love sustained us.

That first year brought us to Virginia and to a new way of defining our family. Two-year-old Matthew, conceived within the marriage of his biological parents, Katherine and Ken, was actively incorporating T. J. as a parent. Having met when Matthew was 13 months old, they now had a remarkable connection. Even today, Matthew loves to recreate the day he met T. J. in 1988, toddling over to her with a book of nursery rhymes.

The move to Virginia included Matthew's father. The four of us worked together to negotiate new pathways for our family. While Matt was in child care, we attended parent–teacher conferences together and had family discussions on topics such as visitations and school activities. Ken now lives in a neighboring state but visits our home monthly to spend time with Matthew.

Our definitions of *family* are flexible, conscious, and negotiated. Our community of friends includes lesbians, gay men, heterosexual and bisexual individuals, and couples and families of all kinds. Matthew has created a vocabulary to describe his family: "I have three parents—two moms and a dad." "There are four kinds of love—two women loving each other, two men loving each other, a woman loving a man, and a man loving a woman." His teachers and classmates know that Matthew has two mothers, and most have welcomed the opportunity to discuss their own ideas and experiences with family diversity.

PLANNING THE PREGNANCY

We began to consider having another child even before we moved to Virginia. Before a moving sale in Texas, we packed away choice baby clothes of Matthew's "just in case." In 1991, we had a commitment celebration and affirmed the importance of our relationship with more than 100 friends and family members. We drew up wills, living wills, and powers of attorney. T. J. was given a permanent medical release in the event Matthew became ill or injured while his legal parents were unavailable. We created the paper trail necessary for lesbian and gay couples, of joint bank accounts, joint investments, and joint home ownership. We spoke to various groups about lesbian and gay families and were active in supporting changes in civil rights legislation. By 1992, we began to talk seriously about having another child.

We agreed that T. J. would carry the child conceived through donor insemination. We considered adoption but decided we did not want to endure the media coverage that would result from such a politically controversial situation in the state of Virginia. Virginia is one of the more restrictive states when it comes to lesbian and gay civil rights.

T. J. also wanted to experience pregnancy and bear a child. The next question was, "Who would be the donor?" After considering several options, we decided to ask Keith, the partner of Katherine's brother, John. Keith and John have been in a relationship with each other for twelve years. We have been close to them as a couple since we got together. Although John and Keith live 600 miles away, we spend vacations together and feel connected to them as a family.

On Thanksgiving night in 1992, we told John and Keith of our plans to have another child and asked them to consider Keith being the donor and the two of them being involved as role-models for the child, just as they are role-models for Matthew. Keith immediately said "yes" and expressed his comfort in the idea of creating a child together. He and John agreed to discuss it further in the privacy of their relationship and with their close friends and to communicate questions and concerns openly with us. We spent time over the winter holidays discussing the possibilities and challenges of what we were going to pursue.

Matthew also participated in the conversations. He was quite logical in his early questions about reproduction, asking, "What does an egg and an egg make?" We responded, "They make a lot of love, but they don't make a baby." He understood that sperm was needed to create a baby. We told him that Keith's body made sperm and that he would help us make the baby that would grow inside T. J.'s body. This made sense to Matthew, and his questions were soon centered on having a new sibling.

We were now ready to attempt pregnancy. On April 25, 1993, we met John and Keith in Washington, D.C., for the March on Washington for Lesbian, Gay, and Bisexual Civil Rights. We signed a donor agreement, which established in writing that Keith would not attempt to gain legal custody of the child nor would he be held financially responsible for the child.

We attempted pregnancy in April, June, and July without success. T. J.'s menstrual cycles were incredibly varied which made ovulation difficult to pinpoint. Each visit, however, provided more opportunity for us to build our connections. Matthew understood the workings of temperature charts and home pregnancy tests and hoped each month that "the egg and sperm got together." By August, we had become somewhat weary in the travels (a 600-mile distance each way) and decided to meet half-way in Hershey, Pennsylvania. Our semester was near, and work schedules had become more rigid. This visit had to be on a weekend. T. J. put away the ovulation kits and made a guess as to the best chance for ovulation: August 20–22. We relaxed and made hotel reservations.

The trip became a vacation. We rode roller coasters and ate chocolate. As we left the museum shops, T. J. said, "Let's get a Hershey bib, just in case." We returned home Sunday night to a meeting of our lesbian community, at which we set a date for the first gathering of the Blacksburg Lesbian Mom's Group. We needed support from other lesbians who had or wanted children.

On September 8, Katherine lectured to undergraduate classes on gender and family diversity. T. J. spoke to Lynn Hill's child care center, Rainbow Riders, about working with lesbian and gay families. And, that was the day we learned that Sharon Bottoms had lost custody of her son to her own mother. The Virginia judge ruled that Sharon Bottoms was an unfit parent on the basis of her sexual orientation. This ruling upheld a 1985 Virginia Supreme Court decision that named a gay man unfit as a parent and awarded custody of his child to his former wife. We were living in a hostile state for people like us. Family and friends called us from all over the country to offer solace.

That evening, we sat around the kitchen table with other lesbian mothers while the kids played cheerfully. We did not want them to know of our fears. We did not want them to have to understand that a child was taken from his mother because she is a lesbian. We called Charlotte Patterson, a psychologist at the University of Virginia and the author of a review of research on lesbian and gay parents (Patterson,

1992). Her review had concluded that the research literature provided no evidence for any significant effects on children that were attributable to parental sexual orientation, and she had shared this information with the court as an expert witness in the Bottoms case. We talked about the case, and she told us that the Virginia chapter of the ACLU was coordinating legal work in support of Sharon Bottom's custody rights. We drafted a letter to the Virginia ACLU and volunteered to help in the appeal.

At 9 P.M., as we made plans for the upcoming Mom's Group meeting, T. J. received a phone call from her doctor. After reviewing the irregularity of T. J.'s menstrual cycles, she prescribed a medication for the regulation of ovulation. T. J. was to begin taking the prescription five days after the onset of menstruation. Relieved, T. J. returned to the table with the information about the possibility of predicting ovulation. Katherine looked over and said, "You look so radiant right now."

Two days after the Sharon Bottoms decision, T. J. felt frustrated, moody, and bloated. That night Katherine asked, "Do you think you might be pregnant?" Believing we had missed ovulation again, it seemed doubtful, yet T. J.'s symptoms did coincide with pregnancy. She took a home pregnancy test the next morning. There was that blue line in the left window—it was as bright as we had imagined it. T. J. yelled down the stairway, "I think we're pregnant!"

WE'RE PREGNANT!

Katherine ran up the stairs crying, full of "happy tears" as Matthew says. We were trembling with disbelief. "It worked!" "This is really going to happen!" We called Keith and John in Connecticut. They were excited and surprised. Keith said it was nice not to hear a disappointing "I got my period" phone call. Just to be sure, T. J. planned to take another test on Sunday and go to the doctor on Monday. We called John and Keith four times that weekend.

T. J. took the pregnancy stick downstairs to Matthew. He knew what to look for and quickly noticed the second blue line. His face erupted in a wide smile. He looked up and said, "You got it, Teej."

We made dozens of phone calls, and with each one, Katherine insisted on giving the news and then handing the phone to T. J.: "You're carrying this baby, I get to tell people." T. J. was overjoyed with Katherine's pleasure. Our friends were happy for us, and several cried on the phone. T. J.'s mother, father, brother, and grandmother were ecstatic.

We spent the day shopping and wandering around in blissful shock, yet it was difficult to completely indulge in the realization of pregnancy until we did a second test. As we ate lunch, Matthew made his only baby-related comment of the day: "If our baby is a boy, we need to tell the doctors not to cut his foreskin off." We assured him that we would tell the doctors not to circumcise our baby, just as he was not circumcised.

The next morning T. J. took another pregnancy test. This time we were looking for a second pink dot—and there it was. Two positive results with two different brands of pregnancy tests. We were ready to indulge in planning for our expanding family.

That Sunday was the first meeting of the Mom's Group. Nine women came for brunch, discussion, and planning. Five were mothers, one was planning adoption, and three were considering children. Several women asked about our quest for a second child, and we told them of the stripes and dots on our pregnancy tests. There was a round of congratulations. We discussed the Bottoms case, scheduled our next meeting, and told of our desires and fears about parenting. The Blacksburg Mom's Group was born.

The next morning, T. J. took a urine sample to her doctor's office for the official result. After waiting ten minutes, the woman behind the desk called T. J. over and drew a plus sign with a circle around it on her chart. Yes! T. J. scheduled her first appointment for the end of September.

We called everyone again to make it official. Matthew called his dad. We left a message on his machine asking him to call us back because we had some news to share. He returned the call later that evening, beginning his conversation with, "Hi, when is the baby due?" He expressed his congratulations and pleasure at the idea of Matthew having a sibling. Katherine wrote letters to members of her family telling them of our desire to have another child, our decision to have that child within our relationship with John and Keith, and our recent success.

THE FIRST TRIMESTER

T. J. has diligently chronicled the events of her pregnancy, particularly during the first trimester. In reflecting on the audience for whom this chapter would be written, she wrote the following narrative in her pregnancy journal:

> Writing this chapter has become a part of the pregnancy. At first, I visualized the audience as students learning about multicultural perspectives using this book as a text. That audience remains with me always, but others emerge, too. At times I write this for my own family, for my son, for the new child to read as she or he matures. A close friend said her eleven-year-old daughter read the first draft aloud on a car trip while she, her nine-year-old daughter, and her husband listened. The girls saw me a few days later and expressed how important the words were to them. They are my audience, too. I also feel, at times, that I am writing so that my wishes and intentions are known. In the event that something should happen to me, I want people to know that all I ever wanted out of life is the love and connection of family, as well as the fairness to which I am entitled. Mostly I write about my family in this way because I know it has to be written. We know very little of the everyday lives of lesbian and gay people. My desire to have a family, to raise children with another woman with whom I share a lesbian relationship, has been twisted and exploited by religious extremists and the far political right. This cannot be ignored. Legal decisions and policies are being made based on such distortions. I want basic protection for my family.

The First Month

In early September, T. J. went to Texas to join her parents in the Gay Pride March of Dallas. Her mother, Pat, is president of the Dallas PFLAG chapter, and both parents are leaders in the lesbian and gay civil rights movement. Her mother carried a sign, from the March on Washington, that reads, "We Love Our Gay and Lesbian Children." T. J. carried her sign that says on one side, "We Love Our Straight Parents," and on the other side, "Proud Lesbian Mother!" It was a very pro-gay, pro-family weekend.

During this time Matthew began to ask a few questions about the addition of a new sibling: "Can we keep it from messing up the computers?" and "Will I get as much attention?" Katherine explained the possibility of a child gate on the doorway to the study and the belief that we are creating more love and attention in our family, not dividing it into smaller portions. He was satisfied with these ideas and later became very quiet about the baby. At dinner one evening, Matthew said, "You know Emma almost had a baby brother or sister and that baby died."

Emma's mother, a close friend and former teacher at Matt's school, had miscarried the previous winter. T. J. explained to Matthew that sometimes that happens, but we hoped our baby would be fine. He returned to laying his head on T. J.'s stomach at night and telling us "what the baby was saying." The baby "said" such things as "Hi," "I like Matthew's voice," and "I want to be born." Matthew continued, however, to be somewhat hesitant in making plans for the baby.

T. J. turned 30 on September 24. We celebrated with friends and "came out" about our pregnancy to many families at the party. We explained the history of our decision and the familial connection with our baby's father. Our friends shared in our joy—wishing us the best, making doctor recommendations, offering maternity clothes. Creating a supportive community is a survival skill for lesbian and gay families (Weston, 1991).

By the end of September, T. J. was feeling nauseated most mornings. Fortunately she had classes in the afternoon and could approach the mornings slowly. On September 29, after her first doctor's visit, she wrote the following in her journal:

After updating insurance information and giving urine and blood samples, I met with the OB-GYN nurse practitioner. Our children went to preschool together so we knew each other. As she looked at the forms she asked how I preferred to list information about the father. I took that opportunity to say, "You know the score with me, don't you?" She smiled and said, "I think I do." I continued, "You know my family is Katherine and Matthew." She said, "Yes." I told her this baby was conceived through donor insemination, that the father was a close friend out of town, and that we all preferred to not list him on official medical forms. I said I could easily find out any family history that was needed.

She asked a variety of questions about my current health then calculated the due date. I pulled out my temperature chart and showed her my apparent days of ovulation. She agreed that conception probably occurred about August 26. The due-date wheel indicated May 19. Unbelievably, this was Matthew's due date in 1987! I would have the same pregnancy schedule as Katherine. It was beginning to seem so real. She gave me a prescription for vitamins and described services available at the hospital.

I told her I felt vulnerable, in light of the Sharon Bottoms ruling. She expressed anger and distrust toward this ruling and said she understood my feelings. She assured me that my chart would reflect nothing about my sexual orientation or the nature of the baby's conception. I added that I knew that I would protect myself most in the medical arena if I looked like a single woman on paper. I added that I wanted my family to be treated as such during care and delivery. She agreed.

Now it was time for the examination. She did the preliminary checks—eyes, throat, pelvic, heart, and then she asked about an STD test. I told her I didn't see this as a risk, but that I didn't mind running the test anyway. She gently explained that these tests were routinely done with single women and that to keep from drawing attention to my chart perhaps I should have it checked. She was looking out for me, yet it seemed inaccurate to call myself a single woman.

After more blood was taken, my doctor came into the examining room. She congratulated me, expressed amazement at hitting ovulation, and suggested we write an article about the process. When I referred to the Sharon Bottoms decision, she expressed disappointment and said, "Oh, I thought of you guys when I heard that." As she left she congratulated me again and smiled. I shook her hand and thanked her for what she had done to help. She said to come back in a month, and we'd try to hear a heartbeat.

We have taken much time, care, and space in this chapter to describe our first visit with medical professionals relating to our pregnancy because we felt so vulnerable with the official forms and conversations. Each new encounter with a formal system outside our family, such as the school or medical system, requires us to come out about who we are as a family. The subsequent doctor visits went very well, and much to our surprise, we were always treated as a family.

The Second Month

In October, T. J. continued to feel a mixture of pride and nausea. Katherine became overwhelmed by fear. She recognized this fear as internalized homophobia. We spoke to three different groups; in each situation, Katherine did not want to reveal the pregnancy. She felt targeted, that we were pushing the limits and would experience retaliation. T. J. felt fortunate to actually be pregnant and was comfortable in explaining the situation to friends, yet yielded to Katherine's cautions when speaking to groups of strangers.

At our second Mom's Group meeting, we collected sixteen signatures for a letter to the Virginia ACLU and Sharon Bottoms. A woman, new to Blacksburg, told of her attempt to place her partner on the university's health insurance policy. The request was denied. A family shared their coming out processes with their daughter's elementary school friends. We planned a panel of lesbian mothers for the university's Women's Week program. Most importantly, we watched five children—some meeting for the first time—play together in the back yard.

The day after National Coming Out Day, *Other Mothers* aired on CBS as their School Break Special. The hourlong program presented a family—a high school boy and his two mothers. The women had been together since the boy was two years old. We watched the show with Matthew and felt encouraged by the parallels to our lives. The audience was carefully made aware of the struggles for this lesbian-headed family—coming out in each new setting, dealing with homophobic parents in the high school, and realizing a lack of support in school personnel. The program also skillfully illustrated the strengths of this family—honesty, reflexive communication, proactive parenting, willingness to educate, and supportive extended family members. We shared the program with students, friends, family, and our Mom's Group.

As we became increasingly confident of the success of our pregnancy, we began thinking about the future. Katherine's legal parental rights were a concern. Our lawyer stated an interest in protecting these rights, and we began to exchange information regarding second parent adoption and the right to provide our dependent child with health insurance. Second-parent adoption of this type—Katherine becoming the child's second parent through legal adoption—has not occurred in the state of Virginia. Arrangements have been made in eleven jurisdictions in Alaska, California, Oregon, Washington, New York, Washington, D.C., Vermont, Texas, New Jersey, Pennsylvania, and Massachusetts (Benkov, 1994). We would have to carefully consider the effects of media coverage in attempting such legalization in our state.

One night, T. J. woke up with the phrase "inherently unfit parents" echoing in a dreamlike voice:

> As I walked to the bathroom I remember this feeling of disbelief. I had intellectualized the ridiculous inaccuracy of this statement in more conscious states, yet now I was feeling nothing but its cruelty. Over and over it had continued in my head. "1985 Virginia Supreme Court Ruling. Gay and lesbian people are inherently unfit parents." I felt so stunned, still half asleep. I have spent years trying to see things from Matthew's point of view: I talk with him and read to him for hours every day, I negotiate his childrearing in detail with his other mother, I serve on the board of directors for his school, I hold him when he is sick in the middle of the night, I cry when I see his feelings are hurt, I cherish him. How can they say I am unfit? He loves me. Why can they threaten to take him away from me on the basis of this cruel belief system?
>
> Although we were beginning to see our baby as a reality, Matthew remained hesitant about counting his chicken before it hatched. After seeing a baby on a commercial, T. J. remarked about its gentleness and asked Matthew if he wanted to hold our baby like that. He solemnly stated, "T. J., you really shouldn't say things like that until we really have the baby." We hadn't realized how serious he was about this potential loss. T. J. explained that in most cases, "once the baby is twelve weeks old inside the mother, then it will be fine." Being very connected to numbers, Matthew began counting the weeks. We were four weeks away from twelve at that point. Every four or five days he would figure the remaining days left for the first trimester.
>
> On October 29, T. J. saw the baby's ultrasound image. The head, body, arm and leg buds, and a beating heart were visible. T. J. was awed by the clarity of the baby. She returned home with a printout to show Katherine and Matthew. They would both attend the next ultrasound.

The Third Month

At our third Mom's Group meeting in November, we learned that a family at Matthew's former child care center was angry about the school's inclusive activity regarding children's families. The daughter of our friends, another lesbian couple, was in the class with the angry parents' child. The parents denied being homophobic, yet insisted that the idea of having two mothers was confusing for their child and requested that our friends' photograph be removed from the bulletin board. Lynn Hill, the director, refused to exclude our friends, attempted to educate the other family, and issued an anti-bias policy to all enrolled families.

As we discussed this situation at home, Matthew overheard us and asked about it. He confidently predicted Lynn's actions. We said, "This kind of thing makes us angry, and it also makes us realize how much we have to help people understand that there are many kinds of love and many kinds of families. Some people just don't like the idea of two women loving each other." Matthew looked at T. J. and said, "What do your parents think about that?" T. J. replied that her parents "understand that there are different kinds of love. They think it's fine. And they spend a lot of time telling other people that it's fine." He then looked at Katherine and asked the same question. Katherine made an "in-between" gesture and said, "They worry that it might hurt you." "It doesn't hurt me!" Matthew stated boldly. "We know that," we said, "and your grandparents are starting to see that, too. They see you, and you are so happy. It is changing their minds."

During November, Katherine's fears of homophobic retaliation began to transform into an empowered position about self and family. She attended the National Council on Family Relations and gave presentations on issues related to sexual orientation and lesbian and gay families that were later accepted for publication (Allen, 1993; Allen & Demo, 1995). Her disclosure about the pregnancy was met with support and discussions among colleagues.

Soon, the pregnancy hit the twelve-week mark. Matthew wanted to stay up until midnight the day before to usher in "November 18, the 12-week day." He began speaking about the baby and making plans. He questioned T. J. about some candy she was eating: "The books say no caffeine. Is it okay for you to be eating chocolate?" When we discussed our holiday plans, we explained that we would be in Dallas for New Year's Eve and asked him if he was ready for 1994. He said, "Yes, because that is when our new baby comes." He began to fall asleep each night with one hand on T. J.'s stomach.

We celebrated Thanksgiving with John and Keith. It was the first time for us to see them since Hershey. A full year ago we had begun the discussion of having a baby. This year we discussed the new pleasures and challenges of our relationship, Keith's desire to spend the summer with us, and baby names.

THE PREGNANCY PROGRESSES

The second trimester of our pregnancy coincided with the winter months. In December, an abnormal blood AFP profile indicated the need to further examine the fetus for chromosomal or spinal abnormalities. We agonized over the decision to have an amniocentesis—realizing that the procedure itself could cause a miscarriage. In preparing for the amniocentesis, doctors conducted two ultrasounds. Matthew marveled at seeing the baby for the first time and was equally impressed with the technology of the equipment: "Oh, that's a great shot of the spine. Can you pause it? Print that one, okay?"

Katherine attended the second ultrasound and amnio procedure with T. J. On the first day of 1994, while visiting T. J.'s family in Dallas, we learned that we were carrying a healthy baby boy. We have named him Zachary.

During January we met with our lawyer to begin legal protection for Zachary. She drafted a contingent guardianship for Katherine, stating our desire for Katherine to be a legal parent for our child. Zachary's heartbeat was strong, and he began to move noticeably. Matthew began to think about the things he would need to teach his little brother. T. J. began to study for her doctoral preliminary examinations.

In February T. J. successfully completed her prelims and began to focus on transforming the guest room into a nursery. The Mom's Group finalized plans for the lesbian parenting panel. At the meeting we greeted new members—another lesbian couple who were expecting a baby boy in May! We planned to take prepared childbirth classes together. Knowing another family in a similar situation made the world feel safer.

Matthew wondered about the questions Zack will ask him. In addition to asking about reading and building with Legos, Matt predicted that Zack would probably ask him, "Hey, am I being raised by two lesbians?" Matthew rehearsed his reassuring reply of, "Yes, and that's great."

As T. J. started to "show," we provided information about our family structure to friends who wanted to explain the pregnancy to their children. We value the opportunity to educate children and their families because it is a way to lessen homophobia. In response to requests by friends, relatives, and the families in Matt's school, T. J. created a sample dialogue explaining our pregnancy, new baby, and the love of our family. We respect children as full human beings and believe they deserve honest answers to their questions:

> You probably already know that there are many different kinds of families. Some families have grown-up kids, while some families just have grown-ups. Some families have one child, others have two, three, four, or more children. Some families have a mom and a dad. Some families have a mom. Some families have a dad. Other people, like grandparents, aunts, uncles, and friends, might be part of a family. Our family has two moms and one child—Matthew. We call women who take care of you and love you like parents do "moms" and Matthew has two of those—Katherine and T. J.
>
> Matthew also has a dad named Ken. Katherine and Ken used to be married to each other. Katherine's egg and Ken's sperm made Matthew. He grew inside Katherine's body. Katherine and Ken decided they would be better parents for Matthew if they were no longer married, so they got a divorce and now they are very good friends. Katherine met T. J., and they found that they loved each other very much, and they both loved Matthew, too. Katherine and T. J. decided to share a home together and be partners. Matthew was two years old when he, T. J., and Katherine started being a family.
>
> Now Matthew is six years old. We have been a family for a long time. Last year, we all decided we wanted to have another child in our family. You may have already learned that it takes an egg and a sperm to make a baby. In our family both of the parents' bodies make eggs, so we couldn't make a baby together. Sometimes families with a mom and a dad have a problem, too. Some men's bodies don't make sperm, and some women's bodies don't make eggs. Anyway, we have a friend named Keith. He is part of our family. He has been partners with Katherine's brother John for twelve years. John and Keith love each other very much. Keith's body makes sperm, and he wanted to help us make a baby. T. J. put his sperm into her body so that it could meet with her egg and make a baby. Now there is a little baby boy growing inside T. J.! We named him Zachary. He will be born in May—very close to Matthew's seventh birthday. We are all excited and can't wait to see

him. Zachary will have a big brother—Matthew. He will have two moms—T. J. and Katherine—just like Matthew does. Keith and John will also be part of our family. Keith is Zachary's father, and he and John want to visit us a lot.

So that is how we are all a family. We will love each other forever. We are glad you are our friend.

HE'S HERE . . . A MONTH EARLY!

Zachary, weighing more than eight pounds, was born a month early on April 25th, 1994. When T. J. was in labor, she glanced over at her bag of supplies and noticed the "March on Washington, April 25th" pin fastened to it. Little did we know the importance of that date a year earlier.

The birth experience was empowering. T. J. had Katherine on one side, Lynn on the other, and her doctor of choice ready for delivery. "Here's your miracle baby," she said as she laid Zack on T. J.'s stomach. The hospital staff honored all requests regarding the treatment of us as a family.

We are still cautious but very proud. The Hershey bib hangs on Zack's mirror, our lesbian Mom's Group is flourishing, and as the big brother predicted, Zachary loves Matthew's voice.

CONCLUSION

Reflecting on this examination of one aspect of our family's journey in diversity, we realize that like any family, we have dealt with the normative transitions of pregnancy: Will we get past the first trimester without miscarrying? Will we like our doctor? Will our older child accept a new sibling? Do we have the emotional, physical, and financial resources to raise another child? Unlike most families, however, we have dealt with other issues that arise on the basis of the sexual orientation of the adults in our family. The lack of legal protection and the need to construct a paper trail to prove our commitment in the absence of a legal right to marry are added stressors we must confront.

We must also work to create the kind of relationship that can handle the contradiction between our joy about having another child and our disappointment with homophobia and heterosexism. Heterosexual couples have many privileges denied lesbian and gay couples: They do not have to hesitate when filling out a medical form, they can provide health insurance to their families, and they do not have to worry about custody of their children. To deal with these institutional barriers, we have developed a therapeutic partnership and friendships with others. This helps to alleviate the external pressure that comes from societal exclusion and oppression.

Our urgency to foster authentic relationships with ourselves and others is a benefit of being in a lesbian-headed family. One characteristic of traditional gendered relationships is the oppressive character of the roles that husbands and wives can fall into if they are not vigilant about preserving the vitality of their marriage (Baber &

Allen, 1992). Constructing an egalitarian relationship that is not rooted in rigid gender roles can be a liberating feature of gay and lesbian relationships (Blumstein & Schwartz, 1983; Brown, 1989; Weston, 1991).

Finally, sharing our story is a way for us to turn our private struggles into educational activism. We write about our lives as a way to make ourselves more fully known to each other and to the world. We resist invisibility and negative definition by claiming our identity, subjecting it to the scrutiny of others, and being willing to commit our perception of our lives and experiences on paper.

We risk these revelations because of the educational value of discussing differences. By writing about our lives, we contribute more accurate knowledge about lesbian and gay families. The irony is that we invite criticism and inspection at the same time that we participate in being more fully known. We are willing to do this, thought not without fear, because we know that our story, like all the stories in this book, has the potential to educate and activate change. It is with a great deal of care, thought, and emotion that we offer this story—much like the process of safely delivering a child into the world.

REFERENCES

Allen, K. R. (1993). Opening the classroom closet: Sexual orientation and self-disclosure. *Family Relations, 44*, 136–141.

Allen, K. R., & Demo, D. H. (1995). The families of lesbians and gay men: A new frontier in family research. *Journal of Marriage and the Family, 57*, 111–127.

Atwood, M. (1986). *The handmaid's tale*. New York: Fawcett Crest.

Baber, K. M., & Allen, K. R. (1992). *Women and families: Feminist reconstructions*. New York: Guilford.

Benkov, L. (1994). *Reinventing the family.* New York: Crown.

Blumstein, P., & Schwartz, P. (1983). *American couples: Money, work, sex*. New York: William Morrow.

Brown, L. S. (1989). New voices, new visions: Toward a lesbian/gay paradigm for psychology. *Psychology of Women Quarterly, 13*, 445–458.

Burke, P. (1993). *Family values: Two moms and their son*. New York: Random House.

Carrasquillo, H. (1994). The Puerto Rican family. In R. L. Taylor (Ed.), *Minority families in the United States: A multicultural perspective* (pp. 82–94). Upper Saddle River, NJ: Prentice Hall.

Goodman, P. (1991, May). *Supporting our gay loved ones: A Parents FLAG perspective*. Paper presented at the American Psychiatric Association Annual Meeting, New Orleans.

Herek, G. M., Kimmel, D. C., Amaro, H., & Melton, G. B. (1991). Avoiding heterosexist bias in psychological research. *American Psychologist, 46*, 957–963.

Laird, J. (1989). Women and stories: Restorying women's self-constructions. In M. McGoldrick, C. M. Anderson, & F. Walsh (Eds.), *Women in families: A framework for family therapy* (pp. 427–450). New York: W. W. Norton.

Laird, J. (1993). Lesbian and gay families. In F. Walsh (Ed.), *Normal family processes* (2nd ed.) (pp. 282–328). New York: Guilford.

Patterson, C. J. (1992). Children of lesbian and gay parents. *Child Development, 63*, 1025–1042.

Peters, M. F. (1988). Parenting in black families with young children: A historical perspective. In H. P. McAdoo (Ed.), *Black families* (2nd ed.) (pp. 228–241). Newbury Park, CA: Sage.

Sollie, D. L., & Leslie, L. A. (Eds.). (1994). *Gender, families, and close relationships: Feminist research journeys*. Newbury Park, CA: Sage.

Weston, K. (1991). *Families we choose: Lesbians, gays, kinship*. New York: Columbia University Press.

Witherell, C., & Noddings, N. (Eds.). (1991). *Stories lives tell: Narrative and dialogue in education*. New York: Teachers College.

CHAPTER 13

Contextual and Multicultural Perspectives on Intervention Services for Families

ELIZABETH B. FARNSWORTH

A s practitioners who provide intervention services—therapeutic assistance to individuals and families facing stressful circumstances—we bring our own personal histories and consciousness of diversity issues into our interactions with others. Reflecting on our own personal experiences is an avenue for exploration that may inform our consciousness of the multiple experiences and needs of others and guide us to become more aware of the roles we play as helpers. Contextual and multicultural theoretical perspectives are open and complex organizing perspectives that increase visibility of multiple family experiences and perspectives (Baber & Allen, 1992; Burstow, 1992; Walker, 1985). They reveal linkages between personal and intellectual knowledge (Thompson, 1992; Walker, 1985).

As a therapist and educator, contextual and multicultural perspectives have increased my consciousness of my own place within the social context of individuals and families and encouraged me to examine myself and my influence on intervention processes. In this chapter, I will address the usefulness of contextual and multicultural perspectives in therapeutic practices with individuals and families, beginning with personal narratives that explore my own awakening to diversity almost a decade ago. These narratives, guided by my doctoral adviser, Katherine R. Allen, first articu-

187

lated my own conversations with myself in the academic milieu, then provided the basis for our conversations as student and adviser. They assist me in extending outwards to others as I become increasingly aware of the value of telling one's stories in the therapeutic process. Listening to the stories of others in therapy broadens understanding and connections between people with diverse perspectives and provides visions of democracy in intervention practices. I will then discuss one context of practice—therapy in early intervention, and offer reflections on my own practice in that context.

AWAKENING TO DIVERSITY

October 13, 1984, was a crystal clear, colorful fall day in Virginia, a day that was to introduce diversity and change into my life in ways I did not fully understand or appreciate at the time. Based on my own perceptions, this opening of heart and mind to family diversity continues today in my collaboration with family scholars who are attentive to and respectful of multiple truths and family experiences. In coming together with the other authors to work on *Affirming Diversity Through Democratic Conversations*, I was inspired to share my own story of family diversity and to reflect on how this personal story has influenced my own practices with others.

Our second child, Thomas, was born on that lovely fall day after much planning, excitement, and anticipation. Less than an hour after his speedy and uncomplicated birth, the obstetrician appeared in my hospital room and somberly announced, "Your baby looks a little funny." I recall feeling stunned, shocked, and unable to respond immediately. Later I felt angry that my peaceful reverie had been shattered and angry about the choice of the word "funny" to refer to my baby, the baby I had nurtured and loved even before birth. As a family scholar now informed with new knowledge, I am conscious of the cultural context within which a parent is informed of a child's disability—a cultural context that dichotomizes normalcy and abnormality, thereby creating a world of "insiders" and "outsiders."

A short while after my interaction with the obstetrician on that lovely and bleak October day, the pediatrician came in to examine Thomas. Blood samples were taken, and about a week later we learned that he had a condition referred to as Down syndrome. Down syndrome results from extra genetic material in the cells and is characterized by physical and mental delays. Many deep feelings welled in me when I learned of my child's condition—anger, disappointment, sadness, disbelief, and fear. Like many parents who learn of a child's disability, I had had little experience with it; I felt inadequate and confused about my new and unexpected role as parent of a child with Down syndrome.

Returning to our own home, a place of safety and care, with my husband, Dave, and 4-year-old son, Michael, we began to restructure and pull together as a family. Thomas quickly and naturally became a part of those experiences. We began to notice the endearing things he did, like batting at the rattle hanging in his playpen and cooing with delight as we played with him.

I began reading everything I could about Down syndrome and made connections with other mothers who had children with special needs. They were people with whom I could be fully myself and with whom I could articulate my fears and concerns during our conversations together. I had many questions: What would Thomas need to grow and learn? Would others accept him? Would I accept him? How would this affect Michael? Cultural contexts and definitions of normalcy seemed to compound the difficulty of adapting to his birth. Negative generalizations on families with a disabled member were and are pervasive in the literature and in U.S. culture serving to diminish our visions of ourselves and our families' strengths (Turnbull et al., 1993).

There were many difficult times—like the day a geneticist at a follow-up clinic announced what Thomas' I.Q. would be and that "these kids" usually could perform self-help skills, but had difficulty reading and writing. Painfully and poignantly, I came to see that a child with a developmental disability lives in a world, a social context, that is "structured for people who have no weaknesses" (Wendell, 1993, p. 51), and it is easy to objectify those who are different from us in some way as "others" with whom we have no common ground. My experiences with diverse people and reflections on our conversations make visible our common ground and forge connections between us. Such experiences help me see people with different contexts as potentially myself and guide me to integrate knowledge with practice. As I continue to reflect and to tell my story over time, I understand that I, too, have objectified people with special needs. Connection with my own stories led me to this recognition and gave me a sharpened perspective from which to draw as I approached my work. This self-critical analysis now enables me to be more conscious of myself in interaction with others.

Listening to the "expert" opinions and predictions of a geneticist did little to help me see Thomas as a unique human being with his own strengths and needs. The geneticist reinforced the notion of the label first, a reification or static picture of Down syndrome, not a person with strengths and needs of his own.

In contrast, I remember people who were helpful by fortifying me with a sense of hope and personal strength. Primarily, these were other parents who had "been there" or astute practitioners who understood the tremendous needs of families to have hope for their children. These were people who held Thomas, played with him, referred to him by name, and virtually ignored the label "Down syndrome." They were people who knew how to *listen* more than talk. I will never forget our primary pediatrician, himself a bereaved parent, who never faltered in his support of our family. He was a professional who listened with care, made time and space for the telling of stories, and gently and lovingly cared for Thomas with the same tenderness and respect he had demonstrated with our older child. Experiences such as these led me to desire that people with whom I work as a practitioner should not leave me without a sense of hope and confidence in themselves as people and respect for their own families' histories and meanings. Almost a decade later, my doctoral experiences have guided me to continue to develop these meanings and articulate their usefulness to my work.

When Thomas was 2 months old, we learned that he had cardiac disease and would require surgery within the first year of life. Sometimes he seemed to be working so hard to stay alive. I breast-fed him, as I had our first child; these special moments provided me with the time and arena to stroke his hair and cheeks, to see his grateful smiles, to hear his gurgles—in short, to see him as a person and to fall in love with him in spite of a culture that denigrated his very existence. Thomas had open heart surgery when he was almost 6 months old. After a month of struggling to survive, of life on a roller coaster, he died at the age of 7 months. I heard and saw so much in the walls of the university medical center—children who had no visitors and never left the hospital, stories of courage and struggle by families, and recognition of personal vulnerability to a greater degree than ever before. It seems so long ago, and yet it seems like only yesterday. Thomas touched many lives during his short life, and he touches mine still—most vividly—sometimes painfully, sometimes joyfully. I did not realize when he died that I would carry the memory of him into my educational and career experiences as a springboard for understanding theory, a foundation for practice, and an epistemological critique of positivism. He taught me patience and compassion and led me to see the overt and subtle marginalization of so many "others" in contemporary U.S. society. Coming to know him and to see life through tear-stained eyes provided an experiential thread for contextual analysis of multiple oppressions—ageism, racism, classism, sexism, and heterosexism (Baber & Allen, 1992).

As a result, my doctoral educational experiences have become rich, more satisfying, and whole as personal and intellectual knowledge have become linked. These linkages dialectically free me to see and affirm many experiences (Baber & Allen, 1992; Belenky, Clinchy, Goldberger, & Tarule, 1986; Greene, 1988; Thompson, 1992), to privilege many stories, to have visions of democracy. Instead of grappling for "the truth," I have become free to affirm multiple truths, to hear many voices, and to honor the self as well as others. I have also come to understand that the path from practitioner to clients or students is not one-dimensional; clients and students also teach me about their lives and my own in an ongoing process. This, to me, is the essence of a multicultural perspective in practice. Through conversations and experiences with others, we come to shared understandings and increased respect for the experiences of others (Allen & Farnsworth, 1993).

EARLY INTERVENTION AND FAMILIES

After Thomas died, my feelings of grief were almost unbearable, the void enormous. I became aware of how quickly a baby becomes a member of a family and felt myself increasingly drawn to people with disabilities and their families, wanting to know them, to shatter the myths of a childhood in the "golden age" of the 1950s, the zenith of traditional family structures and ideals of normalcy (Cheal, 1991; Mintz & Kellogg, 1988). I was ready to reevaluate an early childhood experienced before the national awareness of human rights started escalating in the 1960s, an awareness that continues today in spite of numerous oppositions and obstacles.

About a year-and-a-half after Thomas' death, with my background in psychology and counseling, I accepted a position in an agency as a case manager for adults and children with special needs. Because I had come to know and love my child and met and conversed with other children and their families, I believe I was guided to see each person more completely, with more complexity, and with more honor than I had before having Thomas. Thomas grounded my perspectives in lived experience (Van Manen, 1990). My beliefs, actions, and attitudes were increasingly informed and shaped by my own family experiences. Further collaboration with my doctoral adviser guided me to clarify and privilege the use of the personal in my work and nourished my continual awakening to diversity, a process that is never finished (see Chapters 3 and 10).

I was drawn to the early intervention program that was part of the same agency and eventually became an advocate for infants and toddlers with special needs and their families. The early intervention program served families of various social situations, races, ages, sexual orientations, and structures. The expansion and contraction of individual family boundaries over time was evident to me as I witnessed families adjusting and adapting to changing economic, social, and cultural realities (Baber & Allen, 1992; Stacey, 1990).

As I reflect on the families I have known, it becomes clear that there is no "typical" family in late twentieth-century United States. The diversity of family life was visible to me daily (Cheal, 1991). As Allen and Crosbie-Burnett (1992) pointed out, a wide range of family structures exist in addition to traditional families, many of which have existed for centuries. Some of these structures are "multigenerational families, clans, matrilineal families, dual-earner couples, communal families, lesbian and gay families, single-parent households, binuclear families, and stepfamilies" (p. 9). In spite of the existence of multiple family structures, traditional families have been the standard against which all families have been judged (Cheal, 1991).

If practitioners approach their work with families assuming that one standard is "right" or "superior," they do not effectively address and honor the richness of the many families that make up contemporary U. S. society. Bringing families of diverse structures in to the center of our vision is a way of affirming diversity and moving toward more inclusive practices which honor multiple family experiences (Allen & Crosbie-Burnett, 1992; Baber & Allen, 1992) and create a multicultural climate which is safe and respectful to all. Families with a member(s) with special health and/or developmental needs are an example of families which have been marginalized in American society.

The early intervention program was designed to provide services to address the needs of young children with developmental disabilities and/or at risk for developmental delay due to specific diagnoses. Public Law (P.L.) 99-457, Amendments to the Education of the Handicapped Act of 1986, ushered in changes in the provision of early intervention services for infants and toddlers. Most significant to the current discussion is the move toward a family-centered approach to care, as contrasted with a traditional approach directed toward the child, with little attention to the issues and concerns of the family. P.L. 99-457 provided explicit attention to the interrelatedness of child and family and emphasized change in practitioners' day-to-day relationships and practices with families in ways that address family needs and affirm diversity.

Early intervention programs provide a range of services to families with the goal of minimizing the effect of developmental disabilities and risk factors in children from birth to two years of age, using a multidisciplinary team approach. My responsibilities on the multidisciplinary team were to acquaint new families with the program and pave the way for a positive experience; to provide advocacy and supportive counseling for individuals or families desiring these services; and to facilitate the development of parent networks through information, support group meetings, and family activities.

When a full-team assessment was indicated to gain a more comprehensive view of a child and family's strengths and concerns, a team consisting of parent(s)/guardian(s), psychologist, speech therapist, occupational or physical therapist, child development instructor, and family advocate came together to collaborate in the development of a six-month plan of service. The service plan, an actual document called an Individualized Family Service Plan (IFSP), was an outcome of this collaboration. It identified background information about child and family needs, as well as a listing and frequency of the services agreed on by all members of the team. It is important to note that parents/guardians were at the center of the plan; they were viewed as directors of the plan with full participation in its development and implementation.

Contextual and multicultural theoretical perspectives provide a basis for intervention services that are responsive to families and empower them to change themselves in ways that honor their histories (Burstow, 1992; Morgaine, 1992). Guided by these approaches, the practitioner is not a remote "expert" who dispenses diagnoses and solutions to the concerns of a family, thus changing the family to fit a dominant view (Morgaine, 1992). Rather, the practitioner works to establish a relationship with the individuals in the family, strives to understand their perspectives and concerns through conversations, and interacts to facilitate self-understanding and empowerment of the individuals with whom she or he comes in contact.

Reflexivity in the process involves talking, listening, and sharing diverse perspectives toward increasing self-understanding and respect for the experiences of others (Allen & Farnsworth, 1993; Fonow & Cook, 1991; Thompson, 1992). Through conversations with one another, there is potential for growth of families, as well as practitioners who strive to continually stretch their awareness and sensitivity to contemporary family life.

REFLECTIONS ON PRACTICE

As I reflect on my work in early intervention, I recall many faces, many voices, many stories. I recall single women rearing children in poverty, multigenerational households pooling skills and resources to meet family needs, financially secure married couples adjusting to the unexpected birth of a child with special needs, and foster families who opened their hearts and boundaries to children in need. My experiences as a practitioner linked me conceptually to the idea that there is not one but many families in contemporary American society (Baber & Allen, 1992; Stacey, 1990). These experiences also led me to see the oppression of many women in families and society at large and to articulate a feminist perspective in my work (Baber & Allen, 1992; Burstow, 1992; Faludi, 1991; Okin, 1989). The very real vulnerability of women and children after marital dissolution was visible each day (Weitzman, 1985).

Most important, I realized how little I knew about the circumstances of individuals and families in the absence of a connected, caring relationship with them (Belenky et al., 1986). Knowing the complexity of my own thoughts, feelings, and actions surrounding Thomas' birth, I valued conversations that were supportive and nondominant as a vehicle to respecting and understanding the circumstances of others. One young woman named Rhonda stands out to me during my work as a therapist in the early intervention program.

A Woman Named Rhonda

I am conscious of the fact that my reflections of Rhonda, a married woman with three young children, are my own perspectives of our work together. Does she view our relationship in the same way? This is a question I am unable to answer. My story would be strengthened by further conversations with her to clarify her perceptions; however, when I attempted to contact her, I learned that she had moved and I was unable to locate her.

Rhonda (all names and some details have been changed) was a young woman eager for contact with the early intervention program, and she expressed the desire for individual counseling. On the other hand, her husband, Robert, who was several years older, refused contact with the program. One child, a 10-year-old boy, was diagnosed with learning disabilities; a second child, a 5-year-old boy, had no diagnoses; and the third child, a boy who had been born prematurely and had high-risk medical needs, was receiving developmental services from the early intervention program.

When I met Rhonda, she expressed many concerns about her family situation. In our private sessions, she wove stories of her life, of sexual abuse as a child and current episodic battering by her husband. She had many financial worries, as her partner's employment was irregular and unpredictable. She had never been employed outside of the home and believed that lack of education and the presence of young children prohibited paid work as a goal for her.

She shared feelings of depression and hopelessness and believed that there was no way to improve her situation. She did not have a high school diploma and did not have a driver's license—and could see no hope for attaining them. Extended family on both sides had not been supportive of their interracial marriage, thus these familial relationships were strained and conflictual. Rhonda believed her marriage was marginalized by many people with whom she came in contact, such as teachers, social workers, and medical providers. Supportive relationships for her were essentially nonexistent. She told me that she often believed there was no one she could turn to for help. She believed teachers and social workers generally had a blaming, critical attitude toward her.

Thus informed of Rhonda's negative experiences with other agencies and schools, I was especially sensitive to her needs for support and affirmation. Her expressions of depression and isolation concerned me, as did the periodic abuse she encountered. She was an isolated young woman facing multiple stressors without access to social or financial resources and opportunities. She had left her husband previously but said that she always returned because she had no other place to go, no money, and three children. She also said, "Robert can be loving and charming, and I think he really does care about us." She told me that leaving him was not an option she was willing to pursue, leading me to see stability and change interwoven for this young woman. She wanted change but was unsure how or where to begin.

Guided by respect for women's stories and concerns (Baber & Allen, 1992; Burstow, 1992; Thompson, 1992), I began to ask myself, "How can I be helpful to Rhonda? What can I do that will be useful to her? How can she locate buffers from the stresses she faces daily?" A supportive relationship based on listening, talking, and sharing seemed to be an appropriate path to initiate our time together.

The questions that I posed to myself guided me to build a relationship with Rhonda based on respectful conversations and empowerment, not remote authority (Baber & Allen, 1992; Belenky et al., 1986; Greene, 1988). My initial goal was to understand the contextual (Walker, 1985) circumstances in Rhonda's life, with the idea that her own reflections would provide a vehicle for her to "seek alternative ways of being, to look for openings" and create her own "possibilities" (Greene, 1988, p. 2).

The contextual theory of stress assumes that multiple interdependent levels of the social system interact to influence the degree of stress in individuals and families (Walker, 1985). These levels are the individual, the dyadic relationship, familial relationships, social networks, community, and cultural/historical circumstances (Walker, 1985). Furthermore, the model assumes that stress is constant and that change is always required (Walker, 1985). Reflecting on my own experiences as a family member and listening to Rhonda's changing circumstances over time provided practical connection with this theoretical point.

Whereas Rhonda wanted a better life for herself and her family, she wanted change within her marital relationship—goals which initially seemed contradictory. Guided by respect for women's stories and multiple experiences, I supported her decision to remain within the dyadic relationship with her husband. Rather than marginalize and "blame the victim" for wanting to stay as others had done, I felt it was my responsibility to affirm and support her and to respect the boundaries she drew (Burstow, 1992).

Thus, her lived experiences were honored and treated as the source and justification of knowledge about her life (Burstow, 1992; Thompson, 1992). I could not possibly know of the multiple layers of meaning for Rhonda, the contexts, outside of a connected, concerned relationship with her as an individual (Belenky et al., 1986; Walker, 1985). Conversations provided the basis for these understandings.

We agreed on weekly hourly sessions together while her child was meeting with the speech and physical therapists. During these meetings, Rhonda, as a woman and mother, unfolded to me. Her difficulties seemed to be based on cultural devaluation of women and diverse families and limited access to opportunities (Burstow, 1992). As she located her own voice and desires within our conversations, she began to identify goals, to, in effect, change herself (Morgaine, 1992), and to exhibit a more hopeful attitude toward reaching her goals. She began by identifying the goal of pursuing her GED—her high school equivalency diploma. I provided her with information about registration, and we had conversations about what it would be like to again be a student. She seemed intrigued to learn that I was also a student and expressed the belief that learning is a lifelong process whether we are in school or not. We identified and discussed learning strategies together. She enrolled in the program and started attending classes. When she mentioned having difficulty with math problems, I invited her to bring in some problems that we could work on together. Freire (1970, 1973) elaborated such an approach in teaching Brazilians to read. He believed that it was important to begin with the actual experiences of people's lives in pedagogical practice. Guided by the direct needs of learners, Freire (1970, 1973) found that learning could be made relevant and connected to actual experiences. Russian psychologist, Vygotsky (1978), similarly viewed education as a sociocultural activity and believed that practitioners must participate in their own learning, as well as the learning of others. Practitioners can provide opportunities for people to practice the skills they need to use elsewhere through guided, assisted practice.

To Rhonda, obtaining her high school equivalency diploma was a strong goal that presented an opportunity for me to connect with her concerns and provide support. Rather than paint myself as an expert, I acknowledged my own difficulties with math problems, and we explored solutions in a framework of equality and collaboration (Belenky et al., 1986; Freire, 1973). Rhonda completed her GED and then pursued and obtained her driver's license. She then pursued and completed a nurse's aide training course. With each accomplishment, Rhonda exhibited a sense of pride and mastery, which became a part of our ongoing conversations. In effect, Rhonda was beginning to weave new stories about her life that centered on self-respect.

Rhonda's safety at home was an overarching concern to me. In our conversations, we explored this issue; I provided her with emergency information and strategies to follow if she wanted to leave. I was aware of trying to maintain a balance, that is, not contributing to her fear, but helping her to realistically appraise the cycle of violence. She talked with Robert about her education as a means to get a job and contribute toward improving their lives. As she became empowered, she became less fearful and had goals for herself, and their relationship seemed less strained. Because child care was a need, Rhonda was linked to a program within the agency that provided in-home, trained child-care services for families. This practical assistance helped her focus on her educational and employment goals.

When she was ready to interview for a job, we again practiced together. She used language and activity in the safety and privacy of our relationship that she would then take outside into the public arena. We began where she was—her concerns always provided the basis for our time together. Her meanings and words took center stage. A nonjudgmental, open space in which to dialogue, to become reflexive, and to find her own truths (Greene, 1988) seemed to provide Rhonda with a buffer as she went outside of our relationship. Thus, my perception of my role as a practitioner was a flexible one; I functioned as a teacher, a mentor, a coach, a therapist, a friend—attempting to respond to Rhonda in fluid and diverse ways as her conditions and needs changed and evolved over time. A connected approach to practice involves both change and stability, personal commitment, and sharing of one's own struggles and vulnerabilities (Belenky et al., 1986). Frequently, I was able to reflect on my own experiences (Thompson, 1992) with others who had provided help to me and to imagine what might be helpful to Rhonda. Rhonda did not have sources of privilege accrued by society, but she seemed buffered by sharing her stories and concerns and facilitated to find her own truths (Greene, 1988). She, like Thomas, touched my life; I learned lessons from her about courage in spite of multiple sources of oppression.

Contextual and multicultural perspectives, as open, fluid frameworks, guided me to honor Rhonda's sources of knowledge and to respect her family experiences; I was able to connect with the similarities and diversities in our experiences as women. The devaluation of her family experiences by many people in her social system—teachers, doctors, neighbors, friends, and even some family members, had served to further isolate and victimize her for experiences of poverty and abuse; and this contributed to the stress and isolation experienced by her family (Bronfenbrenner & Weiss, 1983; Walker, 1985).

Contextual and multicultural perspectives provide a vision of how things might be different for families if we approach them in ways that honor their sources of knowledge and bring multiple experiences into the center of our vision.

As Fu articulated in Chapter 1, engaging in conversation with others "enhances the possibility of moving toward what might be or ought to be." Reflecting on my association with Rhonda as one example of contemporary family experience, guided me to think theoretically about providing intervention services. What does it mean to provide intervention services?

THEORETICAL PERSPECTIVES

Theoretical perspectives provide organization and cohesion to our thinking and practices with families. Practitioners, as therapists or teachers, who operate from a positivist paradigm assume that the practitioner is an "expert" who can provide the family with the "best" solutions to their questions and problems. In contrast, practitioners who embrace a constructivist paradigm assume that knowledge is created through "selecting, ordering, and organizing information" (Baber & Allen, 1992, p. 12) individually and in collaboration with others. In teaching, Stremmel (1999) describes a process of mutual involvement between people toward problem solving. These practices are characterized by conversations and reciprocity. As a therapist, collaborative conversations are appropriate strategies for helpful involvement with families.

Constructivist practitioners believe that multiple voices and perspectives should be heard in the process of arriving at new knowledge. A constructivist paradigm of knowledge is sensitive to family diversity and goals of multiculturalism by attending to many voices, diverse family experiences, and multiple systems of meaning based on personal locations.

Contextual and multicultural theoretical perspectives are consistent with a constructivist paradigm of knowledge and are useful conceptual tools for practitioners as they develop relationships with families (Bronfenbrenner & Weiss, 1983; Burstow, 1992; Vygotsky, 1978; Walker, 1985). Practitioners operating from this perspective do not view themselves as "experts" on the lives and circumstances of others; rather they are willing to engage themselves with others to discover answers to questions and problems. In viewing families as the source and justification of knowledge about themselves, we become more reflective about our interactions with them (Thompson, 1992). In reflecting on my association with Rhonda, a feminist perspective guided me to privilege the individual—the woman—in the family, to place her perspectives in the center of vision (Baber & Allen, 1992; Burstow, 1992; Thompson, 1992). Knowing that women's lives have been socially constructed as different from men's lives, under the supervision of men, without access to opportunities and resources, led me to listen and respond to Rhonda as an individual with concerns and interests of her own (Burstow, 1992).

The contextual model of family stress was useful in understanding family stress holistically based on the perspectives of the individual (Walker, 1985). Walker argued that attention to multiple interdependent levels of the social system broadens our understanding of multiple family stressors. Factors on both the microlevel and the macrolevel influence the degree of stress; and the diverse experiences of individuals in families must be considered, as opposed to a family perspective of stress.

Frequently, the experiences of dominant family members are considered the "truth" in the family, rendering invisible the equally important and valid responses of less powerful family members. In Rhonda's case, she was the family member without access to resources and opportunities. When her child entered early intervention services, she voiced her perspectives through a family-centered approach to intervention, which recognizes the link between child and family. Family experience is not viewed monolithically. Individuals make up families, and the perspectives of individuals are important and worthy in the process of assisting families.

CONCLUSION

And now I return to the personal as a vehicle for connected practice inspired by a concern for multiple perspectives (Baber & Allen, 1992). Fu (1999) said, "Every life is a story that is worth telling." I have told the story of Thomas' life from my own perspective as his mother. His story has been valuable for me to share, helpful for me to reflect on as I interact with individuals and families; my stories have evolved and helped me to heal from the stressors surrounding his death. His story is my story, and it continues to take form over time.

I have also reflected on my therapeutic practices with another woman and my perceptions about conversations as vehicles for contextual and multicultural understanding. As a practitioner, I believe it is useful to reflect on and critically examine our own experiences in families. Past and current experiences provide threads of meaning and influence our work with others. As we reflect on our own experiences, we begin to identify these threads of meaning and understand how they influence our interactions with others. More important, I believe these reflections and conversations have made me conscious of how much Thomas and Rhonda have given to me. They were not "passive recipients" of my care as a mother and a therapist; they were creative actors at the center of their own complex social systems who influenced me and interacted in their own ways.

Through telling stories and engaging in democratic conversations, individuals in families begin to locate their voices and sources of knowledge; they become free to pose their own questions to themselves and discover their own ways of making change. As Thomas' mother, I have often said that he planted seeds of change that I did not fully understand or appreciate at the time. Through telling my story and his story, I have come to understand. I continue to clarify myself, my stories, and the meanings of my experiences in an ongoing, dialectical process. This process increases my consciousness of the stories of others, the privilege in the sharing, and my responsibilities as a practitioner to engage meaningfully and with care.

REFERENCES

Allen, K. R., & Crosbie-Burnett, M. (1992). Innovative ways and controversial issues in teaching about families: A special collection on family pedagogy. *Family Relations*, *41*, 9–11.

Allen, K. R., & Farnsworth, E. B. (1993). Reflexivity in teaching about families. *Family Relations*, *42*, 351-356.

Baber, K. M., & Allen, K. R. (1992). *Women and families: Feminist reconstructions*. New York: Guilford Press.

Belenky, M. F., Clinchy, B. M., Goldberger, N. R., & Tarule, J. M. (1986). *Women's ways of knowing*. New York: Basic.

Bronfenbrenner, U., & Weiss, H. B. (1983). Beyond policies without people: An ecological perspective on child and family policy. In E. F. Zigler, S. L. Kagan, & E. Klugman (Eds.), *Children, families and government: Perspectives on American social policy* (pp. 393–414). London: Cambridge University Press.

Burstow, B. (1992). *Radical feminist therapy: Working in the context of violence*. Newbury Park, CA: Sage.

Cheal, D. (1991). *Family and the state of theory*. Toronto: University of Toronto Press.

Faludi, S. (1991). *Backlash: The undeclared war against American women*. New York: Anchor.

Fonow, M. M., & Cook, J. A. (1991). Back to the future: A look at the second wave of feminist epistemology and methodology. In M. M. Fonow & J. A. Cook (Eds.), *Beyond methodology: Feminist scholarship as lived research* (pp. 1–15). Bloomington: Indiana University Press.

Freire, P. (1970). *Pedagogy of the oppressed*. New York: Herder and Herder.

Freire, P. (1973). *Education for critical consciousness*. New York: Continuum.

Fu, V. R. (1999). Stories of we the people: An invitation to join in the conversation on diversity in a democracy. In V. R. Fu & A. J. Stremmel (Eds.), *Affirming diversity through democratic conversations* (pp. 3–13). Upper Saddle River, NJ: Merrill/Prentice Hall.

Greene, M. (1988). *The dialectic of freedom*. New York: Teachers College Press.

Mintz, S., & Kellogg, S. (1988). *Domestic revolutions: A social history of American family life*. New York: The Free Press.

Morgaine, C. A. (1992). Alternative paradigms for helping families change themselves. *Family Relations, 41*, 12–17.

Okin, S. M. (1989). *Justice, gender, and the family*. New York: Basic.

Stacey, J. (1990). *Brave new families: Stories of domestic upheaval in late twentieth century America*. New York: Basic.

Stremmel, A. J. (1999). Developing interpersonal understanding in teaching culturally diverse children. In V. R. Fu & A. J. Stremmel (Eds.), *Affirming diversity through democratic conversations* (pp. 77–91). Upper Saddle River, NJ: Merrill/Prentice Hall.

Thompson, L. (1992). Feminist methodology for family studies. *Journal of Marriage and the Family, 51*, 3-18.

Turnbull, A. P., Patterson, J. M., Behr, S. K., Murphy, D. L., Marquis, J. G., & Blue-Banning, M. J. eds. (1993). *Cognitive coping, families, & disability*. Baltimore: Paul H. Brookes.

Van Manen, M. (1990). *Researching lived experience: Human science for an action sensitive pedagogy*. New York: State University of New York Press.

Vygotsky, L. (1978). *Mind in society*. Cambridge, MA: Harvard University Press.

Walker, A. J. (1985). Reconceptualizing family stress. *Journal of Marriage and the Family, 47*, 827–837.

Weitzman, L. (1985). *The divorce revolution: The unexpected social and economic consequences for women and children in America*. New York: Free Press.

Wendell, S. (1993). Toward a feminist theory of disability. In A. Minas (Ed.), *Gender basics: Feminist perspectives on women and men* (pp. 50–58). Belmont, CA: Wadsworth.

Epilogue

Different Voices, Common Ground

ANDREW J. STREMMEL AND VICTORIA R. FU

uilding on the idea that U.S. culture may be seen as a conversation of different voices, we have sought to focus on the affirmation of multiple perspectives and possibilities while striving for understanding of our connectedness as human beings. We have assumed a social constructivist orientation in which inter-subjective understanding is socially constructed in conversation involving people conditioned by divergent perspectives. We have acknowledged that in democratic conversation, space is created for the telling of our stories. Like all stories, the ones presented here accommodate ambiguity and dilemma and represent an authentic expression of our personal experiences and concerns. Many of the chapters have been written as reflective journeys, involving a process of undergoing change through the experience of conflict or the confrontation of differing views. All of the chapters, however, reflect in some way the notion that in conversation, we open new perspectives, create new understandings, and transcend what is (Greene, 1988).

So what have we learned through democratic conversation? After completing our chapters, we engaged in a collaborative conversation as authors. We discovered that telling our stories required considerable courage, created risks for some, and exposed us all to the possibility of danger. For example, Jim Garrison reminded us that because prejudices constitute our identities and shape the way we view our reality:

> When I say I understand you, that probably means I am not taking any risks at all. I am not going to produce anything new. I understand in my terms, and my identity is not at risk. In a book like this where we are talking about listening, it is dangerous for some to put our identities at risk. When people say they understand, there is no more to discuss. You have been defined—because they know you, understand you. There is no way to go on and say, "but let me tell you more about me, my experience, because you don't understand."

All of us come to a conversation with individual, subjective ways of making sense of what is spoken. The discussion of differing viewpoints may lead to shared understanding. Vygotsky (1978) suggested that development (i.e., change) occurs only when people come to a situation with different understandings or points of view; however, development cannot occur if the initial gulf in understanding is too great, or if one simply agrees or takes a position without understanding the other's viewpoint. But what does it mean when one understands from one's own point of view? Kimball and Garrison point out in Chapter 2 that because one's viewpoint, constructed from personal experiences, influences how one views another's experience or story, prejudices or "pre-judgments" get in the way of attempts to truly understand.

Is total understanding ever possible? To suggest that it is possible is potentially dangerous. Ellsworth (1989) noted that it may be impossible for members of any one group to completely know the experiences of another. Our prejudices make it impossible to know and make sense of the experiences of others outside our own group. Though we can only have or hope to have a partial understanding of another, we must work toward finding points of commonality that can become the foundation for conversation. This has been our challenge.

Where does the courage come from to take the risk of putting oneself in the dangerous position of being understood on someone else's terms, from perspectives that categorize and define and restrict the possibility for further conversation? Unless one can recognize another's prejudices, and understand that his or her knowledge of you will always be partial and potentially oppressive, conversation has no chance of proceeding with possibilities for shared understanding within a context that is safe and liberating.

We take a risk both in trying to understand others and in revealing ourselves to others—both can be dangerous, both require courage, yet both are necessary to conversation. We have compiled these chapters because we believe that conversations are constructive, growth producing, and essential to change. We believe strongly in the notion that "people are the experts on their own lives . . . the only authentic chroniclers of their own experiences" (Delpit, 1993, p. 139).

However, each of us chooses what to reveal, which stories to tell. On the one hand, we have had the courage and have felt encouraged to tell our stories, because we have created a safe environment for sharing; on the other hand, for reasons of self-preservation, we have chosen to withhold portions of our stories because of certain loyalties. For example, C. B. Claiborne mentioned the importance of not saying negative things about your team or your coach in public. Anyone who has been a part of a team, a club, or an organization has no doubt experienced this sense of loyalty. To say something negative would be risking an essential value: "You don't talk about your team." C. B. explains:

> The idea of allegiance to the team is a very essential value that I have that started when I was in the seventh grade, the first time I played ball. To take that away from me is almost more detrimental than to not speak up for my rights about discrimination. Without the value of loyalty, there is no private part.

For others of us, family loyalties have limited our presentation of self. Would we want our families to read our stories? At what risk to our identities? Where does the courage come from to confront our families or our team, to create conflict for the sake of moving forward in thought and understanding?

Reluctantly willing to reveal a part of my own identity (i.e., that of being a father), so often discounted as trivial among academics, it was very difficult for me to write about a brief encounter with my son (Chapter 7), a seemingly minor and easily forgettable incident in the eyes of many. Although I never seem to be at a loss for words when I talk about him with colleagues and friends, to put onto paper something as simple as a brief interaction with him seemed almost like turning myself inside out. Why is this? When we share stories orally, we have the opportunity to clarify points, change our minds, and explain further our points of view. But once committed to paper, it seems so permanent. How will others view what we have written about ourselves and those we care about? Will *they* care? Is it worthy of book-print? These are some of the questions that contribute to our hesitance to share intimate encounters, relationships, perspectives—our stories!!

A point raised by our struggles is whether we believe we have the freedom to be explicitly who we are as citizens. John Dewey (cited in Greene, 1988, p. 3) pointed out that we are free not because of what we are, but because we can be different from what we have been. Our stories can provide a release, a means of freeing ourselves through choice of action, to go beyond the given to what can be. Greene (1988) suggested that when we take risks, we act in our freedom to make a space for ourselves in the presence of others. If we do not reveal any more than that which will do no harm, do we reveal that which will do any good? What we say, in essence, is that our views, our versions of what is possible, are not important, when indeed they are.

So we have chosen to tell parts of our stories, though perhaps we have revealed more than we ever thought we could. As one person asked, "If we don't tell our story, who else is going to tell it? At some point you have got to tell it in a heroic way." If our stories prompt others to sit around a table as we have to talk about their lives, to think without restraint, to see the value of conversation as a means of connecting personal experience to that of others, to help answer, "Who are we?", and to thereby achieve mutual understanding, then we have achieved our purpose. Perhaps it is true that, as Delpit (1993) suggested, it is the group having the most power (we all are academics, and hence part of the culture of power) that must take the initiative and greater responsibility for initiating careful, interpretive listening through democratic conversation.

REFERENCES

Delpit, L. D. (1993). The silenced dialogue: Power and pedagogy in educating other people's children. In L. Weis & M. Fine (Eds.), *Beyond silenced voices: Class, race, and gender in United Sates schools* (pp. 119–139). Albany: State University of New York Press.

Ellsworth, E. (1989). Why doesn't this feel empowering: Working through repressive myths of critical pedagogy. *Harvard Educational Review*, 59, 297–324.

Greene, M. (1988). *The dialectic of freedom*. New York: Teachers College Press.

Vygotsky, L. S. (1978). *Mind in society: The development of higher psychological processes*. Cambridge, MA: Harvard University Press.

Index

community education programs, 45
lifelong education, 38
multiculturalism and, 44, 77, 143, 145–146, 152–154
parents and, 116–117
school experience, 112–114, 116–119, 164
social class and, 111
socieconomic achievement and, 35
understanding and, 26
Vygotsky on, 195
of women, 38
Elbow, P., 22
Elkaim, M., 67–68
Ellison, R., 135
Ellsworth, E., 202
Empathetic listening, 16–22
Empathy, 19–20
Equality, 8, 16
Ericson, Milton, 64
Ethnicity, 69. *See also* Minorities; Race
Eugenics, 138*n*
European heritage, 4
Exosystems, 45

Family. *See also* Intervention services
change and, 33, 34, 86
community and, 45, 49
contextual perspectives of, 34
diversity and, 25, 32, 36–38, 171–184, 188–189, 191, 195, 197
early intervention and, 190–192
feminist perspective on, 25, 32, 34–38, 193, 197
fusion of horizons and, 24–25
gender and, 33, 34, 175, 184
inclusion and, 43–44, 180, 191
marital permanence and, 33–34
microsystems and, 45
postindustrial society and, 34–36
stability of, 35
stories and, 172–173, 184, 188, 192–198
women and, 31–39, 192–193, 195
Family and systems therapy, 63, 64, 65
Feminism. *See also* Women
diversity and, 29–39
family and, 25, 32, 34–38, 193, 197
family and systems therapy and, 63, 64
gender and, 31–33, 37
marital permanence and, 33–34
men and, 36
Ferguson, A., 37
Freedom
control and, 8, 9
democratic conversations and, 3, 8
power and, 151–154
reproductive freedom, 38
self-dependence versus relationship, 10
stories and, 203
Free speech, 8–9
Freire, P., 195
Friedman, E., 70

Fruggeri, L., 64
Fu, Victoria, 143, 196, 197
Funerals, 129–130
Fusion of horizons, 17, 23–25

Gadamer, H. G., 16, 17, 18, 19, 20, 23
Gallimore, R., 78, 79, 82, 87
Garbarino, J., 45, 46, 96
Gardner, H., 82
Garfunkel, A., 8
Garrison, J., 137, 202
Gay men
civil rights and, 174, 175, 178, 179
family and, 32, 37, 171–172, 174, 191
Gender
family and, 33, 34, 175, 184
feminism and, 31–33, 37
marriage and, 37
men and, 31–32, 36
power and, 67
social class and, 107–108, 119
theories influenced by, 64
therapeutic relationships and, 69, 71
traditional roles and, 33
understanding and, 31–33
use-of-self themes and, 66
Gergen, K. J., 65, 66
Gifted and talented programs, 117
Gilligan, C., 10, 26
Gines, B., 47, 49–51, 54
Gomez, M. L., 87, 88, 142
Goode, W. J., 32
Goolishian, H. A., 71–72
Greene, M.
on caring, 99
on community systems development, 47
on freedom, 6, 10, 203
on public space, 8
on stories, 5
Group identification, 4
Growth, definition of, 141
Guided participation, 79, 80, 81–83, 85

Handicapped-accessible community, 44
Handmaid's Tale, The (Atwood), 172–173
Hare-Mustin, R. T., 33
Hawkesworth, M. E., 46
Head Start, 88, 101, 118
Henry, M., 83, 86–87
Hermeneutic listening, 9, 19, 23, 120, 142
Hermeneutics
interpersonal understanding and, 16, 17
ontological hermeneutics, 17–22
social constructionist therapy and, 64, 72
Herrnstein, R. J., 121
Heterosexism, 172, 190
Heuristic research, 127–128
Hill, Anita, 108
Hill, Lynn

collaboration and, 148–151, 155
conflict resolution and, 146–148
family diversity and, 175
freedom and, 151–154
reflection and, 141
stories and, 142–146
Hooks, B., 44
House on Mango Street (Cisneros), 111
Hughes, M., 83
Human development, 5, 52, 93
Hyphenation, 4

Identity
common identity, 45, 49, 51
community and, 50
group identification, 4
prejudices and, 18, 25, 202
stories and, 202–203
understanding and, 26
IFSP (Individualized Family Service Plan), 192
Immigration, 6, 45
Inclusion
community and, 43–44, 45
family and, 43–44, 180, 191
metaphors and, 3–4
social class and, 118
Income, 35, 37
Individualism, 10
Individualized Family Service Plan (IFSP), 192
Individual responsibility, 66
Intentionality, 70, 103
Internalization, 79
Interpersonal understanding
believing game and, 22
choice and, 26
fusion of horizons and, 23, 24
hermeneutics and, 16, 17
prejudices and, 18–19
role of, 80–81
Interpretation
alternative interpretations, 21
believing game and, 22
definition of, 17
democracy and, 4
hermeneutics and, 16, 19
interpretation-action, 64
prejudices and, 26
Intersubjectivity
child development and, 80–81, 83
guided participation and, 80–83
pedagogical relationship and, 95
public space and, 11
responsive teaching and, 85, 86
social constructionist therapy and, 201
Intervention services
diversity and, 187, 188–190
early intervention and, 86, 190–192
practice and, 192–196
stories and, 188, 192–198
theoretical perspectives and, 196–197

Japanese culture, 133–135